Lidia Guzy, James Kapaló (Eds.)

Marginalised and Endangered Worldviews

Marginalised and Endangered Worldviews

Comparative Studies on Contemporary Eurasia, India and South America

edited by

Lidia Guzy and James Kapaló

LIT

Cover image: Afro-Brazilian altar, Niteroi, Rio de Janeiro, Dec 2015, James Kapaló

This publication was supported by University College Cork, College of Arts, Celtic Studies and Social Sciences Research Publication Fund. We thank UCC for this support.

This book is printed on acid-free paper.

Bibliographic information published by the Deutsche Nationalbibliothek
The Deutsche Nationalbibliothek lists this publication in the Deutsche Nationalbibliografie; detailed bibliographic data are available on the Internet at http://dnb.d-nb.de.

ISBN 978-3-643-90644-1 (pb.)
ISBN 978-3-643-95644-6 (PDF)

Verlagskontakt:
Fresnostr. 2 D-48159 Münster
Tel. +49 (0) 2 51-62 03 20
E-Mail: lit@lit-verlag.de http://www.lit-verlag.de

Auslieferung:
Deutschland: LIT Verlag, Fresnostr. 2, D-48159 Münster
Tel. +49 (0) 2 51-620 32 22, E-Mail: vertrieb@lit-verlag.de

E-Books sind erhältlich unter www.litwebshop.de

Content

Preface

Lidia Guzy and James A. Kapaló

The volume you hold in your hands is the first collaborative publication from the *Marginalised and Endangered Worldviews Study Centre* (MEWSC). Based at University College Cork, Ireland, the centre was established to promote the interdisciplinary study of contemporary endangered and marginalised cultures, religions and worldviews. The centre brings together, through its series of international workshops and conferences, scholars from diverse disciplines (anthropology, folklore, study of religions, history, law, environmental sciences) and diverse regions of the world (Brazil, Russia, India and Europe) with the aim of fostering dialogue and exchange on the critical problems faced by endangered cultures and marginalised communities in the contemporary world and the implications for global society of the destruction and impoverishment of human and ecological cultural diversity. The interdisciplinary nature of the centre encourages the different disciplinary voices to challenge one another to 'look again' at shared concerns and questions. The ethos of MEWSC is both collaborative and comparative.

As an academic community, the centre aims to promote engaged and philanthropic scholarship for a more inclusive, integrative and reflective global society. With this goal in mind MEWSC operates as a 'roaming' centre, holding meetings wherever like-minded scholars are inspired to share their varied perspectives and critical insights on questions of marginalisation and the endangerment of cultures and worldviews. The work of the centre is counter-hegemonial in orientation, seeking to challenge and question systems of cultural, economic and political domination through research that is both engaged, in the sense that it 'cries out when something is not right' (Campbell 2015: xiii), but also firmly empirically grounded in the lifeworlds (Jackson 2013) of the communities we research and enter conversation with.

Who are the marginalised?

Marginalisation as a concept is often equated with social exclusion, the systematic relegation of someone or some group to an inferior, less powerful and less influential position in society. Such processes of marginalisation within modern states are often driven by national discourses that value and propagate the ideal of an undifferentiated, unified body of citizens thus underscoring the norms of dominant or majority groups in society (Young 1989). Ethnic, religious, linguistic and indigenous minority groups find themselves systematically disadvantaged and excluded by such discursive practices as they are forced to conform to the social, cultural, political and economic forms of organisation and value systems of majority societies.

An important aspect of the discourses that lead to the marginalisation of minority and indigenous groups relate to the devaluation by mainstream societies of the cultural practices and forms of knowledge of minority communities. Cultures of visuality and performativity that hold and transmit knowledge through dance, ritual spectacle, trance mediumship and other forms of embodied practice are characteristic of many indigenous minorities while linguistic minorities often value practices of orality with performed utterances central to their cultural knowledge systems. In relation to 'writing' cultures, minority cultures therefore are often judged deficient. Discursive regimes that marginalise in this way are marked by the accumulation of pejorative ways of speaking about 'illegitimate' and non-institutionalised forms, for example languages that are classified as patois, pidgin, creoles, and dialects, while religious systems and practices that do not fit the world religions paradigm are designated as magical or ritualistic, their religious texts, beliefs and creeds as superstitions and heresies. The MEWSC scholarly collective advocates an expansion of what we understand by "knowledge" (Taylor 2003: 16) offering a more inclusive comprehension of the diverse, creative and innovative local knowledge systems that are the product of varied historical, ecological and social experiences. As Brabec de Mori asserts as human action in the world "is diverse also the structure and meaning of the world is diverse" (2016: 78).

Who or what is endangered?

The marginalisation of linguistic, cultural and indigenous communities goes hand in hand with a systematic exploitation and degradation of the natural environment upon which so many of them depend. This dependency is not merely economic, it is also the lifeblood of their cultural worlds. Creativity and the production of indigenous knowledge is the product of distinct indigenous epistemologies (Brabec de Mori 2016: 80). Such epistemologies are grounded and sustainable through the material, environmental and ecological worlds inhabited by communities. The products of indigenous knowledge have value for the dominant wider society but there is little recognition of their unique epistemological frameworks that gave birth to such knowledge, the "indigenous explanations" that appear "meaningless for the modern world" (Brabec de Mori 2016: 80-81). The rejection of indigenous epistemologies can be accredited to the devaluation and near extinction of other ontological frameworks than the prevailing western "naturalistic" scientific ontology.

With the ontological turn in French anthropology (Descola 1992; Descola 2005; Descola 2013; Viveiro de Castro 1998) as well as the discourse on neo-animism (Harvey 2005), hegemonic anthropocentric and dualistic perspectives have been broadly questioned. An emerging "new kind of ecological anthropology" (Descola, Pálsson 1996: 2) is blurring the supposed clear demarcation line between nature and culture opening up new approaches to understanding alternative taxonomies, epistemologies and ecologies.

Contemporary indigenous ecological knowledge systems relate to shamanic eco-cosmologies (Århem 1996: 166-184; Kopenawa, Albert 2013) and the non-dualistic perspective on human and non-human agencies in a mutually shared world and cosmos. Ontological pluralities include the diverse perspectives of humans, non-humans and other-than-human elements regarding each other, interconnecting with each other as different personalities in a mutually interconnected world and cosmos (see Viveiro de Castro 2015).

Within the process of industrial extraction of natural resources diverse indigenous communities are deprived of their fundamental human rights for a secured livelihood and the means to preserve their eco-cosmological systems. An industrial neo-colonial intrusion into mineral rich territories of indigenous peoples is taking place worldwide. With ecological degradation, vulnerable indigenous eco-cosmologies, perspectivist ontologies and their associated rituals become critically threatened. These worldviews and local knowledge systems, however, could be a key for finding local and global solutions for a sustainable and philanthropic global world of cultural and eco-biological diversity and mutuality.

By listening to voices representing values and eco-cosmological knowledge systems based on non-dualistic understanding of human, cultural and non-human sustainability and interrelatedness, our Volume aims to contribute to the search for a local and global, cultural and eco-biological sustainable future.

Worldview and Lifeworld

We employ the term 'worldview' in the title of our centre and of this volume as an alternative to religion or religious culture. As with the term 'religion', 'worldview' also carries some Christian theological connotations through its deployment as a hermeneutic tool to grasp the "cosmic and all-encompassing implications of biblical revelation" (Naugle 2002: xv) and how a Christian should live according to Christian perspectives. However, the reality of pluralism and diversity encountered through the European colonial project gave rise to the acknowledgement that alternative worldviews also warranted moral and cultural evaluation in relation to Christianity and its 'worldview'. Our use of the term is informed by its later assimilation within cultural anthropology that emerged through this colonial encounter.

Since the father of ethnographic fieldwork Bronisław Malinowski wrote his now famous words defining *weltanschauung*; "Every human culture gives its members of definite vision of the world, a definite zest for life" (Malinowski 2014: 534), worldviews have been approached in anthropology as "culturally organised systems of knowledge" that include ideas about values, cosmology, and conceptions of the natural and social universe (Kearney 1975: 248). According to anthropologist Michael Kearney, worldviews also always points to a particular class or group and encapsulate the fundamental outlook that works to distinguish 'them' from others. The prevailing "hegemonic worldview" is embedded in values, figures of speech, common sense, and taken for grandness, hence the need for a "meta-worldview theory" to expose the ideological background to theories of worldview (Naugle 2002: 241). There are two principle orientations behind worldview theory in anthropology; cultural idealism and historical materialism (Naugle 2002: 241) and as Naugle summarises "The former point of view has dominated American cultural anthropology, and the latter is Marxist in orientation and progressive" (Naugle 2002: 241). What interests us here is the main question debated by both camps, namely, "do ideas in consciousness cause social conditions, or do social conditions cause ideas in consciousness? (Naugle 2002: 241).

According to cultural idealism, ideas are "the preeminent reality", this "assumes that material conditions are shaped by some immaterial force that operates essentially independent of matter and is responsible for material phenomena" (Kearney cited in Naugle 2002: 241). The idealist approach has dominated cultural anthropology in America and according the Kearney comes down to the fact that in Europe and America anthropology has been dominated by relatively affluent individuals who have "not personally experienced hunger and poverty associated with life lived at survival level. Consequently, living in a world of ideas, they tend to let this preoccupation with mental phenomena shape their anthropological theory and assume that ideas have the same importance in the lives of the people they study" (Kearney 1984: 16).

If we accept the relationship between environment and the epistemological frameworks that produce indigenous knowledge and creativity this cultural idealist perspective is difficult to support. It implicitly positions the diversity of ontological realities in the realm of belief and language and away from existential concerns. The alternative materialist approach gives the prime importance to material and social conditions as the source of how we know the world. Existential conditions, history and ecology are foregrounded as the drivers of epistemologics and knowledge production. If a forest is irreversibly destroyed through logging or the tundra polluted through oil extraction then the material conditions that gave birth to unique epistemologies, ontologies and eco-cultural systems lose their coherence and relevance for the lives of displaced people who then also suffer cultural alienation in addition to material and economic marginalisation. Viewed this way, worldview has a material, existential base. Contrary to the kind of essentialist, cultural idealist understanding of worldview that is criticised for being divorced from "social action and what the world really is" (Heijnen 2014: 53), our approach to worldview encompasses "a lifeworld where people live in and not on" (Ingold 2000: 14-15). It is the relationship with our surroundings, our "struggle for the wherewithal for life" in a world of ever scarcer resources (Jackson 2013: 5) that we can point to as the source of shifting and constantly renegotiated subjectivities and the pressures driving the impoverishment of epistemological frameworks and the ontological underpinnings on which they rely. Therefore, this understanding of the unique and situated "articulation of worldviews" in the "negotiation with lifeworlds" (Bowman, Valk 2012: 5) represents our primary object of enquiry.

The United Nations, the Indigenous and Testimonial, Tribal and Analogous Peoples

Indigenous worldviews are the cultural ideals and values expressed and practiced by indigenous peoples which are the product of epistemologies related to their land and environment, their "territory". The United Nations Working Group on Indigenous Populations defines indigenous peoples as:

> (...) those which, having a historical continuity with pre-invasion and pre-colonial societies that developed on their territories, consider themselves distinct from other sectors of the societies now prevailing in those territories, or parts of them. They form at present non-dominant sectors of society and are determined to preserve, develop and transmit to future generations their ancestral territories and their ethnic identity, as the basis of their continued existence as peoples, in accordance with their own cultural patterns, social institutions and legal systems (Martinez Cobo 1986).

Throughout global history, indigenous peoples have been marked by marginalisation, degrading colonisation processes – on the one hand by European settler societies, on the other hand by local agrarian settler politics (see Lee 2006: 134). Darcy Ribeiro's (1972) anthropological account of the history of the Americas, designates indigenous and Native Americans as "testimonial people", those who – while becoming cultural minorities during the European colonisation project and conquest – witnessed with the arrival of European "transplanted people" the loss of their own local majoritarian societal status, facing new hegemonic power structures, unchanged until today. Given the spread of "an increasingly homogeneous industrial civilization" (Riveiro 1957: 299) and the cultural vulnerability, diversity and smallness of Amerindian indigenous peoples particularly, the cultural survival of indigenous peoples worldwide, but specifically in Brazil, is critically endangered as indigenous peoples often cannot "simply continue as parallel systems" (Riveiro 1957: 299) if their bio-ecological, cultural and spiritual environment is irreversibly destroyed by aggressive and often deadly incursions of farmers, legal or illegal loggers or industrial monopoles (see: www.survivalinternational; www.culturalsurvival).

In the context of India, indigenous peoples are generally called *Adivasi*, a term which is widely used as self-designation for groups of people in India who are also known as "indigenous," "tribals," "Scheduled Tribe's," or "forest dwellers" (*vanvasis*). *Adivasi* satisfy the criteria for indigenous status established by the United Nations, making India home to roughly one hundred million (100.000.000) indigenous people, more than any other country in the world. In the South Asian and Indian context in particular the term "analogous" is also used to stress the culturally, economically and ecologically alternative but contemporary situation of indigenous or tribal people living in South Asia (Kulirani, Misra, Basa 2015). Analogous/indigenous/testimonial/tribal societies represent stateless forms of social organisation and community formation. Indigenous worldviews are based on radically different values to the global, homogenous capitalistic worldview and lifestyle. They thus represent radical – and therefore often devalued – alternative models of humanity.

Despite their cultural diversification, smallness, vulnerability and constant external aggressions, indigenous communities worldwide also show a resistance and resilience to the hegemonic world model of a uniform capitalistic "way of life as consumption." Today the engagement of indigenous communities on the international stage, and at the United Nations in particular, is growing reclaiming their rights as indigenous rights (see Bellier 2008: 125-145; Bellier 2009). Today in many parts of the world "indigenous peoples no longer consider themselves outside the realm of international politics" (Kirsch 2006: 10). With their recourse to indigenous rights, a political "indigenism" and a new indigenous political self-confidence is growing. The recent rise in indigeneity discourses worldwide (Devy, Davis, Chakravarty 2009; Devy, Davis, Chakravarty 2011; Devy, Davis, Chakravarty 2012; Devy, Davis, Chakravarty 2013; Devy, Davis, Chakravarty 2015) can be seen as the contemporary expression of an emerging indigenous civil society reclaiming political, ecological and spiritual rights to existence and self-determination. This book renders respect to the emerging indigenous discourses.

Our volume represents a selection of papers presented at several international MEWSC workshops held in Cork, Ireland (2013 and 2015), Tartu, Estonia (2014), Venice, Italy (2016) and Recife, Brazil (2015). The individual papers are not comparative in the sense that they relate to problems of cultural comparison, however, they represent a selection of approaches and concerns that express common issues that generate debate and that reflect MEWSC's core orientation. The papers are all empirical case studies based on ethnographic fieldwork and cultural-historical research. They offer studies on three geographical regions, South Asia, Eurasia (Eastern Europe and Siberia) and Latin America. The selection of papers and their geographical spread do not constitute an ideological position but reflect the expertise of the network of scholars that have engaged with MEWSC thus far. For this reason, we forego the convention of offering a summary of each paper in our introduction, each paper speaks for itself. The postface to this volume by Arpád Szakolszai, however, offers some necessary reflections on the significance of the MEWSC project and this first volume in particular.

References

Århem, Kaj (1996): "The cosmic food web: human-nature relatedness in the Northwest Amazon", in Descola, Philippe and Gísli Pálsson (eds), *Nature and Society. Anthropological Perspectives*, 166-184.

Bellier, Irène (2008): "Le développement et les peuples autochtones: conflits de savoirs et enjeux de nouvelles pratiques politiques", in Vincent Géronimi, Irène Bellier, Jean Jacques Gabas, Michel Vernières et Yves Viltard (dir.), *Savoirs et politiques de développement. Questions en débat à l'aube du XXIème siècle*, Paris, Karthala – GEMDEV, 125-145.

Bellier, Irène (2009): "Usages et déclinaisons internationales de l'autochtonie dans le contexte des Nations Unies",in Natacha Gagné, Thibault Martin et Marie Pineau Salaun (eds.), *Autochtones: vues de France et de Québec*. Laval-Québec: PUL.

Bowman, Marion, Ülo Valk (2012): "Introduction: Vernacular Religion, Generic Expressions and Dynamics of Belief" in Bowman, Marion and Ülo Valk (eds.), *Vernacular Religion in Everyday Life: Expressions of Belief*. Sheffield: Equinox, 4-19.

Brabec de Mori, Bernd (2016): "What makes indigenous unique? Overview of Knowledge Systems among the World's Indigenous People", in *Past-Future-2016: Seminar on the Protection of Aboriginal Wisdom; Proceedings.* Huailien: National Dong Hwa University, 78-85.

Campbell, Craig (2014): *Agitating Images: Photography against History in Indigenous Siberia*. Minneapolis & London: University of Minnesota Press.

Descola, Philippe (1992): "Societies of nature and the nature of society", in Adam Kuper (ed.), *Conceptualizing Society.* London: Routledge.

Descola, Philippe, Gísli Pálsson (1996): *Nature and Society. Anthropological Perspectives.* Routledge: London.

Descola, Philippe (2005): *Par-delà de la nature et culture*. Paris: Gallimard.

Descola, Philippe (2013): *Beyond Nature and Culture*. Chicago: The University of Chicago Press.

Devy, Ganesh N., Geoffrey V. Davis, Kalyan K. Chakravarty (eds.) (2009): *Indigeneity, Culture and Representation*. New Delhi: Orient Black Swan.

Devy, Ganesh N., Geoffrey V. Davis, Kalyan K. Chakravarty (eds.) (2011): *Voice and Memory. Indigenous Imagination and Expression*. New Delhi: Orient Black Swan.

Devy, Ganesh N., Geoffrey V. Davis, Kalyan K. Chakravarty (eds.) (2012): *Narrating Nomadism. Tales of Recovery and Resistance*. New Delhi: Routledge.

Devy, Ganesh N., Geoffrey V. Davis, Kalyan K. Chakravarty (eds.) (2013): *Knowing Differently. The Cognitive Challenge of the Indigenous*. New Delhi: Routledge.
Devy, Ganesh N., Geoffrey V. Davis, Kalyan K. Chakravarty (eds.) (2015): *Performing Identities. Celebrating Indigeneity in the Arts*. New Delhi: Routledge.
Harvey, Graham (2005): *Animism: Respecting the Living World*. Columbia University Press: New York.
Ingold, Tim (2000): *The Perception of the Environment: Essays on Livelihood, Dwelling and Skill*. London: Routledge.
Jackson, Michael (2013): *Lifeworlds: Essays in Existential Anthropology*. Chicago: University of Chicago Press.
Kearney, Michael (1975): "World View Theory and Study", *Annual Review of Anthropology* 4: 247-270.
Kearney, Michael (1984): *Worldview*. Novato. California: Chandler and Sharpe.
Kopenawa, Davi, Bruce Albert (2013): *The Falling Sky*. Cambridge, MA: Harvard University Press
Lee, Richard B. (2006): "Indigenism and Its Discontents", in Max H. Kirsch (ed.), *Inclusion and Exclusion in the Global Arena*. New York: Routledge, 129–159.
Malinowski, Bronisław (2014): *Argonauts of the Western Pacific*. London and New York: Routledge.
Martinez Cobo, J. 1986. *Study of the Problem of Discrimination against Indigenous Populations.* http://unesdoc.unesco.org/images/0013/001356/135656M.pdf (last accessed in July 2017); also available www.un.org/esa/.../workshop_data_background.doc (last accessed in July 2017).
Kulirani, B Francis, Kamal K. Misra, Kishor K. Basa (2015): *Tribes and Analogous People in India: Contemporary Issues*. Delhi: Gyan Publishing House.
Naugle, David K. (2002): *Worldview: The History of a Concept*. Grand Rapids, Mich./Cambridge: William B. Eerdmans Publishing Company.
Ribeiro, Darcy (1972): *The Americas and Civilization*. New York: E.P. Dutton.
Ribeiro, Darcy (1957): "The Tasks of the ethnologist and the linguist in Brazil" in *U N - E S C O International Social Science Bulletin* IX, 298-307.
Solway, Jacqueline S. (ed.) (2006): *Political Anthropology: Theory and Practice: Essays in Honour of Richard B. Lee*. New York, Oxford: Bergham Press.
Taylor, Diana (2003): *The Archive and the Repertoire: Performing Cultural Memory in the Americas.* Durham: Duke University Press.
Young, Iris (1989): "Polity and Group Difference: a critique of the ideal of universal citizenship", *Ethics* 99, 250-274.
Viveiros de Castro, Eduardo (1998): "Cosmological Deixis and Amerindian Perspectivism", *The Journal of the Royal Anthropological Institute*, Vol. 4, No. 3 (Sep., 1998), 469-488.
Viveiros de Castro, Eduardo (2015): *The Relative Native: Essays on Indigenous Conceptual Worlds*. HAU Press: Chicago.

Engaging Scholarship in Understanding Endangered Societies with special reference to India

Marine Carrin

CNRS Centre d'Anthropologie, Toulouse-Université Jean Jaurès

Introduction

In this paper I explore the conditions for engaging scholarship in the understanding of endangered societies. Like many anthropologists, I have spent most of my professional life working with people whose traditions, language or way of life are opposed by the people in power. We often use the term indigenous to refer to such people, and to contrast them with groups who dominate them in economic and political terms.

As Bowen (2000) writes, current discussions of indigenous people take place against the background of three conceptual frameworks that emerged after World War II: human rights, collective rights, and the rights of the Aboriginal people. American tribes and Aboriginal Australians have served as prototypes for thinking about indigenous peoples. The thrust of the classification promoted by International Labour Organization (ILO), United Nations (UN) and other international agencies is that indigenous peoples constitute a separate category, that they are "indigenous" because they have endured a history of spoliation, and that they consequently deserve special entitlements as members of designated communities, to compensate for prejudice and loss (Karlsson and Subha 2003: 29). Li (2010) reminds us that indigeneity is a mobile term that has been articulated in relation to a whole range of positions and struggles (De la Cadena and Starn 2007).

Today, indigenous people generally want to preserve their distinctiveness and this has often led to associations of indigenousness with cultural authenticity, with spiritual ties to the land, and, in some cases like Brazil, with a powerful set of images about national identity (Ramos 1994), there called "*indigenismo*". Although the characterisation of "indigeneity/ autochthony" and the nature of "peoples" is debated among academics and activists (Bellier 2001: 204-206) we observe that international discourses have an impact on the ground, in the formation of indigenous organisations or the political re-articulation of their goals – particularly since the adoption of the Declaration on the Rights of Indigenous Peoples (UNDRIP) by the UN General Assembly in 2007. "Indigenous peoples" are not necessarily ethnic entities, but groups of indigenous persons which by and large correspond to one or several criteria of the working definition: historical continuity; experience of colonisation; social and cultural divergence with the majority population; economic and social marginality; and a lack of adequate control of the economic and political institutions that determine their living conditions. Proponents of the rights of indigenous peoples take the pains to differentiate their claims from those which can be made for other oppressed communities.

Are indigenous people necessarily endangered communities? The idea that prior occupation of territory confers particular rights on some indigenous peoples may work for groups in Canada and Australia, while similar claims are contested in Indonesia or in India. Theorists in Canada and the U.S. such as Kymlicka (1995) focus on the problem of the political representation of the minorities and the degree of tolerance that states ought to afford them. The term "Native" used here still has a colonial ring, and the term First Nations is often used as an alternative designation. Many designations for particular indigenous people have changed such as Saami for Lapp or Inuit for Eskimo. In the last decades, indigeneity has expanded in its meaning to become an international category referring "to peoples who have great moral claims on nation-states and on international society, often because of unequal, inhuman and exclusionary treatment" (Merlan 2009). There have been rejections of the term indigeneity, and many states including China, India, Myanmar, and Indonesia claim that the category does not apply to their populations. Kingsbury (1995) notes that China and Indonesia, for example, claim that all their people have lived on their lands for a long time, and hence are equally indigenous.

Adivasi communities as endangered societies

An important group of marginalised people in India are the communities which are often called *Adivasi,* and whose members sometimes refer to themselves by this term. The Hindi term *adivasi* is derived from the prefix *adi*, "before", and *vasi*, "resident", and is equivalent to the word "aboriginal", referring to the "original habitants of a given place". Adivasis are not always the first settlers, but the term generally implies a connection between a group and a locality. But this relationship may be problematic: indigenous peoples do not necessarily live only within their original territory. The territory may be lost through a history of dispossession, or people may have had to move: Thus the Santals came to Assam from their home in Chota Nagpur in the nineteenth century to work in tea plantations and are not recognised as indigenous in that region (Carrin, Tambs-Lyche 2008).

Adivasi communities would seem to be endangered since they are stigmatised and exploited.

The Scheduled Tribes of India, referred to as *adivasi*, *janajati*, or "tribe", number about 100 million persons from more than four hundred different groups (2011 Census of India). From a sociological viewpoint, they represent a significant component of Indian civilisation, theoretically separate from the caste system. Any claim for scheduled tribe status today will be measured against the following criteria; social and cultural identity, demarcated occupation and use of primitive technology, lack of relationship to the majority community, practice of endogamy and an animist and totemic religion.

A general problem of States in regard to minorities is to recognize difference while ensuring a degree of redistributive justice. These principles were applied to what became scheduled castes and scheduled tribes, and the principal aim was to promote their 'uplift'.[1] A number of tribal groups have been legally recognised; in some cases, the Constitution has granted them rights to sustain their cultural, religious and linguistic characteristics while this has not been the case for others. Scheduled tribes, however, were defined primarily in respect of their tribal origin, their distinctive and primitive way of life, their remote location and their "general backwardness". While Scheduled tribes were to be developed, they were also to be protected as autochthones or Adivasis (Corbridge 2000).

Besides, even when such formal rights are granted, education, industrialisation, urbanisation and forced migrations due to poverty, change the conditions for the tribal groups. Further, the State has created an environment policy which allows a complex relationship to emerge between communities insisting on their formal rights, socio-economic change at the global level, and political articulation of indigenous peoples, the state, and multinationals. The relative powerlessness of tribal communities has led conventional development theorists to view them as passive objects, rather than as active agents of change.

Caste and tribe in India

Tribal people in India, as well as low castes, have often been marginalised and exploited by dominant groups. By accepting several group–specific rights and devising a set of policies for the recognition of cultural differences in the public domain, which granted autonomy and equal treatment to minorities while seeking to redress inequalities between groups, the Indian constitutional experiment departed from the then current models of Western democracy. In India today, local communities conceive their identity around the terms of caste and tribe,

[1] In India, these principles of redistributive justice emerged between 1946 and 1949, all citizens being declared equal in the Constitution.

though anthropologists have considered boundaries between these assumedly discrete identities as porous, allowing individuals to shift between them. I have been struck, however, by the way tribal people themselves take their identity as immutable, regardless of social dynamics. While not denying that continuity and innovation have equally affected the construction of identities in South Asia, we should not treat them as arbitrary constructions, as has been a trend in post-modern times.

The government acknowledges that Scheduled tribes present unique challenges and assumes that these populations require assistance. But it is not ready to equate the indigenous people category with tribe. The view that identities are basically constructed has also led to a stress on people's own self-definitions in preference to attempts at classifying them in accordance with formal features (Ardener 1972). The flexibility of identity construction reminds us that there are two kinds of identities, those assumed by the people themselves and identities ascribed to them by their neighbors or the state. Ascribed identities have often resulted in negative stereotypes. More insidiously, a pejorative image of tribes entails seeing them as outcaste, which means, in many cases, treating them as untouchables, a negative stereotype which has sometimes been internalised by Adivasis.

Efforts by anthropologists and sociologists to discuss the relationship between caste and tribe on the basis of formal features have not been successful, since the definition of one depends on the other. Béteille (1998) notes a gradual shift from using the term "tribes" to the term "indigenous people" without really asking if these terms are equivalent or can be mutually applied to the same social reality. He sees the role of different agencies and NGOs in promoting this shift and stresses the extreme difficulty in distinguishing tribes from non-tribes in India since it is often hard to decide whether a particular group is to be regarded as "indigenous" or "immigrant". Béteille's argument is that any definition of tribe based on language, culture, or territory is inadequate in the complex context of Indian modern society. He stresses the permeability of the tribe/non-tribe distinction and of the tribe/caste distinction. Virginius Xaxa (1999), who has examined the relationship between the concepts of tribe and indigenous people, stresses that the problem of identifying the latter has arisen because nation and region are not clearly distinguished by scholars discussing these concepts. He asserts that it is the denial of territorial rights and privileges to tribal communities by dominant regional communities which has led tribal people to adopt the idea of indigenous people (1999: 3594).

Adivasi or Janjati in India: an anthropological overview

These communities may also be defined by their ecological adaptation or by their social and political organisation. It seems impossible to provide an overall view of the tribes, insofar as geographical, linguistic, and cultural entities do not necessarily coincide. Among tribal groups, we find different linguistic families. In the north-east live the Tibeto-Burman groups while the Mundari groups are settled in Central India (see Zide 1966). Further south, we find the Dravidian speaking groups mainly living in the Nilgiri Mountains.

Tribes are kinship-based communities that, throughout history, have continued to reproduce their ethnic identity through distinct markers. Tribes that had a formally structured society in the past, and held a dominant position in former kingdoms, were generally sedentary farmers, such as the Raj Gond of central India.

Anthropologists have often considered the tribal populations of India from three points of view: the first considers a tribe as an isolated sociological entity – as illustrated by the works of C. von Fürer-Haimendorf (1985) on the tribes of the sub-continent. A second stance, defended by F.G. Bailey (1960) for the Kondh of Orissa, develops the idea of a tribe-caste continuum, which allows for the various degrees to which tribes have integrated the world of castes by appropriating Hindu values, without necessarily implying a one-way process. The last position, defended by G. S. Ghurye (1959), considers the tribes as castes-to-be in an evolutionary process where they will ultimately lose their original language and adopt a mode of subsistence similar to that of neighbouring castes. This is the situation of the Bhuiya of the plains of Bihar who live in multi-ethnic villages as neighbours of a farming caste, the *kurmis*. It is sometimes difficult to draw an absolute line between "tribe "and "non-tribe" regarding habitat, language, livelihood, or form of kinship (Carrin 1986).

Adivasis have various modes of subsistence: some are hunter-gatherers, such as the Chenchu (see Fürer-Haimendorf 1985), the Yanadi, the Malapantaram of Travancore (see Morris 1982) or the Birhor of Bihar. Other groups living in southwest India practice shifting cultivation, such as the Jena Kurumba (Demmer 2001a, 2001b, 2002), the Urali (Hockings 1989) who live in the forest, as well as some of the Garos of Meghalaya (north-east) (see Karlsson 2011) who nevertheless enjoy relative prosperity in societies which have long been Christianised.

Some authors maintain that the real difference is found in terms of language and religion, since most tribes who still speak their original language practice animism, both considered as paradigms of indigenous culture. This argument implies that the castes, on the other hand, speak one of the regional languages of India and practice Hinduism, the latter being not alien to some tribal communities, but less fundamental than animism.

Since the sixties, the question of the Hinduisation of the tribes has produced a debate among scholars and has influenced the way anthropologists in India and Europe consider "tribe" in relation to caste. Castes and tribes never lived in complete isolation from each other, though there are differences from state to state. In the past, these contacts contributed to the reshaping of tribal identities through Sanskritisation, Hinduisation and various religious movements which developed alongside resistance (Carrin 2012).

The legacy of the past

I shall take as my departure point that "tribes" or "indigenous people" refer to ethnicities which can be explained in terms of culture and history, while not denying that identities may have been reinvented, as Hobsbawm and Ranger (1983) put it. It seems impossible to discuss the idea of indigenous people in India today without considering the historical and social situation of the tribal population. Attachment to the land or claims to the land have been an irreducible component of the idea of indigeneity which characterizes tribes rather than low castes or Dalits. This attachment to the land has allowed Adivasis to maintain historical continuities with colonial and pre-colonial times. I shall briefly explore the legacy of colonial policies in marginalizing Adivasis in the colonial period, to show how tribal groups were treated during the Independence period, before considering the Adivasis of Middle India as a main example.

Colonial discourse often responded by labeling groups as "tribes", when they were seen as vulnerable, or having a different mode of life such as hunters-gatherers or pastoralists. A common approach to the land question in the colonial period was to separate people who were designated to become competent market citizens in possession of their land from those who should be protected from the risk of dispossession by consolidating their attachment to the land on a collective basis. The division was often wrought on a spatial axis since lowland people were often considered as tax and rent paying subjects with individual or family tenure, while upland people were treated as collectivities which needed to be protected. Dividing populations and enclosing bounded groups on limited land offered colonial officials an efficient solution to several problems at once: clearing land for plantations and settlement and enabling efficient taxation, administration, and indirect rule. Colonial policies established administrative arrangements that confined tribal populations to tribal districts in which the laws applying to the general population were suspended and where the rule was enforced by agents, commissioners and missionaries exercising a form of authority influenced by customary law (Ghosh 2006).

In Middle India, from the nineteenth century onwards, "tribes" forced their way onto the historical scene with a series of rebellions that may be perceived as political acts, though they have been interpreted in various ways as revolts or insurgencies presenting agrarian claims. Among them, we can mention the Paharia violence (1772-1780), the Santal uprising of Tilka Manjhi (1780-85), the Bhil rebellion of 1819, the Munda revolt in Palamau (1819-1820), the Chuar rebellions

(1820s), the Bhumij rebellions of 1832-1833, the Kol uprisings of 1830-1832, the *sardar* movement which lasted four decades, the Santal rebellion of 1855, and finally the Birsaite Munda rebellion of 1895.

At Independence, the Indian Congress Party adopted the policy of assimilation of tribal populations rejecting the isolating approach of the British on the ground that it prevented social change (Corbridge 1988). Post-Independence approaches to governing the relation between "tribal" populations and land in India maintain what Corbridge (1988) calls "the ideology of tribal economy and society," initiated in the colonial period and still intact, according to which tribes occupy bounded space, sharing equitably access to land and forest, and stand united in their commitment to a communal and subsistence-oriented way of life.

I would like to stress that perceived "tribal" characteristics have been influenced by a history on which social anthropologists, colonial administrators and Christian missionaries have left their mark since the early nineteenth century. According to the different contexts, the claims of the weak have been violated by the strong – sometimes dramatically, like in colonial encounters, sometimes more insidiously in the case of internal colonisation of weaker communities. Indigenous peoples themselves insist on their socio-economic distinctiveness. This leads us to the expression of identities based on self-definitions, a process which has been mediated by a series of factors since the nineteenth century. Some communities have not been recognised as Scheduled Tribes by the State, a situation which endangers them both culturally and economically, since they are often exploited by more powerful groups. At another level, Adivasi as a concept has emerged as a powerful form of political imagery since the term has become an indicator of political modernity.

Recontextualising Adivasi societies

We can define Adivasi as a marginalised group located in a world that was transformed by colonialism, and today, by the postcolonial Indian state. But Adivasi experiences and identities need to be recontextualised: whilst their histories can be written with Adivasis as vulnerable subjects of 'progress' and development, Adivasi also need to be seen as agents able to negotiate with the structures of power and dominance.

In Middle India, the forms of social organisation are varied depending on the size and scale of the population including small bands of food gatherers in contrast to larger tribes of settled agriculturist such as the Santals, the Munda and the Ho growing into chiefdoms and kingdoms (Carrin 1986, Das Gupta (2011). Hunter-gatherers, such as the Birhor of Jharkhand, have experienced close symbiotic relations for centuries with other Mundari speaking communities, practicing settled agriculture (Adhikari 1982). I cannot detail the variations in social organisation, but briefly, when considering the level of political organisation with chiefs, participating in modern village councils, we find many kinds of variations: matrilineal or patrilineal kinship organisation, clans and lineages, rules of residence, succession and inheritance as well as variations concerning the position of women, the transmission of knowledge and skills between age groups, and the various types of religious specialists.

Tribal villages are often grouped in federations, including 5, 10, or 30 villages, as among the Munda, Santal, and Bhumij. In some larger unions, known as the *patti* system, the strongest among the village headmen becomes the *patti* chief. The village was the unit of ancient Munda polity, and the chief was a *primus inter pares*. During the colonial period, these chiefs often became Hinduised and acted as rent collectors. Some chiefs, like the *pargana* among the Santal, were surrounded by symbols of royalty, sometimes reinvented today.

Interactions between Adivasis and Hindu castes were often conflictual since Hindu zamindars and Hindu moneylenders exploited Adivasis who were often dispossessed of their lands and ancestral forests and gradually marginalised in regional politics by a predominantly Hindu elite (Damodaran 1997). By the nineteenth and the early twentieth centuries, as a result of increasing interventions by a modernising colonial state, Adivasi culture in Middle India had gradually been reduced to the status of a 'minority culture' by the dominant, resulting in a growing Adivasi consciousness and a sense of an authentic Adivasi identity.

The identity crisis has led the Mundari groups, often called animists by others, to use the word Sarna for their religion. Sarna, the sacred grove, is a piece of virgin forest left untouched when the village was founded. Felling its trees is taboo. In this reinvented religion, the supreme being is seen as self-created, omniscient, and as the source of life. Other important concepts are *buru* and *bonga*. The two words are often joined, *bonga* being a gloss of *buru*. Buru is a hill, where sacrifice is often performed: Buru *bonga* denotes one of the village spirits. Maran Buru, the chief deity worshipped by the Santals, means "Big Mountain". Even today, the power of the mainstream religion is reflected in the fact that Scheduled tribes may be counted as Hindus unless they have adopted Christianity. No doubt, tribal religion covers a great variety of forms but it is striking that the larger tribes like the Santal or the Munda have tried to escape Hinduism, or have consciously distanced themselves from the Hindu way of life and Hindu values, identified as "casteism". Despite this trend, there has been over the centuries an interpenetration of Hinduism and Animism in all parts of the country (Carrin 2012).

Hindu influence on tribal religion is clear, and many Munda, Oraon, Kharia and Ho invoke Ram, Ganesh, or Jagannath. Many Oraon are *bhagats* of Vaishnavite sects. Some Hindu charismatic figures have both tribal and Hindu disciples, and elements of Sarna religion are shared with Hinduised communities. The

Hindu Goddess is found in multiple forms. Often, she reveals herself by leading the devotee to her shrine (Carrin 1997).

In the nineteenth century, reformist movements inspired by Adivasi gurus contributed to the reinvention of tribal religion, articulating the new cults alongside the political claims of the Adivasis. Christian missionaries arrived in the 19th century under five denominations – Lutheran, the Anglican Society for Propagation of the Gospel, Baptist, Seven Day Adventist and Catholic – which have strongly influenced the life of tribals. The social history of Christianity in Jharkhand has brought in its wake "new conflicts, new jealousies and, therefore, new political formations and communities, (which) have marked local memory in most profound ways" (Ghosh 2006; see also Carrin, Tambs-Lyche 2008). For the tribals, conversion partly implies a strategy to oppose the exploitation of Hindu landlords and moneylenders. Christian education in Jharkhand began in 1860, but developed considerably from 1905 to 1920. The ideal of Christian justice was recognised by the tribals, who felt they had lost the egalitarian values of their ancestors. Santals were converted by the Lutherans from 1870 onwards, and the literary activity they initiated reinforced Santal identity.

The Sarna Dhorom "the movement of the sacred grove", called Adi–Dharam among the Munda and the Ho, was rooted in the Jharkhand movement that led to the creation of Jharkhand State in 2000. It implies both a reformist ethos and a political dimension, but opposes Hinduised sects. The term Sarna evokes the sacred grove where the tribal deities reside, but also alludes to the idea of sacred sites as symbols of the unity of the indigenous people, which in turn associates it with ecological issues. Through the reinvented Sarna religion, hunting and agricultural rituals such as the annual Flower Festival (Baha Bonga) have been reframed as regional cults (see Schulte-Drooesh 2014; Carrin *forthcoming*), patronised by Adivasi political leaders and intellectuals. Similarly, pilgrimages to sacred sites enshrined in the landscape have revived both the feeling of belonging to the land and the environmental claims (Carrin 2015b). The gurus of the Sarna Dhorom movement developed cultural activities such as village theatre, while equally promoting the diffusion of the new Santal script (*ol' chiki*), the protection of the Santali language and the development of literature (Carrin 2002, 2013, 2015a). Other cultural reinventions concern the religion of the Sacred Grove, adopted by all the Adivasi groups in Central India and linked to various ecological movements, which are not just ethnic but insist that all Adivasis are citizens of the forest (Carrin, *forthcoming*).

The Jharkhand Movement which led to the creation of the Jharkhand state in 2000 has adapted itself to the Indian State's stance towards the political recognition of cultural identities. It started off as a movement for a separate tribal state but gradually extended its membership to non-tribal communities, and asked for a new state to be carved out of South Bihar so that development could be administered in the interest of the regional inhabitants (Stuligross 2008). The Indian state's policy of positive discrimination for tribal communities has had an important bearing on the Jharkhand Movement. It has also led to the rise of a tribal middle class which has benefited from the reservation system and played an influential role in regional politics. From the early seventies, an alternative idea of class, inspired by Communist ideology, began to be voiced by leftist parties, bringing the Jharkhand Movement into a phase of more radical redistributive politics. This version of politics mobilised against local grievances over land and forest rights until the emergency (1975-77), when most of the activists were arrested or forced to go underground. Then, from the 1980s, as economic liberalisation took over in the mainstream economy, the extreme Hindu right introduced the rhetoric of majoritarian identity as an alternative to the mobilisation of tribal minorities.

In this context, while the leftist regional parties adopted a political agenda which was more compliant with the state's neo-liberal development vision, radical redistributive politics continued underground in the form of the Naxalite Movement (Shah 2007). The political discourse developed by the Jharkhand Party, before the foundation of Jharkhand state, involved the idea that indigenous people had rights over the land as well as representing indigenous knowledge. These ideas have contributed to creation of the political space of Jharkhand, in which Adivasi populations have emotionally invested in asserting their identity, although other factors related to the exploitation of natural resources (forests, mines) have brought continued dispossession and exploitation.[2]

It is important to stress the on-going state of insurgency amongst *Adivasis* in India, and how central the image of the primitive rebel has been to the larger Indian political perspective. Here, we have a different view, onc that sees peripheral populations as active agents controlling their engagement with the outside world, and with non-Adivasi populations. It seems clear that Adivasis are increasingly aware of their exploitation and try to assert their rights as citizens, promoting the idea that they are competent to manage their own resources (Corbridge 2002; Corbridge, Jewitt, Kumar 2004). This has been discussed in Sundar (2009) where the contributors examine rights, laws, and policies on land, forest, water, and mining. On the one hand, Adivasis have been able to give local meaning to alien ideas and institutions; on the other hand, they have resisted them. But this awareness does not imply that they have achieved their goals: their struggle is still going on.

2 Mining has been at the heart of the development debate since officials and middle-class spokesmen assessed that the surest way to development was to intensify mining. Adivasi labor in the coal fields has a long history (George 2009). The Forest Act of 2006 at least acknowledges some of the everyday violence that forest laws impose on Adivasi existence (Carrin 2009).

Adivasis as promotors of ecological sustainability?

A number of organisations, both governmental and non-governmental, are involved with welfare and research among tribal groups. Many of them reflect a cultural stereotype of the backward and primitive tribal whose way of life needs to be protected, or uplifted, in order to find a place in the developed world.

This implies that Adivasi societies are endangered societies. But as anthropologists, we need to rethink our approach in order not to reproduce the hegemonic discourse of the powerful groups. We must avoid reproducing the paternalist approaches of earlier days, whether of anthropologists, NGOs or the State. How can we be of use in assisting the efforts of indigenous peoples to assert themselves?

We cannot deal with this subject without commenting on the current discourse on biodiversity. It is not by chance that this current concern in a globalizing world has invested hope in 'tribal practices', regarded as sustainable. But biodiversity also comes with the promise of an alternative lifestyle, contrasting with the homogenised consumerism that dominates today's capitalist economy. Such alternative lifestyles, usually focused on a reinvention of traditional institutions or values, generally depend on the control of resources and territory, as when forest people try to regain control over the forest economy. What indigenous people try to avoid, by these means, is above all the destruction of their culture and social organisation that comes with migration for work elsewhere.

Adivasi societies have often developed a policy of resisting global capital and savage and corrupt industrial exploitation. Indigenous people try to resist such exploitation by finding new niches in the market with the help of Non-Governmental Organisations. Such resistance, though obviously limited by the forces of the capitalist order, may imply reorganisation of production in the form of cooperatives, micro-finance, or other local initiatives. The Indian State legitimizes its current policies for liberalisation by promising economic growth and prosperity to the poor. Among different models of welfare, sustainable development appears today as the most influential. As noted by Baviskar (1997: 195-196), this idea contains two key concepts: that "overriding priority should be given to essential needs and that ecological sustainability is inseparable from social equity." But she deplores that despite the appeal of this ideology for activists, Adivasi assertion has taken a different direction altogether, towards "a kind of minority identity politics which is ambivalent in its orientation towards the principles of sustainable development." This can be explained, as Baviskar does, by the fact that middle class activists and tribal leaders, though they share some common concerns, have competing views of the "tribal" and of the environment. On the symbolic level, indigenous people tend to assert the value of local knowledge in order to defend their environment, often arguing in terms of eco-sustainable development but also expressing symbolism of the soil and the forest through narratives and using the terms that environmentalists use.

Adivasi societies do not necessarily have more ecological wisdom than other segments of Indian society. Class formation in Adivasi societies and other social conflicts should warn us against ecological romanticism, as Prasad (2003) shows for the Gond of Chattisgarh. Ingold (2000) makes us understand that the sophisticated knowledge of plants does not refer to a mystical bond linking indigenous communities to nature, as environmentalists often think, but rather to a form of knowledge embedded in experience. In such a perspective, indigenous knowledge represents a resource. In some circumstances, however, Adivasis prioritize other objectives and forget their skills, when they commodify nature, and through capitalistic extraction and market exchange commodify nature (Karlsson 2012: 258).

Understanding being indigenous

The analytical framework I am suggesting here is based on a Universalist normative framework in which consideration of equality and self-governance should serve as key values. But ideas of groups, localities and regions differ across the world. In India, the return of Adivasi people to their old forms of polity in Jharkhand have been perceived as a strategy to differentiate themselves from the State. Mundari and Santal people try to promote their old ideas of chiefdoms while they hesitate to accept the State institutions (Shah 2007; Carrin 2009). Similarly, in Indonesia the concept of the "*adat* ", community, has provided a source of legitimacy for groups seeking to act in the name of society against the State (Bowen 2000:15). There are other examples which retrace the reinvention of indigenous people's cultures. Hanson (1989) shows how Maori culture was invented successively at the turn of the 20th century, when the primary aim was to assimilate Maoris into "the White life" – and in the present day when Maoris rather seek to maintain their cultural distinctiveness and to assume a more powerful position in society. This suggests that indigenous people are often able to stage their own resistance and redefine their identity.

The construction of the Adivasi past

The construction of a past becomes a project that selectively organizes events in a relation of continuity with a contemporary subject, thereby creating an appropriated representation of a life leading up to the present, that is, a life history fashioned in the act of self-definition. Identity, here, is decisively a question of empowerment.

I would like here to recall the work of the Subaltern Studies Group which, in my view, has helped Adivasi communities to think of their own history. Ranajit Guha, the founder of the group tried to align historical reasoning with larger movements for democracy in India. The subalternist project had much in common with the history from below developed in English historiography by Thompson, Hobsbawm and others. These Marxist historians acknowledged a debt to Gramsci who was trying to move away from Stalinist readings of Marx. But, at the same time, Guha signals certain key points that would distinguish the subalternist project from English Marxist historiography.

First, as stressed by Chatterjee (2002: 8), subalternist historiography entailed a relative separation of the history of culture from universal histories of Capital. Second, subalternist historians started questioning the relation between power and knowledge, a paradigm which harbored a potential criticism of the Marxist concept of alienation of the masses. The subalternist project led these historians to write a kind of history which could bring more social justice and express democratic ideals (Chakravarty 2000). They have developed narratives of exploitation showing how Adivasi cultures have been deprived since the beginning of the colonial period (Guha 1983). Further, they demonstrate how narratives on marginalised communities finally recognise *adivasis* as active participants in the making of their own history (Haynes, Prakash 1991).

Performing indigeneity as a form of empowerment?

By the second half of the twentieth century, the mainstream Indian political discourse tended to identify Adivasis with their cultural heritage. The identification was institutionalised in different contexts, such as the Republic Day parade or fairs and markets. The cultural rights argument remains a powerful resource for mobilisation, and is often used by Adivasis themselves to assert their identity.

Berger (2014) distinguishes three types of indigeneity among the Gadaba of Odisha: the first kind, or indigenous indigeneity, turns on local sacrificial practices, processes where indigeneity is constructed. This type of indigeneity is local, symmetric, relational and created by the Gadaba themselves. By contrast, various forms of ascribed indigeneity are assigned unilaterally to the Gadaba, and the relationship here is asymmetrical and monolithic. The third type of indigeneity, the one that is claimed, is as yet nascent, as only a few Gadaba voice an indigenous identity in the larger political field; no cultural performances are staged and no political organisations exist to support such a claim. In some cases, the staging of indigeneity implies some ideological trap, as Prevost argues (2014) for the transformation of a Gond ritual into a dance competition, promoted by the government, in order to absorb the tribal people into Hindu society. But as he also stresses, the Gond resist this strategy by appropriating the stereotypes projected on them, through their musical performance.

The presence of Adivasis on the larger cultural scene takes various forms and implies different degrees of control by members of their own communities. Rousseleau (2013) shows that bronze art made by the Kondh is now promoted at the regional and federal levels as authentic Kondh art, but most of the brass images are now produced for foreign or urban Indian clients, taking inspiration from traditional Kondh models but also from the better known Bastari or Bengali dhokra bronzes. Similarly, the Sora and the Warli sell their paintings in the market under government initiative, but do not always benefit from the commercialisation of their art.

Santal writers today strategically transform selective contents of oral tradition into forms of counter-culture and expressions of protest against exploitation. When they show mine accidents on the stage, however, neither the companies nor the State accept it: often, they call for repression. It is clear that indigeneity may be displayed and even encouraged by the State, which provides support for some ethnic groups to build their own museums and encourages a variety of music and dance performances. This staging of indigeneity has certainly contributed to make the Adivasi more visible in the public sphere. But has it helped the Adivasi to feel less marginalised? All the groups are not able to perform indigeneity to the same extent, and State patronage is sometimes ambiguous as we have seen for the Gond dance. But when the government of Jharkhand recently acknowledged the animist cults as Sarna religion, the sacred groves came under the protection of the temple act, and the Adivasis realised their aim that higher castes would no longer be allowed to defile them.

The role of the anthropologist

Anthropologists should be explicit about their assumptions and try to interpret the way in which a community tries to stage its own assertion. Fields of research such as indigenous knowledge or the politics of representation must be central here. Other possible scholarly engagements concern the cultural rights argument, which remains a powerful resource for mobilisation. Anthropologists do seem to be able to dialogue with Adivasi, NGOs and even government institutions to help the diffusion of engaged tribal art and literature. They must listen to Adivasi voices, but desist from imposing their own categories. We have some universal ideas of what indigenous people's rights should be, but we must be aware of who speaks for whom. The idea of universal applicability of the rights of indigenous peoples should not preclude the realisation that there is a temporal element in the rights discourse.

Societies have different ways to historicize their struggle. This means that we, as anthropologists, should realise that local communities have their own strategies. The fact that cultural elements such as language, material culture or traditional institutions are endangered, does not necessarily justify our activism. We may deplore that Mundari youth sometimes forget their own language, but any program of language revitalisation should first try to identify the local demand. For example, when I published with Soren and Andersen the translation of Santal texts which had been written by Santals in the second part of the nineteenth century, we felt that the book had become an incentive for educated Santals who were trying to awaken their children's interest in their language and mythology. People's cultural choices are their own, though sometimes, of course they are not in a position to articulate these choices.

In some cases, anthropologists may be able to help bring about sustainable development, by analyzing, together with activists, the decisional processes which often escape the control of Adivasis. Anthropologists should work with villagers towards building a model of economy and polity which should be autonomous and satisfy the subsistence needs of the population without entering the ever rising spiral of consumption demand, which could not be sustained from an ecological point of view. Anthropologists cannot interfere directly in these decisions, but they can work at furthering the acknowledgement of indigenous knowledge.

Different assumptions have been made regarding the nature of indigenous knowledge, but I use the term to label indigenous understandings of the natural and social world. We should be concerned here with the issue of rights, since indigenous knowledge has become an entity subject to statutory recognition. But the environmentalist representations of indigenous people cannot alone define indigenous knowledge, since it is also informed by myths, narratives, symbolism and art.

The idea that knowledge may exist within different subsystems that are variously linked to each other suggests an important role for anthropologists. Through a better understanding of local knowledge systems, social scientists can work at identifying those truly specialised parts of local knowledge which are in danger of imminent loss, so as to focus resources on work to preserve endangered sectors of knowledge, like horticulture (Brodt 1999). Today, indigenous knowledge often represents a meaningful source of assertion. It is therefore becoming crucial to identify the sources from which such representations of indigenous knowledge emerge.

Another recommendation may concern the memory of indigenous societies, since it is crucial that endangered societies can reflect on their own past (mythical and historical), to experience a sense of belonging which may help them to make sense of their struggle, as did the Kwaio of New-Guinea, when they revived their concept of custom. As Keesing (1992: 238) wrote: "It is worth underlining again that although in a colonial situation the cultures and politics of subalternity are inherently oppositional, structured by 'a series of negations' they may be structured by 'affirmations' as well."

In order to resist assimilation indigenous peoples need to build local and translocal relationships to promote their cultural institutions or their art and to defend indigenous rights. The difficult issue seems to be to articulate local ideas of peoplehood with regional identities or even ideas about citizenship. The work of International Workgroup for Indigenous Affairs (IWGIA) and Survival International has been very important in publicizing the claims of indigenous peoples and the debates on associated legal issues, as well as bringing to the public eye atrocities committed against such groups. But anthropologists in dialogue with indigenous peoples must go further in analyzing the various entanglements of hegemony and domination. Anthropologists may contribute to the emergence of counterhegemonic thought among endangered societies, by paying attention to the dialectic of symbolic representation that the discourses of indigenous resistance provide.

Bibliography

Adhikari, Ashim Kumar (1984): *Society and World View of the Birhor.* Calcutta: Anthropological Survey of India.

Ardener, Edwin (1972): "Language, Ethnicity and Population", *Journal of the Anthropological Society of Oxford,* 3 (3), 125-132. Reprinted in E. Ardener (1989) *The Voice of Prophecy and Other Essays*. Oxford: Blackwell, 65-71.

Bailey, F. G. (1960): *Tribe, Caste and Nation: A Study of Political Activity and Political Change in Highland Orissa.* Manchester: Manchester University Press.

Berger, Peter (2014): "Dimensions of indigeneity in highland Odisha, India", *Asian Ethnology* 73 (2), 19-37.

Baviskar, Amita (1997): "Tribal politics and discourses of environmentalism", *Contributions to Indian Sociology* (n.s.) 31 (2), 195-233.

Bellier, Irène (2001): "Misunderstanding of autochthony vis-à-vis the question of indigenous peoples", in Q. Gausset, J. Kenrick, R. Gibb (eds.): *The Uses and Misuses of 'Indigeneity' and 'Autochthony', Special Issue of Social Anthropology* 19 (2), 204-206.

Béteille, André (1998): "The Idea of Indigenous People", *Current Anthropology* 19 (2), 187-191.

Bowen, J. R. (2000): "Should we have a Universal Concept of 'Indigenous Peoples's Rights'? Ethnicity and Essentialism in the Twenty-first Century", *Anthropology Today* 16 (4), 12-16.

Brosius, J. Peter (1997): "Endangered Forest, Endangered People: Environmentalist representations of Indigenous Knowledge", *Human Ecology* 25 (1), 47-69.

Brodt, Sonja (1999): "Interactions of formal and informal knowledge systems in village-based tree management in central India", *Agriculture and Human Values* 16 (4), 355-363.

Carrin, Marine (1986): *La Fleur et l'Os: symbolisme et rituel chez les Santal*. Paris: Cahiers de l'Homme, EHESS.

Carrin, Marine (1997): *Enfants de la Déesse, dévotion et prêtrise féminine au Bengale.* Paris: Editions du CNRS et MSH.

Carrin, Marine (2002): "Le retour du bosquet sacré. Réinvention d'une culture Adivasi", in M. Carrin, C. Jaffrelot (eds.), *Résistance et autonomie dans la société indienne, Purusartha* 23. Paris, 233-264.

Carrin, Marine (2012a): "The World of Tribes, Revolutionary Movements and Ethnic Withdrawal", in Chrisrophe Jaffrelot (ed.), *Contemporary India.* London: Penguin, 543-568.

Carrin, Marine (2012b): "The Hinduization of the tribal indigenous groups in India", in K. Jacobsen, H. Basu (eds.), *Brill Encyclopedia of Hinduism* Vol II. Leiden: Brill.

Carrin, Marine (2013a): "Jharkhand, Alternative Citizenship in an Adivasi State", in Peter Berger, Frank Heideman (eds.), *The Anthropology of Modern India.* London: Routledge: 185-198.

Carrin, Marine (2013b): "The Santal as an Intellectual", in Carrin Marine, Gérard Toffin, Pralay Kanungo (eds.), *The Politics of Ethnicity in India, Nepal and China.* Delhi: Primus, 77-99.

Carrin, Marine (2015a): *Le Parler des Dieux: Le discours rituel Santal entre l'oral et l'écrit.* Nanterre: Société d'Ethnologie.

Carrin, Marine (2015b): "Performing Indigeneity on a sacred hill, Logo Buru", *Anglistica AION: An Interdisciplinary Journal* 19 (1), 37-50.

Carrin, Marine (*forthcoming*): *Santal Local Knowledge and Sensitivity: beyond the Indian debate.*

Carrin, Marine and Tambs-Lyche (2008): *An Encounter of Peripheries: Santals, Missionaries and their Changing Worlds, 1867-1900.* Delhi: Manohar.

Carrin, Marine, Gérard Toffin, Pralay Kanungo (2013): "Introduction", in Carrin Marine, Gérard Toffin and Pralay Kanungo (eds.), *The Politics of Ethnicity in India, Nepal and China.* Delhi: Primus.

Census of India 2011 http://www.censusindia.gov.in/2011-common/census_2011.htm

Corbridge, Stuart (1988): "The Ideology of Tribal Economy and Society: politics in the Jharkhand 1950-1980", *Modern Asian Studies* 22, 16-42.

Corbridge, Stuart, Sarah Jewitt, Sanjay Kumar (2004): *Jharkhand: Environment, Development, Ethnicity.* Delhi: Oxford University Press.

Chatterjee, Partha (1994): *The Nation and Its Fragments: Colonial and Postcolonial Histories.* Delhi: Oxford University Press.

Damodaran, Vinita (1997): "Environment, Ethnicity and History in Chotanagpur, India 1850-1970", *Environment and History* 3, 273-298.

Damodaran, Vinita (2005). "Indigenous Forest Rights, Discourses and Resistance in Chotanagpur, 1860-2002", in Gunnel Cederlof, K. Sivaramakrishnan (eds.) *Ecological Nationalisms: Nature, Livelihoods, and Identities in South Asia.* Delhi: Permanent Black, 115-150.

Das Gupta, Sanjukta (2011): *Adivasis and the Raj Socio-economic Transistion of the Hos, 1820-1932.* Hyderabad: Orient Black Swan.

De la Cadena, Marisol, Orin Starn (eds.) (2007): *Indigenous Experience Today.* Oxford & New York: Berg.

Demmer, Ulrich (2001a): Always an Argument: Persuasive Tools in Jēnu Kurumba Death Rituals. *Anthropos* 96: 475-90.

Demmer, Ulrich (2001b): The Social Structure of the Jēnu Kurumba. In G. Pfeffer et al. (eds.), *Contemporary Society, Tribal Studies* 4. New Delhi: Concept Pub. Co., 234 – 265.

Demmer, Ulrich (2002): *The Rhetoric and Poetics of Ritual Performance: The Jenu Kummba*. An Interactive CD-ROM. Munich: Dept. of Anthropology, Munich University.

Fürer-Haimendorf, Christoph von (1943): *The Chenchu, Jungle Folk of the Deccan.* London: Macmillan.

Fürer-Haimendorf, Christoph von (1985): *Tribal Populations and Cultures of the Indian Subcontinent.* Leiden: E. J. Brill.

George, A.S. (2009): "The Paradox of Mining and Development" in Nandini Sundar (ed.). *Legal Grounds, Natural resources, Identity and the Law in Jharkhand*. Delhi: Oxford University Press, 158–88.

Ghosh, Kaushik (2006): "Global Flows and Local Dams: Indigenousness, Locality and the Transnational Sphere in Jharkhand, India", *Cultural Anthropology* 21 (4): 501-34.

Ghurye, G. (1959): *The Scheduled Tribes*. Bombay: Popular Prakashan.

Guha, Ranajit (1983): *Elementary Aspects of Peasant Insurgency in Colonial India.* Delhi: Oxford University Press.

Hockings, Paul (ed.) (1989): *Blue Mountains. The Ethnography and Biogeography of a South Indian Region.* Delhi: Oxford University Press.

Hockings, Paul Stuligross, D. (2008): "Resources, representation and authority in Jharkhand, India", *Asia Pacific Viewpoint* 49 (1), 83-97.

Hosbawm, Eric J. (1964): *Labouring Men. Studies in the History of Labour*. London: Weidenfeld and Nicholson.

Haynes, Douglas E., Gyan Prakash (1991): *Contesting Power: Resistance and Everyday Social Relations in South Asia*. Delhi: Oxford University Press.

Ingold, Tim (2000): *The perception of the environment. Essays in livelihoods, dwelling and skill*. London & New York: Routledge.

Karlsson, Bengt G. (2011): *Unruly Hills: A Political Ecology of India Northeast?* Oxford & New York: Berghahn.

Karlsson, Bengt G., Tanka B. Subha (2006): *Indigeneity in India.* London: Kegan Paul.

Keesing, Roger M. (1992): *Custom and Confrontation: The Kwaio Struggle for Cultural Autonomy*. Chicago: University of Chicago Press.

Kingsbury, Benedict (1998): "Indigenous peoples" in International Law: A Constructivist Approach to the Asian Controversy", *American Journal of International Law* 92 (3), 414–457.

Kymlicka, Will (1995): *Multicultural citizenship: a liberal theory of minority rights*. Oxford: Clarendon.

Li, Tania Murray (2010): Indigeneity, Capitalism and the Management of Dispossession. *Current Anthropology* 51 (3), 385-414.

Merlan, Francesca. (2009): "Indigeneity: Global and Local", *Current Anthropology* 50 (3), 303-333.

Morris, Brian (1982): *Forest Traders, A Socio-Economic Study of the Hill Pandaram*. New Jersey: The Athlone Press.

Munda, Ram Dayal, S. Bosu Mullick (2003): *The Jharkhand Movement Indigenous People's Struggle for Autonomy in India.* Copenhagen: IWGIA Document N0108.

Prévôt, Nicolas (2014): "The 'Bison Horn' Muria: Making it 'More Tribal' for a Folk Dance Competition in Bastar, Chhattisgarh", *Asian Ethnology* 73 (*Special Issue: The Bison and the Horn: Indigeneity, Performance, and the State of India*) (1/2): 201-231.

Ramos, Alcida Rita (1994): "From Eden to Limbo: The Construction of Indigenism in Brazil", in George Clement Bond, Angela Gilliam (eds.), *Social Construction of the Past: Representation as Power.* New York: Routledge, 74-88.

Ranger, Térence (1993): "The Invention of Tradition Revisited: The case of Colonial Africa", in T. Ranger, Olufemi Vaugham (eds.), *Legitimacy and the State in Twentieth Century Africa.* London: Pergrave McMillian.

Rousseleau, Raphaël (2013): "Tribal Artisans and artists in Odisha/ Between Craft Promotion and 'Ethnic Tourism'", in Carrin Marine, Gérard Toffin, Pralay Kanungo (eds.), *The Politics of Ethnicity in India, Nepal and China.* Delhi: Primus, 121-134.

Rycroft, Dan, Dasgupta Sangeeta (eds.) (2010): *The Politics of Belonging in India: Becoming Adivasi.* Routledge: Abingdon.

Schulte-Droesch, Léa (2014): "Fertility or Indigeneity: Two versions of the Santal Flower Festival", *Asian Ethnology* 73 (*Special Issue: The Bison and the Horn: Indigeneity, Performance, and the Sate of India*) (1&2),155-180.

Sharma, Aradhana, Akhil Gupta (eds.) (2006): *The Anthropology of the State: A Reader.* Oxford: Maiden, M A and Blackwell.

Sundar, Nandini (2009): *Legal Grounds. Natural Resources, Identity, and the Law in Jharkhand.* Delhi: Oxford.

Prasad, Arshana (2003): *Against Ecological Romanticism, Verrier Elwin and the Making of an Anti-Modern Tribal Identity.* Delhi: Three Essays.

Thompson, E.P. (1963): *The Making of the English Working Class*, London: Pantheon.

Xaxa, Virginius (1999): "Tribes as Indigenous People of India", *Economic and Political Weekly* 34 (51), 3589-95.

Zide, N. (ed.) (1966): *Studies in Comparative Austro-Asiatic Linguistics.* La Haye: Mouton.

Hints of Ontology in Eastern Gujarat: Structures of Space in Rathva Cultural Practices

Gregory D. Alles
McDaniel College[1]

Abstract

This essay explores what I am calling hints of ontology in cultural practices associated with Rathva traditionalists. Rathvas are the dominant ethnic group in the eastern half of the new district of Chhotaudepur in Gujarat state, India. Although some have received formal education and are now joining Hindu *sampradayas*, this essay focuses on cultural practices among those who have not done so. It would be difficult to identify ontology among Rathva traditionalists in the sense of an explicit account of being such as one finds in some Indian and European philosophers, such as Adisankaracarya, Nagarjuna, or Heidegger. It is, however, possible to tease out ontological implications from what Rathvas have traditionally said and done. While many ontological themes are worth pursuing – for example, structures of time, concepts of speciation, and the boundary between persons and things – this essay concentrates on implicit Rathva conceptualisations of space. Sources for such conceptualisations include traditional mantras and stories, material religious structures, ritual activities, and Rathva paintings, which have started to make their mark on the international art market. In all of these products Rathva space transcends the rigid, bounded structures associated with the kind of three-

[1] I first visited Chhotaudepur *taluka* in July 1998 on a day trip organised by the Bhasha Research and Publication Centre, Vadodara, at the invitation of Ganesh Devy. I am indebted to them and to the Adivasi Academy in Tejgadh for abundant and gracious hospitality over the years. It is difficult to list all in the area who have contributed to my knowledge of Rathva culture, but at the least I should acknowledge the help of the following: Babubhai Harijan (Moti Sadhli), Arjun Rathva (Moti Sadhli), Ashvinbhai Rathva (Kanalva), Dashrath Rathva (Kocvad), Desing Rathva (Rangpur), Haribhai Rathva (Malaja), Kanubhai Rathva (Chhotaudepur), Kocar Rathva (Gabadiya), Mansing Rathva (Malaja), Naranbhai Rathva (Tejgadh), and Subhash Ishai (Chhotaudepur). Research visits were made possible by the generous support of the Fulbright program, U.S.A. (2009), and the Faculty Development Committee of McDaniel College.

dimensional Euclidean and Newtonian space that many North Americans and Europeans unreflectively presume are "normal." Specifically, Rathvas employ concepts of both superimposition and collocation to imagine that the space which we ordinary human beings inhabit is open. This openness in turn allows Rathvas to interact with beings who inhabit other realms, most importantly, *devs, devis,* and ancestors.

Presumably we all operate with implicit convictions about what is real and what is not. Most of the time we simply take these convictions for granted, and this is probably a good thing. Doing so makes it possible for us to survive in a way that constant questioning about reality would not.

But what exactly are we taking for granted? It is often difficult to say. For example, it is easy enough to talk about a worldview of hegemonic, globalizing modernity, dominated by the natural sciences as epitomised by contemporary or more probably classical physics. Yet a number of different ontologies are more or less compatible with this modern worldview, and careful philosophical discussions of them may bear little resemblance to what many of us non-philosophers take the natural scientific worldview to be, namely, materialistic reductionism. In fact, these discussions can quickly leave many of us scratching our heads or teetering on a wobbly perch. Here is an example from David Chalmers' book, *The Conscious Mind* (1996). In this book Chalmers defends a position that he calls property or naturalistic dualism by arguing that even though phenomenal experiences may in fact be naturally supervenient on microphysical processes, they are not logically supervenient on them (see further Chalmers 2010). From this he draws the following conclusions:

> The ontology that this leads us to might truly be called a double-aspect ontology. Physics requires information states but cares only about their relations, not their intrinsic nature; phenomenology requires information states, but cares only about the intrinsic nature. This view postulates a single basic set of information states unifying the two. We might say that internal aspects of these states are phenomenal, and the external aspects are physical. Or as a slogan: Experience is information from the inside; physics is information from the outside. (Chalmers 1996: 305)

A section heading of the book, obviously inspired by computer science, states the position more succinctly: "It from bit" (Chalmers 1996: 302). On this view, what is fundamentally real is not matter or matter conceived of as convertible into energy and vice versa; it is information.

I do not want to consider the worldview – or as I would prefer to say, worldviews – of globalizing modernity in any detail here. Instead, I want to explore what is arguably a worldview that is in the process of being marginalised and endangered by global modernity's expansion. It is the worldview implicit in traditional cultural practices among *adivasis* (indigenous people) in eastern central Gujarat known as Rathvas.[2] Specifically, I want to try to uncover implicit convictions about the structures of space within these practices, convictions that I am calling hints of ontology. As a preliminary to this endeavor, the previous paragraph gives us two warnings. First, it warns us against drawing contrasts too quickly with what we assume is "the" dominant, Western ontology. It is all too easy to schematize the marginal and the dominant, the traditional and the modern, the oral and the literate, or the natural and the cultural in terms of binary opposites. This schematisation is one that needs to be resisted.[3] Second, the previous paragraph also warns us against expecting inevitably to find a single, coherent ontology within the practices that I will be examining. While there is a natural rhetorical tendency to favor the presentation of larger, more coherent systems rather than smaller fragments, there is no reason for marginalised or endangered worldviews to be any more unitary and coherent than those associated with hegemonic, globalizing modernity.

Who, Where, and What

Rathvas (Rahwa's) are the dominant ethnic group in the easternmost *talukas* (sub-districts) of Chhotaudepur District in the state of Gujarat, India. Because Chhotaudepur District was only created from the eastern half of Vadodara District in 2013 – that is, after the last Census in 2011 – firm population statistics for it are sometimes difficult to come by. For example, population statistics for the various *adijati* (*adivasi* or tribal groups) are not publicly available at any level lower than the District, with the result that 2011 statistics present the populations of what are now Vadodara and Chhotaudepur Districts together. Just how dominant the Rathvas are, then, is not clearly quantifiable. Nevertheless, it is still possible to say a few things about them.

The Rathvas whom I know live primarily in Chhotaudepur and Kavant *talukas*.[4] The population of these *talukas* is overwhelmingly rural; it is also over-

2 *Adivasi* is a construct in modern, Sanskrit-based languages with the root meaning "original inhabitant." It is a self-designation that many *adivasi* people prefer. Although the government of India does not recognize the existence of indigenous people, *adivasis* think of themselves as indigenous. In legal terms the people whom I will be discussing belong to what are known as "Scheduled Tribes," hence the term "tribal," which is also a designation which the people themselves use.

3 In the field in which I was trained, the history of religions, the paradigmatic exemplar of this schematisation is Mircea Eliade. This is not, however, to deny differences, sometimes profound differences, between indigenous and non-indigenous worldviews. An excellent, recent exploration of these differences is Cadena 2015.

4 Chhotaudepur is the name of a district, *taluka* or sub-district, a town which is now the seat of the district government, and a former princely state roughly co-terminous with Chhotaudepur and Kavant *talukas*.

whelmingly tribal. According to the 2011 Census, out of the 241,377 residents of Chhotaudepur *taluka*, only 10.7% (25,787) lived in a town (Chhotaudepur town). The population of Kavant *taluka* was even more rural: only 4.5% of the population – 9,553 residents out of 210,002 – lived in a town (Kavant town). In addition, *adivasis* were more heavily represented in rural than in urban areas. While they accounted for only 24.7% and 42.2% of the populations of Chhotaudepur and Kavant towns, respectively, their share of the rural population was much greater: 95.1% for Chhotaudepur *taluka* and 96% for Kavant *taluka*. *Adivasis* who live in town engage in a variety of occupations; as an educator, I know educators – primary, secondary, and tertiary – the best. Most rural households support themselves through agriculture or manual labor. Agriculture is still customarily done with a bullock-drawn, single-furrow plow.

Literacy among the rural population, and so among rural *adivasis*, remains low. In 2011 only 31.7% of the rural population of Chhotaudepur *taluka* and 36.4% of the rural population of Kavant *taluka* were counted as literate (rural male literacy: Chhotaudepur *taluka* – 38.3%, Kavant taluka – 45.2%; rural female literacy: Chhotaudepur *taluka* – 25%, Kavant *taluka* – 27.5%).[5] Nevertheless, literacy is improving, and especially those with formal education find various proselytizing Hindu *sampradayas*, such as the Sat Kaival and Swaminarayan movements, attractive. People who join such movements are known as *bhagats*. They give up eating meat and drinking alcohol, adopt new ways of worship, and in theory at least become acquainted with various formalised teachings.[6] They are not my concern here. In this essay I will focus instead on *jagats*, that is, on *adivasis* who have not joined such movements. They are seen locally as maintaining – or retaining – *adivasi* traditions.

In another article (Alles forthcoming) I have suggested that Rathva *jagats* construct ritual places rather than sacred spaces. To borrow a term from postcolonial cultural analysis, Rathva rituals take place at "contact zones" (Pratt 1991; Clifford 1997; Carrasco 2004; Chidester 2008), but these are not places where *adivasis* encounter and interact with other human groups. I am using the term instead to identify a fundamental aspect of Rathva ritual. Rituals are performed at places where human beings can contact *devs* (gods), *devis* (goddesses), and *purvajo* (ancestors),[7] and they involve a distinctive dynamic. First, borders are constructed as sites of ritual practice, whether by amplifying previously existing borders such as

5 I do not have access to literacy statistics for different age cohorts. These days, however, Rathva villages are served by a strong school system, and Rathvas are very conscious of the need for education. Over time, as older generations give way to younger ones, these figures should change.

6 In some cases this acquaintance is quite extensive. See, for example, Rathva 2015a, 2015b.

7 The English term "ancestor" seems rather unproblematic as a translation for *purvajo*, that is, one's forebears who have died. *Dev* and *devi* are more problematic, and I prefer to retain the original. For brief commentary, see Alles 2013.

mountains or walls or by building new ones. Then the constructed borders are breached through ritual practice. The breaching occurs when gifts are sent across the borders to *devs, devis,* and ancestors and when, in return, *devs, devis,* and ancestors cross the borders to possess ritualists known as *badva*. In an attempt to make sense of this activity, I pointed in part to the kinesthetic image schemata identified by Mark Johnson (Johnson 1987, 2007) and utilised by George Lakoff (Lakoff 1987), but what is of greater importance here is a consequence of the analysis: these ritual practices do not require Rathvas to have any concept of an explicitly ordered sacred space, whether as a sanctuary, a *temenos*, an Eliadean cosmos, or some other form. In Rathva rituals, the border stands at the center, metaphorically but at times literally as well. There is no need for a well-demarcated periphery, such as a fence or wall, and frequently there is none.

How, then, do *jagats* conceive of – or perhaps more accurately, "pre-conceive" of – space? By "space" I mean roughly the framework within which organic beings of whatever sort live and inorganic objects subsist. I use the verb "pre-conceive" because, so far as I know, Rathva *jagats* have no systematic, detailed, and explicit ontological accounts such as one finds in Indian and European philosophers like Adisankaracarya, Nagarjuna, and Heidegger. Nor do *jagats* generally engage in abstract discussions about the structure of space. In this respect (and many others), they are not unlike most people. Nevertheless, hints about space are implicit in what Rathvas have traditionally done and said, and in this essay I want to try to tease them out. I readily admit that doing so leaves unaddressed many other ontological questions, among them questions about time (cf., briefly, Clifford 2013: 21-27), the distinction between persons and things, and speciation (cf. Hallowell 1960; Harvey 2006; Cadena 2015). Space is, however, an expansive enough topic for one essay.

Framing the Question

Jagat religious practices center on visible physical borders. Common examples include:

- free-standing structures two to three feet high consisting of two uprights and a crossbeam and usually thought of as gateways, either as *darvaja* (more massive) or *toran* (less massive);
- a line of *kalam* and *kalo* branches, temporarily constructed in an empty field, that forms the backdrop to the various forms of a major outdoor ceremony known as Ind *puja* (Alles 2015);
- a wall on which has been painted a depiction of the *dev* Babo Pithoro's wedding procession, itself surrounded by a border with an opening painted at the bottom center – the widely discussed Pithora paintings (see esp. Shah 1980; Jain 1984; Pandya 2004; Ishai 2008, 2015b; Tilche 2011, 2015);

- relatively massive posts, often carved from teak, known as *khunta*, again about two to three feet in height, that mark places where *devs, devis,* and ancestors may be addressed, often placed in a row, whether in *devsthan* ("*dev* places") on untillable land or *khatris* (shrines to ancestors) on the borders of fields (Stiglmayr 1963);
- and *thamblio*, thinner posts set against a wall or corner in a house, usually in the kitchen, for addressing the family's *devs, devis,* and ancestors.

While these structures mark and construct spatial barriers and discontinuities, they do not separate a sanctuary from the surrounding territory, as in the case of an ancient Greek *temenos* or the territory around Mecca. To put it more abstractly, they do not isolate and protect the sacred from the profane, as someone working in the tradition of Émile Durkheim (1965) or Mircea Eliade (1959) might expect. It would be wrong to say that barriers separating the sacred from the profane are entirely unknown among Rathvas. For example, occasionally stone walls surround village *devsthan*, as at Ganthiya, Chathawada, and Bedvi, and I once saw a rather flimsy, *ad hoc* fence set up around the branches at Ind *puja*.[8] In my experience, however, barriers of these sorts are rare, and they are not necessary. In most cases the space immediately in front of ritual borders merges seamlessly with the space around it. What counts ritually is the border between human beings and their *devs, devis,* and ancestors.

Here, then, is our first hint of ontology: Rathva space is not closed but open. By "closed space," I mean space that is self-contained. In terms of Mark Johnson's schema of the container (Johnson 1987: 30-40), it is all inside with no outside. Closed space does not absolutely preclude the existence of other spaces, but if the space that we inhabit is closed, it is the only space that we human beings have access to. The implication is not that, if we travel far enough in closed space, we will eventually encounter a wall or other barrier that obstructs all forward movement. Such a boundary would imply, kinesthetically as well as logically, the existence of something on the other side. A better example of closed space would be the two-dimensional surface of a sphere, such as the surface of the earth on which we live. No absolute physical barriers prevent us from circling the earth, but we are still bound in its finite space. In order to escape from this space, an additional dimension is required: up/down. Although our minds have a hard time

[8] Other *devsthan* may be surrounded by stone walls as well. There are 275 recognised villages in Chhotaudepur and Kavant *talukas*, and I have only visited a fraction of them, the majority within proximity of the Chhotaudepur-Alirajpur road. I have only seen a fence erected around the Ind *puja* branches at the celebration of Gamshahi in the village of Manka on the night of January 7-8, 2009. At a dedication of a Pithora painting at Ambala village on the night of January 23-24, 2013, the Ind *puja* branches were similarly surrounded by a fence, but at a Gamshahi celebration in the village of Kachchel on the same night they were not. I know about the celebrations at Ambala and Kachchel from photos shared by Subhash Ishai.

visualizing it, it is possible for three dimensional space to turn back on itself the way the surface of a sphere does and so be closed, too.

In contrast to closed space, open space somehow permits something or someone to traverse its boundaries; as a result, it provides access to other spaces. This, too, is hard to visualize, although science fiction films, with their tesseracts, worm holes, and portals have certainly provided us with some visual images to associate with it. The point I want to make is that the space one encounters in Rathva rituals is open, not closed. The ritual borders that Rathvas construct do not separate two different parts of our space, the way village boundaries separate what lies within the village from what lies outside of it or the way the walls of a sacred precinct demarcate the sacred interior from the profane exterior. In Rathva rituals, the space on all sides of the constructed borders, whether a Pithora painting or Ind *puja* branches or a border of some other kind, belongs to the space that we inhabit. But the borders suggest, kinesthetically and imaginatively, that at these places people have access to another space where organic, person-like beings of a different order live: the space – or spaces – of the *devs, devis,* and ancestors.[9]

The observation that Rathva space is open, not closed, leads to further questions. How, for example, do Rathvas imagine the various spaces as being structured? How do they imagine them as relating to one another? I do not think that there are any definitive answers to these questions. Rathvas do not think explicitly about ontology any more than the rest of us do, unless we happen to be philosophers specifically interested in the topic. But the mind inevitably operates with implicit assumptions, even if they are not clearly articulated in concepts; indeed, it often seems to operate with assumptions that run counter to our explicitly formulated convictions (cf. Slone 2004; more broadly Kahneman 2011). Several kinds of evidence from Rathva cultural practices contain hints of these implicit assumptions. Here I want to examine hints found in two distinct kinds: physical, visible representations in Rathva rituals, and verbal representations in Rathva stories, songs, and mantras – what in earlier days we might have called myths. Let me emphasize again that there is no reason to expect these hints to result in a coherent system, or even in two coherent systems, one for rituals and another for stories. It is not uncommon for people to maintain two or more positions that, strictly speaking, are mutually incompatible. Consider Christians who think that their relatives are in heaven with God immediately after death, but who also maintain that there will be a judgment at the end of time to determine the eternal fate of all people, presumably including their relatives. Note, too, that the extent to which the implicit assumptions about space that we find in Rathva rituals and stories are present in everyday thinking needs to be determined by other means, such as the

9 For convenience I will speak of the space rather than the spaces of the *devs*, *devis*, and ancestors. I will also occasionally employ the phrase "space of the *devs*," which is, of course, sexist, but which also reflects Rathva ways of speaking.

story-recall tasks utilised in the study of religions by Justin Barrett (e.g., Barrett and Nyhof 2001).

Visible Representations in Ritual

Let us start with what I consider to be the most vivid representation of interaction between *devs* and human beings in Rathva ritual, *darvaja* and *toran* (gateways), especially when these are fitted out with terracotta figures. A particularly impressive example sits on a ledge halfway up the sacred mountain (or tall hill) of Vaghasthal, across the Orsang River from Chhotaudepur town.

This location, which I visited a number of times between 2009 and 2013, is the subject of ritual attention on special occasions, such as the *mela* held at its foot on the fifth day of Holi (*rangpanchami*), as well as on Thursdays in the early afternoon. The ledge on which the *darvajo* sits is roughly 22 feet long, running more or less north and south along the western side of the mountain (cardinal directions only approximate), and it has been paved smooth with concrete. The entrance is on the northern end, and although the width varies, it is perhaps 17 feet wide where the *darvajo* sits on the southern end, perpendicular to the north-south axis. The *darvajo* itself is a rich complex consisting of the following:

- in front, two stout *khunta* (posts), carved octagonally in cross-section, just under three feet tall and nine to ten inches across[10]; the posts sit five feet apart and are painted in vertical stripes of red, dark green, and light yellow-green with decorations in white;
- close behind the posts, two more upright posts, roughly 30 inches tall and five inches in cross-section, surmounted by a cross-beam, roughly four and a half inches square in cross-section, that arches gently up in the middle; these posts and the crossbeam are painted with the same colors as the *khunta* in front of them, and the crossbeam is decorated with tailless arrows pointing to the left;
- twelve inches behind the posts with the crossbeam, two more freestanding *khunta*, similar to those in front; these, however, are not painted (or perhaps are no longer painted; they seem to be an earlier installation), but they sport *tipna*, orange-red dots applied while reciting mantras;
- twenty inches behind the second set of *khunta*, two more upright pillars with a crossbeam, also unpainted but with *tipna*; and finally
- roughly two feet behind the second set of upright pillars with crossbeam, a low wall made of flat stones with pointed tops, set upright against the face of the mountain; it marks the end of the ledge.

---

10 All measurements were taken in January 2012 at a time when the area was deserted except for me and a Rathva friend. The size of the ledge and the posts of the installation should be relatively constant. The images mentioned below vary over time in size. number, and design.

This elaborate complex enables interaction with the world of *devs, devis,* and ancestors in a particularly powerful way. While the personal beings themselves are not represented, their vehicles are – in the form of terracotta figures placed in a line at the front of the complex and in rows between the various posts. These figures face the viewers, so that they seem to be coming through the gates and, if they could move, out onto the ledge. They consist mostly of horses between nine and 23 inches tall,but they also include other figures, such as *dhaba* (miniature "temples" where *devs* may live, somewhat resembling stupas but with openings on their sides for entrances), horses and riders, an elephant, and a tiger. The figures are purchased from non-*adivasi* potters, and they are often left unglazed, but white, black, and green glazed figures are generally present as well. To perform *puja*, one faces the complex – and so the figures – and places burning oil lamps on small piles of rice in front of them; one also offers flowers, incense, coconuts, and perhaps *mahua* liquor. (I have not seen animal sacrifice at this site.) In doing so, one greets the figures as they come into our world. When *puja* is not being performed, the figures remain, striding out to meet whoever happens to visit.[11] There is nothing particularly unusual about the figures themselves. They are commonly found at *darvaja*, *toran*, and free-standing posts of all kinds. What distinguishes this particular site are not the elements from which it is constructed but rather the degree of elaboration with which they have been combined.

Consider what this structure implies about space, specifically about the space within which *devs, devis,* and ancestors exist and how it relates to our own space. Somehow, these two spaces exist in a state of collocation; they are proximate to one another. Of course, collocation and proximity can only be taken metaphorically here. Literally they apply to objects that exist within the same space, not to two different spaces. But by its very structure, the elaborate *darvajo* hints, as do all *darvaja* and *toran* and other ritual borders, that it is possible to bring these two spaces together, whether permanently or temporarily, so that they overlap or at least open out onto one another.

As a simple contrast can help us see, however, the *darvajo* on Vaghasthal hints at a spatial relationship that is more specific than mere collocation. It has been customary for Christians and Muslims to locate their god in a space they call heaven and to envision it in terms of verticality: heaven is above the earth. One sees indications of this conception of space not only in common phrases ("Our father in heaven") and stories (Jesus's ascension; Muhammad's Miʿ raj) but also in built environments, such as the many churches whose ceilings have been painted or otherwise decorated to depict or suggest the heavenly realm, and, more abstractly, the domes of mosques under which people pray. Of course, today most Christians and Muslims are well aware that the earth is a sphere, and that the

11 I am, then, presuming an exchange model of Rathva ritual, but I will not elaborate on it here.

space which we humans experience as "above" actually surrounds the earth in every direction. This awareness has not, however, stopped them from using vertical images to point to the unique realm of the divine. Mircea Eliade even made this verticality into an archetype that underlay all religion. He called it the *axis mundi*.

There is some hint of verticality in the constructions on the ledge at Vaghasthal. After all, they are located halfway up a mountain. On Babo Tundvo, another ritually significant mountain some distance to the northeast of Vaghasthal, the main locus for ritual is not halfway up the mountain but actually on the summit (Alles forthcoming). Aside from these two sacred mountains however, very little in Rathva ritual practice actually seems to employ vertical references as a means to hint at the presence of an alternative space.[12] As on the ledge at Vaghasthal, the experience of the presence of the *devs* is primarily an experience of horizontality, of a space that lies adjacent to our own and on the same level. One way to contrast this kind of alternative space with a space like heaven is in terms of the primary physical and social experiences upon which the two depend. The Christian and Muslim conception of heaven signals the presence of an alternative space by metaphorically extending the range of "over" (cf. Lakoff 1987: 416-459). Rathva ritual, however, does not do this. Instead, it signals the presence of an alternative space by imaginatively extending the horizontal space that meets our eyes as we stand upright and survey our world. Perhaps it is even better to say that it metaphorically extends the human experience of meeting other people and other organic beings to include the human encounter with *devs*. One may wonder about the effect of these two different means for imagining alternative spaces upon the manner in which the beings who inhabit them are also imagined. In one sort of space there are beings who stand over and above human beings; in Christianity and Islam, these beings are, of course, God and angels. In the other sort of space there are beings whom we humans meet on our own level, if not exactly as equals. To what extent these characterisations provide insight into any Rathva ways of thinking about *devs*, *devis*, and ancestors I am not at the moment prepared to say.

The dynamic of collocating spaces also appears in the best known element of Rathva culture, Pithora paintings, although with a couple of twists. A Pithora is a painting that fills the wall separating the verandah of a house from its interior rooms, generally a kitchen and a sleeping room. It takes its name from its central element, the *jan* or wedding procession of the *dev* Babo Pithoro, depicted as a line of at least five horses and riders riding from right to left. Different people assign different names to the various riders, but a Pithora is generally said to represent at least Babo Pithoro, his step-mother Rani Kajal, his wife Pithori, and the *dev*

12 Exceptions would be Koraj Hill north of Tejgadh (cf. Tilche 2011), and, farther away, Pavagadh in Panch Mahals District and Mount Abu in Rajasthan.

Ganeh, sometimes taken to be Ganesh. Unlike *darvaja*, *toran*, and various posts, then, a Pithora is a visual representation of both the world of the *devs* and the *devs* themselves.

The rest of the Pithora depicts the space in which the *jan* takes place. Along the edges is a rectangular border, which follows the edges of the wall itself – at least until it reaches the doorway to the interior, which is usually on the right. I have heard this border identified as both a village border and the border of the world. At the bottom center is an opening, sometimes depicted as a *toran*, which provides access to the space of the painting – ritually as well as visually, because it is here that the bloody severed necks of sacrificed animals are daubed. The remainder of the space is filled with juxtaposed groups. They represent divine and legendary beings, such as the fates and Raja Bhoj (a king of Malwa in the 11th century), scenes from human life, such as milking, fetching water, plowing, and hunting, and certain hybrid beings, the most prominent of whom is probably a man with twelve matchstick-like heads who is often identified as Ravana. Different painters paint the groups of figures in blank spaces that happen to be available when they decide to paint them, and this has an inevitable effect on the composition of the painting. Although the painting constitutes a unity, it is not a unity that creates an overall sense of perspective. For the most part Pithoras look like two-dimensional flatlands: various two-dimensional or quasi-three-dimensional groups strewn across a blank white field.

Pithoras lack, then, the kind of perspective that European paintings developed in the Renaissance; they most definitely lack the perspectival trickery that characterizes *trompe l'oeil* paintings. Furthermore, their figures are painted in solid colors – red, blue, green, yellow, whatever colors are available in the market – with dark outlines but without shading or shadows. As a result, no one would mistake a Pithora for the visible world or even for a photographic image of that world. Nevertheless, Pithoras have something of the same effect as *trompe l'oeil* paintings: they offer visual glimpses into a different space, the space where *devs* live. They are, however, more windows than doors: we see into that space, but we do not enter it, and its beings do not enter ours. While the horses and other animal figures at *darvaja* and *toran* appear to be coming into our world, most of the figures in a Pithora are shown in profile, facing left. They remain firmly fixed in their own space. The principal exceptions are two tigers that are often painted on either side of the opening in the bottom border – the entrance to the space of the painting. With huge grins, these guardians look squarely at the viewers, addressing anyone or anything that would care to enter. Thus, Pithoras do not visually signal interaction between the two spaces, as *darvaja* and *toran* do with their terracotta figures. Instead, they juxtapose the space of the *devs* with our space. The general effect is, once again, one of collocation, and once again horizontal. We do not look up to perceive it; we look straight ahead.

This observation, however, is not sufficient, for Pithoras present us with two further ontological twists. As visual depictions of the *devs* and the space they inhabit, Pithoras can introduce elements that *darvaja* and *toran* cannot. One element that they introduce concerns the structure of the space itself. They suggest that the space of the *devs* has two tiers; it consists of both earth and sky. For example, it is customary to paint a wavy line above the wedding procession, which is said to be a canopy (*achad*). Its placement, together with that of the sun and moon above it, visually links the top portion of the Pithora with the space of the sky. Appropriately, this is where we encounter the horses of the rains. Other figures hint at this vertical dimension, too. The most common is a spider portrayed with a thread that hangs down vertically. From the Rathva perspective, this is no ordinary spider and no ordinary thread. The spider is Mama Kolya – "mama" means maternal uncle, not mother – and the thread is the thread up which various heroes, such as Dudho Raval and Babo Pithoro, are said to have climbed to heaven (Rathvi *haragu*; Gujarati *svarg*). To judge from a Pithora, then, the structure of the space of the *devs* parallels that of our own.

Pithoras also introduce yet another ontological twist that is not found in *darvaja* and *toran*, one that concerns not the structure of the space of the *devs* but how it relates to our own space. They depict the *devs* alongside people engaged in the activities of daily life: fetching water, plowing, milking, churning, and so on. These figures may be taken as our *Doppelgänger*. In this case, the *devs* would inhabit a universe that is completely parallel to our own. It is also possible, however, to read Pithoras in another way and take them as showing *devs* intermingling with us. On this reading a Pithora would be more like a mirror than a window; on its surface one sees reflections of beings who are present in our world, but who are not ordinarily visible to the naked eye. In other words, the space of the *devs* is not located next to our world; it is superimposed upon it.

Both the structure of Pithoras and their use in Rathva rituals would seem to reinforce this sense of the superimposition of one space upon the other. For example, during rituals Pithoras receive *puja*, rendering them both wall-painting and *dev*. That is to say, the painting itself superimposes the space of the *devs* – its content – upon the space of the wall, the space in which we live. In doing so, it makes visible aspects of space to which human beings do not ordinarily have access.

At least one other visible aspect of Rathva ritual, a more dramatic one, also hints that the space of the *devs* is superimposed upon quotidian space. I am thinking of occurrences of ritual possession, in which a *dev* takes over a human body. A classic instance occurs in the dedication of a Pithora. After a Pithora is painted, Rathvas perform an all night ritual in the course of which various *devs* and *devis*, including Babo Pithoro himself, enter the body of a ritual functionary known as a *badvo*. In this possessed state the *badvo* identifies the various figures in the Pithora, corrects any mistakes that the painters may have made, performs various dances in the person of various *devs*, and holds consultations with various persons as if he were himself the *dev*. *Badva* get possessed in similar fashion in front of the Ind *puja* branches.

A *badvo*'s possession is accepted and expected, but it is not the only form of possession that Rathvas know. On Thursday mornings at Vaghasthal, women become possessed and make entreaties concerning personal and familial welfare. In the eyes of many Rathvas, this form of possession violates social norms, and they consider the women who get possessed to be witches who should be avoided. Such normative judgments do not, however, alter the ontological implications of their practice. In both cases, the possession of *badva* and that of women, *devs* are superimposed upon the human body. At least for as long as the possession lasts, the spaces in which human beings and *devs* exist overlap one another.

Let us summarize the hints of ontology that we have found in Rathva ritual practice. As one might expect, they largely concern the relations between the space of the everyday world and the space populated by *devs*, *devis*, and ancestors. These relations are of two basic types. A variety of ritual representations, notably *darvaja* and *toran*, represent these two spaces as collocated. They stand next to one another and are linked, so to speak, by portals, across which certain kinds of movement from one space to the other are possible. This collocation differs, however, from the collocation familiar from traditional Christian and Muslim notions of heaven. It is horizontal, not vertical. That is, one encounters the space of the *devs* not by looking up, but by looking straight ahead. Other ritual representations suggest a second type of relationship, namely, superimposition. Pithora paintings and possession experiences suggest that the space which *devs*, *devis*, and ancestors inhabit is superimposed upon our space, whether permanently or temporarily. It is all around us; it is simply not accessible to ordinary perception. There are relatively few hints about the internal structure of the space which *devs*, *devis*, and ancestors inhabit – or ours, for that matter – but Pithora paintings contain at least one hint: the world which these other beings inhabit has significant vertical extension. Like our world, it is divided into two tiers, earth and sky.

Verbal Representations in Songs and Stories

To this point we have examined ontological hints that have come from a phenomenology of mind-body experience centered on Rathva rituals and their settings. Inasmuch as our conceptions of space seem to be primarily shaped by the movements of our bodies within it (cf., e.g., Johnson 1987, 2007; Tweed 2006; Vásquez 2011; Gill 2012), this approach would seem to be appropriate. As already noted, however, hints of ontology appear in several cultural practices, mantras, *gayna* (*bhajan*, songs), and stories among them. Word limits do not permit a detailed examination of these practices here, but they deserve at least a quick glance, because they contain ontological hints that are not entirely commensurate with those that we have found in rituals. I take as my example *gayna* currently being prepared for publication by Subhash Ishai (S.N. College, Chhotaudepur).[13] These *gayna* were recited in 1999 by Chuniya Biliya Rathva, a *badvo* of Moti Jher village (Chhoteudepur *taluka*) in Ishai's house in Chhotaudepur. They are, then, artificial recitations rather than live performances at rituals, but they do represent detailed traditional accounts from an old, respected *badvo* who has since died. They are also recitations that I know well, inasmuch as I have been advising Ishai on translation into English (Ishai 2015b). The *gayna* comprise a narrative cycle that begins with the arising of Dharti Madi (Mother Earth) and Meghraja (the Rain King) and continues through the generations of Dudho Raval, his son Indraj and daughters Kali Koyal and Rani Mokher, and culminates with Kali Koyal's son, Babo Pithoro.

In terms of ontology, these *gayna* allow for richer commentary on topics related to speciation and time than on those related to space. To take just one prominent example: it is not entirely clear to what extent Pithoro's mother, Kali Koyal, is literally a black cuckoo, which is what her name means, and to what extent she is a human-like person. Characteristics of the two intermingle. When she sweeps out Raja Bhoj's cowshed with a golden broom, she seems quite human (aside from the broom); after all, *we* know Raja Bhoj as a historical king from the 11th century C.E. She seems similarly human when her belly swells in pregnancy. After delivery, however, her characteristics shift toward the avian. She flits to and fro upon the branches of various trees, and as she does, trickles of her blood lend to various fruits their distinctive coloration. Such a blurring of the lines of speciation is, of course, hardly unique to the Rathvas, but we cannot pause to consider it in further detail here.

The geography of the narratives is somewhat more determinate. Some spaces appear to be clearly localised on earth. When Bhoola Bharvad is born, he walks to Indore. During the ninth month of Jahurani's pregnancy, she and Dudho Raval walk through Indore and Dhar. After Kali Koyal gives birth to Pithoro, she flees to Dhar. (She flees because Pithoro was conceived as a result of a rape, and she has hidden the pregnancy from her brother Indraj.) Clearly the region of Dhar and Indore, now two contiguous districts in Madhya Pradesh that lie on the opposite side of Alirajpur District from Chhotaudepur District, are significant in the narratives, as is Raja Bhoj, whose capital was at Dhar. Other stories mention several other "actual" places. In the story of Dharti Madi, Bhagwan's wife (she is not named) attempts to see the earth as it is coming into being. In her attempt, she travels to Pavagadh (a locally famous mountain in Panch Mahals District, Gu-

13 The story of Megharaja from this collection has been published in Gujarati in Ishai 2015a.

jarat), Mt. Abu, Junagadh (a city in Saurashtra), and the Ratanmahal hills (located just north of where Rathvas live). Rani Mokher, in her eponymous story, bathes on the banks of the Narmada River. When she is assaulted by Hanyo Punyo Nahalo, Vahi Lakhari (the goddess of fate) quickly writes a letter in Kashi (Varanasi). I have referred to these places as "actual" places, with quotation marks, because to us all of the places mentioned are easily located on a map. Perhaps Chuniya *badvo* thought of them in the same way, but since he has died, one cannot say with certainty.

Other terrestrial places are less easily localised. They seem to be clearly somewhere on earth, but it is not clear where. The palaces that abound in these narratives are good examples: Bhagwan's palace in the story of Dharti Madi, the palace(s) of the various Kanbi brothers in the story of Meghraja, Jahurani's palace in the story of Dudho Raval, and the palace of Indraj in the story of Kali Koyal. The precise location of these palaces is not known, but looking for their location may be to demand that the stories tell more than they really need to do. The important point is that beings of the sort the stories are about are the sorts of beings who dwell in palaces, not ordinary houses or huts. That is true even if they are personally responsible for menial tasks, such as grazing cattle and fetching water, that one would ordinarily expect servants of palace dwellers to perform. Similarly indeterminate is the location of several forests named in the stories of Dudho Raval and Kali Koyal, the Rinza, Kajaliya, and Bhupiya forests. They are not described in any great detail, but once again, the narratives do not need to describe them. What is important is that they denote territory that is distinct from land used for growing crops and grazing animals.

Other places in the stories are celestial; they are located in heaven (Rathvi *haragu*, Gujarati *svarg*). Understandably, heaven is the location of the sun, the moon, various stars, and various rains, but it is also the location of Dhudho *badvo*'s house, Mama Kolya's palace, and the midwife Harja's abode. From the perspective of other religions, some of heaven's features may be unexpected. For example, when a human being is first created, he begins to recognize the roads in heaven. The narratives do not, however, present a full description of this realm; they are more interested in the ability of the characters in the stories to ascend to and descend from it in a way that we human beings do not – at least, not without serious technological assistance. Dudho Raval ascends to heaven in a dream, receives advice from Dhudho *badvo*, and descends on a filament spun by Mama Kolya. When Jahurani goes into labour, Dudho Raval goes to heaven to summon the midwife Harja to oversee the delivery. In a later generation, Pithoro, in search of his uncle Indraj, climbs the spider's thread to heaven. When Indraj flees to earth, Pithoro descends on the thread in hot pursuit.

What emerges from this all too quick glance at the geography of Rathva stories seems to be the following: the narratives are clearer than ritual practices about the structure of the space *devs* and *devis* inhabit, but they are less clear about how this space relates to our own. This difference in clarity is hardly surprising. While the purpose of rituals is to enable interaction between our world and that of the *devs*, the purpose of the narratives is to relate stories about the *devs* and *devis*.

The principal structural characteristic of the space of the *devs* is already familiar. Similar to what one finds in Pithora paintings, but unlike what one encounters in *darvaja* and *toran*, the space of the *devs*, *devis*, and ancestors has a significant vertical extension. It is defined by two tiers, earth and heaven (*haragu*, *svarg*). In describing the actions of *devs* and *devis*, however, the narratives add a further dimension at which the static representation of the Pithora can give only the vaguest of hints. While the principal residence of beings like Dudho Raval, Rani Kajal, Kali Koyal, and Babo Pithoro seems to be on earth, these beings, unlike us, move rather effortlessly between earth and heaven. They do so by means of an instrument that those with the requisite cultural knowledge recognize in Pithora paintings: the thread spun by the spider, Mama Kolya.

The representation of important *devs* such as Indraj and Babo Pithoro as residing primarily on the earth would seem to support the view that the space of the *devs*, *devis*, and ancestors is superimposed upon our space. After all, the Ratanmahal hills, the Narmada river, Pavagadh, Indore, Dhar, Mt. Abu, Junagadh, and Kashi – these are all "actual" places. There are, however, at least two considerations that complicate this position. First, while all of these places are actual places, none of them is an actual place in the space that Rathvas traditionally inhabit. The Ratanmahal hills and the Narmada River define the boundaries of the traditional Rathva territories (although the area just north of the Narmada is populated principally by Bhils). The other places mentioned all lie at a greater distance, Varanasi (Kashi), the home of the goddess of fate, being the farthest. In other words, places associated with the *devs* and *devis* are not coterminous with the space in which Rathvas live. They are, in a manner of speaking, collocated with that space.[14]

There is a second consideration that complicates the notion that this narrative cycle presents the space of *devs* and *devis* as superimposed upon our own, and it is one that I have so far ignored, time. To what extent should we take spatial hints in the narratives as corresponding to what exists today, and to what extent do they characterize a situation that no longer prevails? There is some reason to prefer the latter alternative, although it is not absolutely compelling. For example, toward the beginning of the cycle, the narrative of Dharti Madi states, "With the old earth was the earth of the gods." The narrative cycle ends with Raja Bhoj making the first Pithora and Ind *puja* celebrations and, arguably, establishing the world as we know it today:

---

[14] We should perhaps note that the narratives do know sacred places. The narrative of Dharti Madi explicitly mentions the organisation of *devalay*, "houses of the gods." But *how* these places are organised – what they look like, what takes place at them – is left unexpressed.

There was famine in every direction. The fields and gardens withered. Money and silver were lost. Gaay Gavli became barren. Kali Kadvi became barren. Hari Bakri became barren. Peri Kukdi became barren. Raja Bhoj took the *aarti*, the golden pot, and the gold coins in his hand and he made a vow. He took the vow of Pithoro and Indraj. He took the vow of Hedapale and Khetapale. He fulfilled the vow and happiness spread in every direction. Hatubai, Medubai, Rani Mokher, Rani Kajal, Rahi Rupen – they all began to be happy. Raja Bhoj's sixteen fields became green. Gaay Gavli became fertile, and Hari Bakri along with her. Kali Kadvi became fertile. The fields got better.... Money got better. Silver got better. Grain got better. Wealth got better. Business got better. Children became healthy. With Raja Bhoj happiness spread throughout the entire world.

In this time before our time, the world certainly seems different from the world in which we live now. For example, are Babo Pithoro and Raja Bhoj two different kinds of being, one mythical, the other historical, or are they of one and the same kind? It is difficult to say, but in any case the narratives envision a world in which the characteristics of species shift, species boundaries are fluid, and all manner of beings – gods, animals, and humans – easily interact with one another. Today, by contrast, human beings inhabit one spatial framework, *devs, devis,* and ancestors another. The two are able to interact principally because ritual joins the two distinct spaces together.

As seen in the cycle of narratives recited by Chuniya Biliya Rathva, then, space assumes somewhat different forms than it does in Rathva rituals. On the one hand, the structure of space is clearer: the *devs* and *devis* inhabit a two-tiered universe, but they are able to move relatively easily from earth to heaven and back again. On the other hand, the relation of the space of the *devs* and *devis* to the space that we inhabit is less clear, perhaps because the narrative cycle does not in fact talk about the space that we inhabit but about a prior space. In any case, it would be worthwhile to examine a much more extensive set of narratives from a variety of different narrators, preferably recorded in "live" performances, to see what other ontological hints they might contain. This is not, however, a project for the present context.

A Closing Caution

What we have seen is this: For Rathvas, space is open, not closed. We human beings are not bound within a closed three (or four or x) dimensional universe but through ritual can interact with beings who inhabit other spaces, notably, *devs, devis,* and ancestors. Representations of these spaces in ritual tend to give more specific hints about the relations between them; these two spaces are presented as both collocated horizontally and superimposed. Representations of these spaces in narratives – at least the narratives briefly examined – tend to give more specific hints about spatial structures; like our space, the space of the *devs* and *devis* consists of two tiers, earth and heaven, but movement between these spaces does not present the challenge to them that it does to us. Of course, these generalisations can be taken too far. Some ritual practices, such as the Pithora painting, hint at the structure of the space of the *devs*, while the stories we examined also hint vaguely at relations between the two spaces. Add to these qualifications the many potential questions about space that we have not addressed.

I want, however, to close with another crucial point. In a rather recent discussion of pantheons, Bruce Lincoln (2012: 17-29) has pointed out the dangers that come from formalisation by both indigenous and exogenous scholars. Implicit pantheons, Lincoln says, are fluid, changing, unsystematic, and never complete. Explicit pantheons are systematic, comprehensive, and schematic. "Exogenous theorists," Lincoln writes, "deceive themselves when they believe too strongly in their own pantheons and mistake these artificial scholarly constructions for faithful re-constructions of anything that had more than potential or evanescent existence" (Lincoln 2012: 20). Indigenous formalizers, too, whether operating from a critical distance or not, inevitably fix and alter their topic. Lincoln's principal example is the impact of Snorri Sturluson's account of the god Ullr.

These comments apply, *mutatis mutandis*, to the features of space that I have sketched. It would be claiming too much to say that, in uncovering these hints of ontology, I have identified the worldview of Rathva *jagats* when it comes to space. It would be more accurate to say that I have used certain Rathva cultural practices to begin to sketch a road map for thinking about *jagat* conceptions of space. But maps come in a variety of forms and styles, and they are always corrigible. Furthermore, cultural production is always fluid. The most one can expect is that the preliminary road map that I have sketched can provide us some initial guidance as we wend our way through Rathva cultural space – and perhaps others.

Fig. 1: Vaghasthal, Chhotaudepur taluka, 8 February 2009. Photo Gregory D. Alles.

Fig. 2: Vaghasthal, Chhotaudepur taluka, 8 February 2009. Photo Gregory D. Alles.

Fig. 3. Pithora paintings, Boradha village, Pavi Jetpur taluka, 14 March 2013. Photo Gregory D. Alles.

References

Alles, Gregory D. (2013): "Are *Devs* Gods or Spirits? Some Quick Thoughts on Categories in the Study of Religions", *Din* 2013 (1), 111-118.

Alles, Gregory D. (2015): "Work and Play in Gamshahi: Performing the Indigenous Village in Eastern Gujarat", *International Quarterly for Asian Studies/ Asienforum* 25 (1-2), 103-125.

Alles, Gregory D. (forthcoming): "Ritual Space as Borderland: Building and Breaching Ritual Borders in Eastern Central Gujarat", *International Journal of Dharma Studies*.

Barrett, Justin L., Melanie A. Nyhof (2001): "Spreading Non-natural Concepts: The Role of Intuitive Conceptual Structures in Memory and Transmission of Cultural Materials" *Journal of Cognition and Culture* 1 (1), 69-100.

Cadena, Marisol de la (2015): *Earth Beings: Ecologies of Practice across Andean Worlds*. Durham, N.C.: Duke University Press.

Carrasco, David (2004): "Jaguar Christians in the Contact Zone: Concealed Narratives in the Histories of Religions in the Americas", in Jacob Kehinde Olupona (ed.), *Beyond Primitivism: Indigenous Religious Traditions and Modernity*. London: Routledge, 128-138.

Chalmers, David J. (1996): *The Conscious Mind: In Search of a Fundamental Theory*. New York: Oxford University Press.

Chalmers, David J. (2010): *The Character of Consciousness*. Oxford: Oxford University Press.

Chidester, David (2008): "Dreaming in the Contact Zone: Zulu Dreams, Visions, and Religion in Nineteenth-Century South Africa", *Journal of the American Academy of Religion* 76 (1), 27-53.

Clifford, James (1997): "Museums as Contact Zones ", in ibid., *Routes: Travel and Translation in the Late Twentieth Century*. Cambridge, Mass.: Harvard University Press, 188-219.

Clifford, James (2013): *Returns: Becoming Indigenous in the Twenty-First Century*. Cambridge, Mass.: Harvard University Press.

Durkheim, Emile (1965): *The Elementary Forms of the Religious Life* (J. W. Swain, Trans.), New York: Free Press.

Eliade, Mircea (1959): *The Sacred and the Profane: The Nature of Religion*. New York: Harcourt, Brace & World.

Gill, Sam D. (2012): *Dancing Culture Religion*. Lanham, Md.: Lexington Books.

Hallowell, A. Irving (1960): "Ojibwa Ontology, Behavior and World View", in S. Diamond (Ed.), *Culture in History: Essays in Honor of Paul Radin*. New York: Brandeis University Press, 19-52.

Harvey, Graham (2006): *Animism: Respecting the Living World*. New York: Columbia University Press.

Hofweber, Thomas (2014): Logic and Ontology. *The Stanford Encyclopedia of Philosophy (Fall 2014 Edition)*. Retrieved from http://plato.stanford.edu/archives/fall2014/entries/logic-ontology/.

Ishai, Subhash (2008): "Bābo Piṭhoro", *Ādilok* 1 (1):,10-11.

Ishai, Subhash (2015a): "Rāthvāonī maukhik paraṃparāmāṃ Megharājā", *Ādilok* 7 (5): 14-20.

Ishai, Subhash (2015b): "Tribal Rituals and Beliefs: A Study with Reference to the Pithoro Festival of Rathva Community in Gujarat. Report of a University Grants Commission Minor Research Project, 2013-2015". Unpublished.

Jain, Jyotindra (1984): *Painted Myths of Creation: Art and Ritual of an Indian Tribe*. New Delhi: Lalit Kala Akademi.

Johnson, Mark (1987): *The Body in the Mind: The Bodily Basis of Meaning, Imagination, and Reason*. Chicago: University of Chicago Press.

Johnson, Mark (2007): *The Meaning of the Body: Aesthetics of Human Understanding*. Chicago: University of Chicago Press.

Kahneman, Daniel (2011): *Thinking Fast and Slow*. New York: Farrar, Straus and Giroux.

Lakoff, George (1987): *Women, Fire, and Dangerous Things: What Categories Reveal About the Mind*. Chicago: University of Chicago Press.

Lincoln, Bruce (2012): *Gods and Demons, Priests and Scholars: Critical Explorations in the History of Religions*. Chicago: University of Chicago Press.

Pandya, Vishvajit (2004): "Rathwa Pithoro: Writing about Writing and Reading Painted Ethnography", *Visual Anthropology* 17, 117-161.

Pratt, Mary Louise (1991): "Arts of the Contact Zone", *Profession,* 33-40.

Rathva, Navinbhai Kanubhai (2015a): "Śrī Pragaṭ Puruṣottam Satsaṃg Śibir-7 viṣe ciṃtan", *Sri Purushottam Prakash* 4 (2), 4-32.

Rathva, Navinbhai Kanubhai (2015b): "Śrī Pragaṭ Puruṣottam Satsaṃg Śibir-7 viṣe ciṃtan." *Sri Purushottam Prakash* 4 (3), 4-23.

Shah, Haku (1980): "The Ritual Painting of the God Pithora Baba: A Tribal Ritual in Central Gujarat", *Ethnologische Zeitschrift Zürich* 11, 7–62.

Slone, D. Jason (2004): *Theological Incorrectness: Why Religious People Believe What They Shouldn't*. Oxford: Oxford University Press.

Stiglmayr, Engelbert (1963): "Die Kultpfähle der Rathwa-Bhilala", *Festschrift Paul Schebesta zum 75. Geburtstag, gewidmet von Mitbrüdern, Freunden und Schülern, Studia Instituti Anthropos 18*. Vienna: St. Gabriel-Verlag, 371-380.

Tilche, Alice (2011): *In Search of an Adivasi Worldview: Identity, Development and the Adivasi Museum of Voice in Western India*: Ph.D. dissertation, School of Oriental and African Studies, University of London.

Tilche, Alice (2015): "Pithora in the Time of Kings, Elephants and Art Dealers: Art and Social Change in Western India", *Visual Anthropology* 28, 1-20.

Tweed, Thomas A. (2006): *Crossing and Dwelling: A Theory of Religion*. Cambridge, Mass.: Harvard University Press.

Vásquez, Manuel A. (2011): *More than Belief: A Materialist Theory of Religion*. Oxford: Oxford University Press.

Shamans and Oracles of Tawang and Nafra Circle (Arunachal Pradesh, India)

Stefano Beggiora
Ca'Foscari University

Abstract

The area stretching from Tawang to the Nafra Circle in India, through the high mountain passes of the eastern Himalayan ridge, is a territory with a high density of tribal population. At this cultural crossroads, the authority and charisma of religious figures such as brahmins, pūjārī, lamas, oracles and shamans is mutually acknowledged within their communities. This paper seeks to offer a study of the local shamanistic and animistic tradition, which possesses a complex hierarchical grid of magico-religious ritualism, with particular reference to the Monpa ethnic group. In particular, I will also refer to a lineage of *kutens,* or Himalayan oracles, well known in the *nyingmapa* monasteries of western Khameng and the Tawang district, apparently first instituted by the *tulku (sprul sku)* Tijin Rinpoche at the end of the seventeenth century within the ethnic subgroup of the Tawang Monpas. Despite the fact that this tradition clearly has its origins and contemporary practice within the shamanic substrate of the area and continues to communicate with it, on the other hand it was formally recognized as an official lineage by the sixth Dalai Lama Tsangyang Gyatso, who was himself a member of the same ethnic group.

Introduction

The Monpa group is one of the most significant and culturally important indigenous communities of the state of Arunachal Pradesh, in northeastern India. With permanent and shifting agriculture-based techniques of subsistence and supplementary activities of hunting and gathering among minor subgroups, the Monpas occupy a territory that stretches through the districts of Tawang and West Kameng in India, with minority populations also recognized over the border, in Tibet. In his monumental work on the *Scheduled Tribes* of India, Singh recalled that the name comes from the combination of two words: *mon* meaning low country and *pa* meaning belonging to; Monpa was therefore a generic term for those ethnic groups, today recognized as tribals by the Indian state, who live in these areas (Singh 2001: 818-829). The designation of lowland is justified perhaps only from a Tibetan perspective that views the Himalayan slopes as descending gradually towards India. According to tradition the name comes from the ancient kingdom of Monyul which flourished between the first centuries before and after Christ, in an area between southern Tibet, India and eastern Bhutan, which in the course of history gradually came under the influence of Tibetan culture (Savada 1993: xxi, 254; Chand 2009: 25-28). During the colonial era, the British claimed a large part of the area including it within the McMahon Line (according to the Shimla Accord of 1914) that cut across the Monpa territory (Goldstein 1991: 307). The border issue remains a contested matter between China and India (Athwal 2008: 20-26, 121-123).

According to the latest data available from the Census of India the Monpas number 43,709 people with a very slight upward trend (Chaudhury 2013: 149-152). They are divided into several subgroups: the most important is that of the Tawang Monpa (7,133 people) who consider themselves the highest group perhaps because they live in the proximity of an important Buddhist historical center (Singh 2001: 828-829). Other subdivisions are But, Dirang, Lish, Panehan Monpas, and other minor groups such as Chug and Kalaktang. When we talk about Monpa there come immediately to mind the traditional Himalayan clothes and the typical yak hair hats with long distinctive tassels that make them truly unique come immediately to mind. This mode of dress is widespread in the area of Tawang, but every area displays not only aesthetic but also substantial cultural differences: such as different degrees of assimilation of Buddhism, varieties of shamanic practices, specific celebrations of spring and the languages spoken that, while descending fairly evenly from Tibeto-Burmese stock, they have different inflections (Hyslop 2009: 3-21; Singh 1995: 216-217).

My study focuses in particular on the area of Dirang (7,172 people) and But (225 people) Monpas living in the valley of the town of Dirang and in the mountainous area known as Nafra Circle in West Kameng District. My fieldwork is mainly based on an ethnographic survey project carried out in 2001 and 2002[1] followed by several other separate visits to the eastern Himalayas to collect further data.

As with other regions of the North Eastern frontier, this area has always been characterized by the culture of indigenous peoples and by their strong sense of identity. The patronage of Hindu institutions in the lowlands and the strong prevailing Buddhist presence in mountain areas has contributed over the centuries to

1 Research missions in Arunachal Pradesh were funded by University Ca' Foscari of Venice (Italy).

the creation of a 'shadow zone', where religious traditions are intermingled, and the boundaries are constantly redefined. The relation between the pre-Buddhist Tibetan tradition and shamanism is well known today. What is referred to as reformed *bön* represents a kind of 'straightening' operated in the past by Buddhism and it has a predominantly ritualistic character. But the unreformed *bön*, on the other hand, survives today under its shamanic guise in Monpa culture. Nevertheless, shamanic practices today also seem to be increasingly subsumed within Buddhist structures and legitimized by Buddhist hierarchies. This study aims to explore the complex ways in which the various kinds indigenous shamanic practitioner relate to Buddhist cosmological ideas and find accommodation with Tibetan Buddhist institutional actors.

The Dirang *dzong* and the heart of the demon

A gigantic portal, surmounted by a carved architrave representing the majestic horns of a *mithun*, the mountain bison (*Bos frontalis*) symbol of the region, is the first entrance gate to the State of Arunachal Pradesh. The long and winding road that passes through it soon leaves behind the open landscape of the Assamese plain, diving into the jungles that cover the Himalayan slopes climbing the mountain range towards the districts of Tawang and West Kameng. This immense rocky amphitheater, with peaks covered with eternal snow, surrounds and protects the extreme offshoot of India, on the border with Bhutan. It is a wild landscape, where the dense vegetation of the foothills, crossed by rushing streams, gives way to a bleak land, surrounded by the silence of the mountain passes that often reach above 4000 meters.

The ancient caravan and pilgrimage routes climb through this natural windswept bulwark, linking the northeastern border of India to Lhasa in Tibet. From an anthropological point of view the area is certainly very interesting and still poorly studied. Many indigenous communities such as the Mijis, the Akas, the Sherdukpens, the Buguns, live in the valleys of these districts (Singh 1995: 13, 20-21). Among these, the most important group consists of the Monpa, an ethnic group which includes within it different lineages of Tibetan origin.

One of the most important cultural and religious Buddhist centers of the northeastern borderlands, located a few kilometers from the border between India and China, is the famous Tawang monastery in Arunachal Pradesh. Dating back to the XVII Century, it can host more than five hundred monks and is one of the most important monasteries in South Asia. The nearby library preserves a rich collection of ancient texts besides paintings, sculptures and ritual art objects of fine traditional workmanship (Singh 2009: 88-89). The entire area also occupies a prominent place in the history of the region; in these valleys, Tsanyang Gyatso (*tsang dbyangs rgya mtsho*), the VI Dalai Lama was born in the XVII Century

(Biswal 2000: 48-49). It is interesting to observe the Buddhist religious buildings from various periods, *gonpas*, *chortens*, *stupas*, shrines, monasteries, temples and so forth, scattered amongst the small villages of the local communities, that dot the area along the ancient pilgrimage route to Tibet. In Dirang, right at the entrance of the valley that leads to the Se La Pass, the last pass before the Tawang monastery, stands an ancient *dzong*. This is a kind of fortress, or rather a fortified village in Tibetan style (*rdzong*) (Bernier 1997: 53ff.; Chakravarty, Rai 1997: 242). I infer that, if the Tawang monastery is presently the cultural heart of the region, in the past the *dzong* would have represented the last Buddhist outpost, or rather a fortified village, situated at the entrance of this gateway to Tibet.

Perched on top of a cliff, the fortress has an almost quadrangular configuration; a high wall made of square blocks of rock surround the town and has, as an opening, a finely decorated portal overlooking the steep access road. The structure dates back to the late medieval period (about XVII Century) and over the centuries has been a legislative and administrative center of the region. With the increasing population of the village, the houses that once stood just inside the wall, are distributed today across the valley at the foot of the *dzong*.

Having lost its defensive value as a fortress over the centuries, the entire structure has undergone an incontrovertible process of decay. Here, as in other parts of India, the stones that made up the complex of this national artistic heritage, have been used by the local population to build houses or other buildings. The southern section of the *dzong* is the most damaged because of time and abuse, while the upper section is better preserved. It is interesting, however, that some houses inside the *dzong*, for reasons of space and prudence in the use of materials, were constructed leaning against the perimeter wall, which, in this case, constitutes one of the main walls of the house. The internal structure is usually wooden, while the walls of the house are built with square stones resting on each other. The front opening is commonly surmounted by a double wooden lintel often decorated. At the back of each house, then, there are structures in bamboo and straw woven according to traditional use for the storage of agricultural tools.

In recent years, after finding that the Dirang Dzong is actually one of the only – if not the only – example of this type of architecture, set in Indian territory, the Government is promoting a project of archaeological recovery and conservation of the area (Mizuno, Tenpa 2015: 32-55).

From a religious point of view, Dirang is a Buddhist center of some importance. The *gonpa* located outside the walls is traditional: rich in ritual art objects, it hosts many monks, novices and lay attendants. It is interesting to note that within the fortress lies a second *gonpa*, smaller and square shaped, probably dating from the same period as the *dzong*. Local legend tells how the master Padmasambhava, on arriving here, found a terrible demon infesting the region. After confronting and defeating it, the teacher tore out its heart and inserted its body into the mountain (Sen 2005: 149-152).

In the Tibetan tradition the figure of Guru Padmasambhava appears to be the crucial actor in the harmonisation of human events with the characteristics of the Tibetan world at this particular time. Thus he might be interpreted both as a symbolically meaningful hypostasis of a doctrinal principle and as an actual person, according to the inclination of his devotees. In other words, although it is difficult to establish with certainty whether the figure of this 8th Century Indian Buddhist master existed in ordinary human form or not, there is no doubt that he occupies a prominent place in Tibetan Buddhism, so much so that he is worshiped exactly like a kind of Buddha across all the regions of Himalayas. He is thought to have planted certain spiritual seeds in the vast fields of space and time which he prepared to bring to fruition in various places in future times in order to refresh the teaching, to renew the presence of *dharma,* of its transmission, and of his blessings. In this doctrinal framework Guru Padmasambhava appears, among many other readings, which of course are always possible in Buddhist matters, as a kind of symbolic figure who tilled, plowed and prepared deep furrows in which to plant the seeds of *dharma* that would sprout over a long period of time in a vast area and bear ripe fruits for the Tibetan people to harvest. The best known 'seeds' sown by Guru Padmasambhava in the furrow of Tibet's future are the *gter mas*, the so called 'concealed treasures' (Tulku Thondup 1986). Padmasambhava's lively exploits, not in fact a single episode, whereby in order to do this he travelled the whole of the Himalayas and the Tibetan plateau subduing gods, demons, ogres, spirits and any kind of beings dwelling in the subtle dimension, consecrating the land as a whole, consecrating practice places, and hiding texts and devotional objects to be rediscovered in later times, are renowned in his biography (Dalton 2004: 759-772; Bellezza 2005: 72). It is in this complex spatial – and prior to that, temporal – grid, composed by a sacred geography of places, that the significance of the tradition of Dirang Dzong is to be read.

If the teacher of Buddhism Padmasambhava, the destroyer of demons, is seen as a sacred figure that defeats the supernatural agencies, perhaps the gods of the previous (shamanic or Bön) religion (Bellezza 2005: 20ff.), the *genius loci* of the mountains, and subjugates them to the doctrine, the present case of Dirang Dzong would appear to be different. In fact, here the evil entity is completely destroyed in a battle that can be imagined unfolding in a psychic dimension. After the defeat, however, the body of the demon seems to materialize crystallizing in the form of a stone. At the back of the temple there is a hole in the ground a few meters wide. In the bottom of the cavity it is possible to see an unusual rocky formation, as if it were a section formed by the intrusion of some other material. With a vaguely anthropomorphic shape, it is considered by the locals to be the petrified body of the defeated demon. Therefore the monastery arises in the space in front of the place of this epic battle. Moreover, the monks showed me a secret relic jealously guarded in a container in turn placed in a chest stored in the most inner section of the *gonpa*. This is a dark stone, composed of a red burnished material of a few kilograms in weight that is perfectly cardiomorphic in shape. This peculiar object is considered the heart of the demon: nobody touches it directly, but it is handled carefully using cloth and prayer flags, a sign that it is regarded as an object of great power. This has been preserved to this day as a prodigious relic (Fig. 1).

In addition to the *ringsel* (*ring bsrel*) relics, a sort of miraculous realization found at the place of cremation (*śmaśān*) of spiritual teachers (Germano, Trainor 2004), inexplicable and wonderful objects can frequently be found, especially in those holy places linked to the cult or meditative experience of Padmasambhava, and which are here unequivocally inscribed upon the spirituality of the place.

Lamas and *ku tens* at Se La Pass

It is possible to infer that, if the *dzong* represented in the past the last outpost at the entrance of this gateway to Tibet, the monastery of Tawang – with its almost five hundred monks and its treasured library – was indeed the cultural heart of the region. According to a traditional perspective, the various peoples who live in the area, belonging to the Monpa ethnic group – more or less warlike in the past, more or less close to the Buddhist *dharma* today – were considered as a kind of *dvarapālas*, the 'guardians of the door' to Lhasa (Pommaret 1994: 46-62; Nébesky-Wojkowitz 1993: 10-11).[2]

Getting to the heart of the matter, the Tawang monastery is a major *gelugpa* (*dge lugs pa*) center. Here the lamas and monks of the *gonpa* told me that the whole valley is considered sacred. Conversely, all the surrounding areas, particularly the range beyond the Se La Pass towards India, and the so-called Nafra Circle are considered dangerous and corrupting areas due to the presence of black magic practices. This seems to be a clear reference to the shamanic substrate of the tribes, whose cults usually require bloody animal sacrifices, the phenomena of possession and so forth.[3] Between them – almost a link between the two opposites – we observe the presence of several *nyingmapa* (*rnying ma pa*) school adherents who, unlike the *gelugpas*, usually communicate by means of a particular ritual flexibility with Bön and shamanic traditions. The *nyingmapa* monks interact with the villagers, exerting the cultural influence of their ancient tradition. They do not possess the faculty to self-induce a state of trance, nor the authority to oust the

[2] Nébesky-Wojkowitz noted that the traits of the traditional dress of the Monpa populations are frequently replicated in the attributes of the local *dharmapālas*.

[3] For a general discussion on the Asiatic shamanism I refer to Åke Hultkrantz, (1996: 1–31). For a more critical discussion on this topic I suggest V.N. Basilov (1999: 17-40) and Hoppál (1992: 117–131).

local shamans from the role of religious guides of the community, they merely install them or, in other words, they legitimate the shamans as *pūjārīs* of the villages. This re-consecration, which often includes the formal donation of *mantras* and Buddhist rosaries, however, commonly involves the worship of gods, such as *dharmapālas* or *lokapālas*, which are considered nobler and of a higher status than the entities worshipped in the shamanic world. The latter are generally understood as potential pollutants, since they expose the operator to a ritual contact with the souls of the dead or other potentially dangerous or terrifying entities (Mizuno, Tenpa 2015: 57-111).

In the surrounding valleys inhabited by the Monpas, whose culture blends with that of many other groups that migrated from Tibet and Nepal, as well as Hindus from Assam, four traditional figures of operators of the sacred can still be identified today: *lha jukhans*, *bonpos*, *yunmins* and *phramis*, that is oracles, shamans, experts in magic and divination and lastly ordinary village ritualists who are repositories of the myths and legends of the tribe. The first term (*lha jhukan*), is of uncertain etymology, but appears to be comparable to the Tibetan *kuten* (*sku rten*), or oracle. The last term (*phrami*) clearly indicates a priest of the ordinary type. The terms *yunmin* and *bonpo* refer instead to shamanic figures that may present a certain hierarchy and, as we shall see, some variations in the names are common. The word *bonpo* does not appear in relation to monks of the Bön religion, but rather derives from the term *bombo* that in Tibet and among the Tamang of Nepal indicates precisely a shaman. Equally popular is the Nepali term *jhāÞkri* (Bellezza 2005: 33-34). This rather fluid hierarchy has been permeable to the influence of Tibetan Buddhism, which, in some cases, has tamed the local representation of the sacred. In other cases the religious backgrounds were partially incompatible (Sidky 2010: 213-240).

In 2002 I had the opportunity to research a Tibetan oracle, a *kuten*, and to spend some time at his home near Sapper, the village that inherited its name from a unit of the Indian Army stationed close to Dirang Dzong. Standing at an altitude of around 1,900 metres, this place in the eastern Himalayas is located on the same ancient road that winds from the Brahmaputra plain in Assam and Bengal up through the Se La pass (4.300 m) to the Tawang valley and on to Lhasa. This particular lineage of *kutens,* well known in the *nyingmapa* monasteries of western Khameng and the Tawang district, was first instituted by a *tulku (sprul sku)* called Tijin Rinpoche at the end of the seventeenth century within the ethnic group of the Tawang Monpas; he was formally recognized by the sixth Dalai Lama Tsangyang Gyatso *(tsang dbyangs rgya mtsho)*, himself a member of the same ethnic group (Filippi 2008: 11-35). Interestingly, during a long series of interviews I had with him, I noticed the presence of strongly shamanic traits in most of his experience, starting from the time of his initiation, when he spontaneously fell into a trance and the guiding spirit of his father appeared to him, until the day in which the monks themselves, recognizing him as a medium, introduced him to the nearby Sarong Gonpa (*sa rong dgon pa*) near the village of Jhanda for his long apprenticeship.

His name is Geleg Choi Jang and at the time he was 27 years old. At the death of his father, Leikunjo, in 1997 the present *ku ten* experienced great pain when, for the first time, he was possessed in a dream by an entity, which would be his guiding spirit for a certain period of time. Geleg Choi Jang had no doubt that the 'spiritual guide' of this uncontrolled possession — which subsequently occurred also when he was awake — was the spirit of his father, Leikunjo. The description of this first phase of spontaneous possession can have a double interpretation. The phenomenon of possession by a predecessor recalls a kind of mnemonic metempsychosis that is typical of the passage of powers from one *tulku* to his successor; however, the episodes could also be read as complying with what is commonly documented upon the first calling of a shaman.

As *lha jukhan*, the 'echo of the gods' in the Monpa language,[4] a term that indicates the oracle, he is the means of evocation of Karma Thinle (*karma 'phrin las*) a form of the Tibetan god Pe har. There is not much information about this deity but he would be "A deity either identical with *Pe har* or an 'emanation' of this *dharmapāla,* is the god *Karma 'phrin las* or *rGyal chen karma 'phrin las.* Hanbury-Tracy describes in his book *Black River of Tibet* (London (1938), 66), the trance of an oracle-priest who became possessed by *Karma 'phrin las*" (Nébesky-Wojkowitz, 1993: 129).

In connection with the ritual, there is a specific liturgy that leads the oracle into a trance. I witnessed that the sessions are divided into two different phases. The first stage is always the same and consists in the recitation of a long formula of invocation of the deity. This is the keystone of the entire ritual because it leads the *ku ten* into communication with the pertaining divinity; then anything can happen. I was shown and allowed to photograph a Tibetan text titled *chos skyongdpon blon rnams kyi sku gsol spyan 'dren skor* which, when sung, induced Geleg's trance. This was a thin badly-preserved book, the last two pages of which had been so severely worn and thumbed that they had been transcribed in a much more recent period onto normal sheets of paper from an exercise book (Sanders 2006: 381-403).[5]

For a correct interpretation of the use of this liturgical book we need to return to a more general perspective on Tibetan tantric Buddhism. As stated earlier, when the great master Padmasambhava was about to enter the land of snows for the first time, the local demons obstructed him fiercely. To remedy their in-

[4] Language code, ISO 639-3: twm. (Sino-Tibetan, Tibeto Burman, classification). This is an interpretation of the term I have no further evidence. Uncertain etymology.

[5] Based on this photographic documentation, Sanders – who was with me at that time – has published this first translation into Italian.

domitable insolence he undertook, therefore, a meticulous work of consecration of the Himalayan territory that led him to walk every inch of that harsh land, subduing the gods and demons of several places through the power of his spiritual realization (Drema 2004: 209-222). The powerful master subjugated them, forcing them to take a vow to protect the Buddhist *dharma* and its practitioners. Later his Tibetan disciples taught the appropriate methods to control these subtle beings: the visualizations, the invocations and the offerings to be made, the *mantra* to force them to obey. The tradition considers some of these instructions to have been passed down orally from master to disciple, sometimes becoming lost, sometimes surviving the passing of generations (Nébesky-Wojkowitz 1993: 416-423). In some cases the rituals were drawn up in the form of *sādhana* texts (*sgrub thabs*), namely that *corpus* of literature that contains instructions on the method (*thabs*) of ritual and meditative practices aimed at achieving spiritual realisation (*sgrub*) (Sanders 2006: 383).

This is the case of the text that I found, in manuscript form, which unfortunately does not report any publishing information, does not have a colophon and does not indicate the name of the author or amanuensis: not even the officiating Lama, and neither could Geleg Choi Jang, the depositary of the book, provide any information about it. He merely asserted that these sudden painful and violent episodes of possession that he experienced led him to seek out advice at the *nyingmapa* monastery of Sarong, in the valley of Tawang. Interestingly this *gonpa* has overseen and instructed the *kutens* belonging to this hereditary chain of oracles since the days of Tsangyang Gyamtso. From what Geleg said, it was not possible to develop a clear idea of the instruction and training that he received there given that it was obvious he still did not have any deep and extensive knowledge of Buddhism. Undoubtedly, Geleg Choi Jang was prepared for the performance of his oracular and therapeutic role, leaving doctrinal questions to the *nyingmapa* monks who since then have constantly monitored the ritual aspects of his function. Over the next two years, the spontaneous possessions decreased in number and ultimately disappeared, with the young Geleg now entering a trance solely as a result of the monks' ritual invocations. At the end of the second year of retreat the Rinpoche of the Sarong *gonpa* officially invested him as a *ku ten*, endowing him with the ritual garments and paraphernalia of an oracle. From the above, it is clear that this investiture took place in the year 2000.

The ritual I witnessed took place from morning until night. The morning time was used for the preparation of offerings and for the various arrangements. Gradually, all the participants in the ritual gathered in the house of Geleg. Some families seeking responses mainly about health issues, arrived followed by two officiating monks, a translator from classical Tibetan and the *rin po che* called to celebrate the liturgy. The presence of a translator seems very important as evidenced by a phenomenon of glossolalia. I was told that once the possession had taken place, the gods would speak through the mouth of the oracle. Since they are entities belonging to the *gyalpo* class, or kings (*rgyal po*), the language spoken by them would be noble and not a vernacular or a popular/tribal idiom. This language was identified as the classic Tibetan, khams (*Khams skad*),[6] unknown to the people of the area, but of which nonetheless Tawang is a center of liturgical studies. For this reason the presence of a Tibetan teacher was required as interpreter. It is also interesting to note that at the end of the ritual, Geleg claimed not to know the language of the gods, nor to recall events that occurred during the ritual.

In order for the ritual of possession to take place, as well as the recitation of the liturgy, the formal investiture with the paraphernalia of the oracle is required. In addition to a shamanic robe, a disc of mother of pearl with the syllable hum, and a sword, at the crucial moment of the rite a cap is also placed on the oracle's head. This is not a heavy metal helmet as in the case of the Tibetan state oracle of Nechung (Sidky 2011: 88; Nébesky-Wojkowitz 1993: 411-412), but is a silk hat with three embroidered eyes that recall the iconography of Karma Thinle. At the moment of possession the attendants put the hat in place, tightening it with a string under the chin almost sufficiently to cut off the medium's breath, as this would serve to hold entities inside their human vehicle. Conversely when the possession ends after the formal dismissal of deities this kind of noose is loosened and the oracle collapses to the ground unconscious. During the phase of possession, which lasted about an hour, the main session was that of consultation whereby one by one the applicants remained bowed at the feet of the oracle whilst the interpreter translated requests and responses. After that, however, other minor deities, who were considered to be the retinue of Karma Thinle, manifested themselves: the 'secret consort that generates pleasure', that is, his śakti and dignitaries of his court. From a subsequent study in situ, with the help of audiovisual footage,[7] I concluded that these entities could be distinguished from changes in the oracle's tone of voice and the forming of the different benevolent or wrathful attitudes.

During this phase, the village is reprimanded for its failure to fulfill sacred occasions or for breaking taboos, or otherwise warned about possible future dangers. In particular, the figure of the śakti of Karma Thinle seemed interesting: She is known as the doctor of the gods. "Peaceful at the right hand, [is] the *sman ma*, powerful wife. Dressed with the garment of a goddess, elegant and pleasant, the head adorned with precious gems, the right hand holding an arrow with multicolored silk fringes and the left hand holding a jar [full of nectar] of long life, She rides a blue water horse; the outer garment is adorned [with the image] of the winner of the plagues inflicted by the *ma mo*" (Sanders 2006: 390-391). The

6 L anguage code, ISO 639-3: khg. (Sino-Tibetan classification).

7 We successively produced a film-doc: Beggiora S. Fabian S. (2004), *Un oracolo himalayano*, Venetian Academy of Indian Studies, University Ca' Foscari of Venice (25 min.; language: Italian).

ma mo are a local class of female subtle creatures, generally described as very ugly and fierce and equipped with a bag full of diseases (*nad kyi rkyal pa*) (Nébesky-Wojkowitz 1993: 18; Bellezza 2005: 106, 237). The *sman ma*, often too *sman mo*, literally 'medicine women', are a class of female subtle creatures native to Tibet whose knowledge certainly dates back to the pre-Buddhist Bön tradition. They are generally considered benign and their invocation brings benefit; when disturbed they can sometimes be dangerous (Nébesky-Wojkowitz 1993: 198ff.). These entities seem to form a central figure around which, as we shall see, the tradition of many other shamanic figures of these valleys revolves. The thaumaturgical theme is closely linked to the function of the medicine-men, who according to the traditions of the mountain people are recipients of a call from the world of the spirit. In a play of overlapping levels, Buddhist monks unambiguously categorize all entities falling outside the Buddhist *dharma* as *rākṣasas,* demons and fearsome spirits endowed with the power of possessing human beings. However, in the folklore of the villages, some of these spirits also fulfill an initiatory function. In the sub-Himalayan mountain ranges stretching from Nepal to Arunachal Pradesh, the *ban jhā̃kri* or 'wild shaman' is a kind of *yeti* who abducts young shamans into the forest as part of their training/educational journey. These ancestral spirits are often accompanied by a female paredra known as *ban jhā̃krinī, ban boksī* or *raksī bompo.* With their irascible temperament, these female entities are ambiguously dominated by lustful and cannibalistic instincts for human male prisoners. But according to local traditions, even those who are not abducted and only receive an oneiric call narrate 'love' encounters in dreams with beautiful witches, the *boksīs*, who teach them the pharmacopoeia of Himalayan plants. Hereafter, I will describe the thaumaturgical-therapeutic functions through a series of case studies.

Shamans and *bonpos* of Nafra Circle

The Nafra Circle belt is a mountainous area with deep gorges and dense subtropical forests. It is one of the most backward areas of Arunachal Pradesh. The only road that connects Bomdila with the local headquarters is mostly of dirt and the area remains completely isolated during the rainy season (Subba, Ghosh 2003: 285-286). Here, among the Monpa subgroup of Butpas (Chaudhuri 2013: 150), for some time I visited a shaman named Chetang Ropu, a *bonpo* of the village of Jerigaon (Fig. 2). This society has handed down shamanic traditions with strong regional features, but maintains a certain permeability with neighboring cultural environments, in particular with Buddhism. The But shamans use a rich *paraphernalia* featuring showy headgear consisting of a red scarf tied on two wooden supports arranged like horns. The body is covered by a red blanket, the traditional dress of the area, and a bandolier of bells that resonates when the shaman enters into a trance. The ritual object of greatest interest is a wooden tablet, which the shaman uses to interrogate the spirits.

The jaws of a tiger are fastened to the center of the tablet upon which the blood of sacrificed animals is poured. Around the jaws the remains of other animals such as eagle claws, the hooves of a *mithun* (*bos frontalis*, the local species of mountain buffalo), mandibles of other felines and sometimes giant hornbill beaks are arrayed. It is clear that every object of the tablet has a great symbolic value. The elements which derive from birds and raptors are undoubtedly representative of the uranic dimension and the shamanic flight, while the other wild animals, *mriga* in Hindu terms, symbolize the surrounding forest and the incarnate forces of nature. Perhaps the most striking parallel, however, is that of the tiger and the buffalo, represented here by the *mithun*. This element has a strong presence in the Hindu environment too, as well as in the folk/vernacular religions of the Subcontinent: the tiger and the buffalo represent the feminine and masculine principles, *Prakṛti* and *Puruṣa*, which attract and repel each other in the play of the cosmic manifestation.

In the spatial terms of Hindu vocabulary, this theoretical antithesis can be represented by the concepts of *vana* and *kṣētra* (Sontheimer 1994: 117-174): the forest and the field. The tiger is the driving force embodied in the jungle, incarnating the dimension of the wild, the realm of spirits and animals, of dynamic potentialities and creative chaos. She is opposed to the 'field', or rather the tamed space of the village, the dimension of order, inhabited by men and domesticated animals, including the buffalo/*mithun* (*paśu* in Hindu terms). I do not intend here to say that there is a direct link between the Hindu traditions and the tribal heritage of Nafra Circle. However, in a region that has historically had the patronage of the Hindu institutions officiating tantric and Śākta cults, there clearly now exists a sharing of elements and symbols, as a result of a continuous interchange. The buffalo and the tiger – or their local substitutes – are present in the shamanism of these areas. During the ritual, *chau ji*[8] Chetang Ropu wears the shamanic horns and pours the blood into the tiger's mouth with the intention of feeding her and obtaining her power.

This power, in the Matchopa Nagnoo[9] dialect of Butpas, is called *Juhung*. Chetang stated that it was indeed a tiger – a psychic entity capable of possessing him during the trance and acting as a spirit guide. Through *Juhung* – whom

[8] The term *chau ji*, in Matchopa Nagnoo (see note below), indicates the shaman among the But Monpas, while the compound word *chau phu* indicates the trance. The expression sounds similar to the Tibetan *chos rje* which however translates the Sanskrit *dharmasvāmin*, an honorific title of high spiritual level that cannot be afferent to the shamanic practice. But I remember how the shamans of Nafra Circle were often proud holders of honorary titles as *guruji*, or *lamaji* even used outside of their usual context.

[9] Language code, ISO 639-3: onp. (Tibeto-Burman classification).

Chetang informally called the 'big cat that catches fish' – he was able to perform exorcism, and to hunt demons and evil entities while preserving the well-being of his community. The custom of the tribe requires that the tablet is handed down from generation to generation through the shamans of the *khang* (the local clan with patrilineal descent) and that it is possibly enriched with new elements. The initiation rite is called *rukten* and it has been confirmed to me that in these cases it was possible, through a kind of initiatory hunt, to kill an animal normally considered taboo, such as the tiger or the leopard. Unfortunately, the following year, when I returned to the house of Chetang, I noticed that he was wearing a Buddhist *mālā* and the *lungta* (*rlung rta*) of the *nyingmapas* were waving upon his house. To my surprise he denied any relationship with the tablet (which was still kept in the house), a clear sign that he had embraced a new religion, while remaining a leading figure in the community in his village (Sanders 2013: 333-343).

A more flexible attitude was demonstrated by other shamans I met during research in the area, such as *guruji* Wang Di, hailing from the same ethnic group and his mentor *lamaji* Chapok from the village of Salari (Fig.3). The latter claimed to be a Buddhist lama, without being one, but apparently he acted as a kind of cultural point of reference for ritual operators of the valley, a repository of knowledge of stories and legends of Nafra Circle. He lacked any ability to induce himself into a state of trance, but enjoyed, nevertheless, a certain respect in the area. Despite the clear attitudes, the non-liminality of this tradition with Buddhism was confirmed by Wang Di's practices, as he nourished the jaws of his tablet with the blood of sacrifices and showed evident characteristics of shamanic *bonpos*. The *bonpos* of the area, or even the *jhāPkris* (cf. Lecomte-Tilouine 1987: 57), as Chapok called them, customarily utilised the *vajra* and the *gaṇṭhā* bell, but the usage of these ritual tools is inverted as compared to the Buddhist routine: this fact suggests a special relationship of this type of shamanism with Bön (Dutta, Tripathy 2008: 274-286). It is the cadenced sound of the bell, more frequently than the sound of the drum, that leads the shaman into a state of trance through long sessions of rhythmic chanting.

Among the *bonpos* I had occasion to meet in Nafra Circle, I should also mention Chek Cha *lamaji*[10], who welcomed me into his home. He seemed the most free from formal issues, belonging to the Khoitam community, he benefitted from his great charisma in the village of Salari. He was able to summon all the gods of the sacred geography of the area and contact ghosts and spirits of the dead. The Khoitam are a group of a small number of people settled in small villages in the area above Salari, between Jerigaon, Ralung and Khoina (Fig. 4). They are a community of hunters and gatherers encapsulated within a more sedentary group of

[10] Here again *lamaji* is an expression of respect, he was not definitely a lama.

Monpa (Chutia 2010: 56-67). As I was able to observe some small vegetable gardens near the settlements, I can testify that the techniques of subsistence are based mainly on fishing and collection of timber and minor forest produce. During the period that I stayed in Check Cha's home, I was impressed by the extreme poverty of these people: there was never anything to eat except occasionally some dried fish and a homemade grain distillation called *arah* (or *rakshi*, cf. Singh K.R. et al. 2007: 25-36). Concerning his shamanic experience, Check Cha said he received the call when he was still a child at the time of the premature death of his father, who after passing away began to manifest himself to him in a spirit form. Check Cha showed clear awareness of this transmission of power via the patrilineal lineage: in fact, when he introduced his little son to me, he stated that he would teach the knowledge of *bonpos* to him, but only after his own death. Over the years, the figure of a female spirit became of central importance in Check Cha's apprenticeship, a kind of subtle teacher he called Nampaye. This entity used to kidnap him and take him into the forest[11], guiding him in the knowledge of the spirit world. Nampaye seems in some ways to have a function similar to that of Chetang Ropu's Juhung, but she was described as having the celestial features of the doctress of the gods. Moreover, the knowledge of medicine is a fundamental aspect of shamanic initiation.

Check Cha described a theory of twenty-four uranic deities presiding over the conspicuous heavenly Monpa pantheon and celebrated various rituals in their honor.[12] Below them he described a multitude of spirits and demons that inhabit the world of men. Nampaye seems to manifest herself between the shaman and these subtle entities.

Opening an excursus, I remember that his wife, Jokarmu – his earthly wife in the flesh –, tried to prevent Check Cha from revealing to me the names of the twenty-four deities. As justification, she asserted that the mere pronunciation of these names would have immediately led him into a state of trance and possession that she would struggle to contain. She actually began to argue so heatedly with her husband that during one of the interviews she intervened, tipping the whole mash of fermented grain on his head! With the passing of time I was able to make friends with the older woman who in any case hosted me in her home. Each daily occasion was however a pretext for the married couple to stage theatrical quarrels. She accused him of spending the little money obtained from the collection of

---

[11] He asserted, indeed mimed, to be lifted on her shoulders and so, astride, soaring above the mountains, in a clear allusion to shamanic flight.

[12] An attempt of transcription on phonetic pronunciation of the *bonpo*: *Ganga Dema*, *Beghnanin Chomo*, *Jomrava*, *Jundolin Dema*, *Donlinbuti*, *Jumriti*, *Raton Dema*, *Jumkamsam*, *Kamiam Dema*, *Jumaripti*, *Pumarimsam*, *Pukamiang*, *Tangori*, *Nima Dema*, *Pusapchang*, *Dibonabseng*, *Pulasaum*, *Karchaumjong*, *Pupor ji*, *Bonjum Dema*, *Solayung ji*, *Secerum Dema*, *Rammum Dema*, *Chummusinga Sangam*

firewood on alcohol, and he came one day to tell me that the woman was dead, although this was not true. Nonetheless, during the celebration of the rites I realized that actually the role of women was of central importance, and she acted as assistant to the shaman coordinating all the technical phases of the ritual, from dressing to the preparation of the offerings. Jokarmu used to speak with patients welcoming them and listening attentively to the requests of the community. She then explained to me by showing in detail many plants used in rituals, which give off smoke and intense fragrance when thrown on the embers and which are used to evoke the various entities. A discussion on this issue, however, would require more space.

In the ordinary sessions, Check Cha subdivided the sacred space in front of him into twenty-four sections.[13] Having put on a heavy ochre colored cloak fastened with a silver brooch with turquoise, he then intoned a long litany accompanied by the bell in which he summoned the twenty-four deities offering dried fish and *arah*. In a particular session, I documented that he was possessed in a particularly violent way by four different deities and then he consecrated a kind of thread-cross for ritual use. The sign of a positive response from these entities should have been evident from the fact that he could make a metal *vajra* stand up alone on one end. Something seemingly impossible, but after a series of frustrating attempts he invariably succeeded in so doing.

Conclusion

In conclusion, I think it might be appropriate to give an account of my meeting in the area outside the ancient *dzong* of Dirang with the old Pema Dragpa who claimed to be one of the last *phramis* of the Monpas, the custodians of the corpus of the myths of the tribe which he considered to be endangered. Pema Dragpa, too, was not capable of self-inducing a state of trance but could perform rituals with the preparation *gtor ma* and *mdos* in honor of the deities. As the custodian of Monpa knowledge, he had a clear conception of the overlapping dimensions that compose the cosmos and, although unable to see spirits, he confirmed precisely a number of details, probably belonging to the local tradition, analogous to the above as asserted by *bonpos*. Some spirits in pain, as if to emphasize their state of suffering outwardly, present beastly deformations, such as dog or monkey heads, while others were described as lacking a head, with eyes, nose and a big mouth on the stomach. *Bonsharamira*, according to Pema Dragpa, was the first Monpa shaman to settle in Dirang and Nafra Circle in ancient times, giving rise to the

[13] In detail he prepared twenty-four seats (with pieces of wood used as stools or simple cloths lying on the ground) by placing them in a clockwise direction in front of him. Later he explained that in a ritual, depending on the particular situation, a number of different spirits can respond to the call.

lineages of the greatest *bonpos*. Moreover, in the inner area of the *dzong* we met the old Pema Dondu, another shaman of the place. Of indeterminate age between seventy and eighty years he was almost always drunk and I could practically never obtain information from him. Pema Dondu also stated that, within the *dzong*, the authority of the monks had now overtaken that of the *bonpos* of which he himself claimed to be the last custodian. So according to this *bonpo* in order to access genuine traditional shamanic knowledge I would need to return to Nafra Circle and frequent the area of Butpas.

Finally it is interesting to dwell on the figure of an old traditional doctor (cf. also Ibata 2004: 232ff.). Still inside the *dzong* I had occasion to meet Pema Phutso, an octogenarian doctor who was known for being for years the medicine man of the area. In his house, not far from the central *gonpa*, this man did not follow Tibetan medical science, but carried out a singular technique seemingly of the alchemical-metallurgical type, applying metal objects, coals, heating, cooling or applying pressure to the diseased parts of the body of the patient. He did not recognize the aforementioned classification of the Monpa operators of the sacred, considering his function to be humble and exclusively mechanical or based on a practical understanding. However, when I asked him where he had learned that unique technique he told me that he had been kidnapped at a young age by three beautiful goddesses, the doctresses of the gods (*sman mo*), who, having carried him into the forest, initiated him into the knowledge and application of natural remedies and medicinal plants (Namsa et al. 2011: 7-31). He indicated a particular place, a minor ridge dominated by a large tree visible in the distance from inside the *dzong*. In this place, nighttime meetings would take place with the goddesses, thus in a kind of ecstatic or dreamlike dimension: these meetings were not only to be understood as having a propaedeutic nature, but also as having strong sexual connotations. Without the slightest embarrassment Pema Phutso asserted that he continues to this day to spend time with these celestial figures in pleasant loving activities. About the three goddesses, considered the guardians of the place and of the specific surrounding mountain passes, inscribed in *sman ma* class, he specified the names of 'Manpa Chenten Droma' (*sman ma mchod rten sgrol ma*), 'Renchin Bhu' (*rin chen phug*) e 'Yashe Droma' (*ye she'i sgrol ma*)[14].

[14] I try some possible interpretation of the phonetic pronounced by the old practitioner: *sman ma mchod rten sgrol ma* corresponds to a name of Tārā deity (*sgrol ma*). Otherwise instead of *sman ma* could be *nang pa* = inside-er o Buddhist. For the second name rin chen = jewel; phug = cave, the result looks more like a toponym instead of a proper name. At last *ye she'i sgrol ma* can be *jñāna* (knowledge) and again Tārā. Possibly *ye she'i sgron me* = light of knowledge (?).According to Pema Phutso these three goddesses refer to a male deity, 'Phu Bangle' (*phu dbang las*?) over which unfortunately I have no more elements, if not the fact of acknowledging that indeed the *sman ma* are the minor deities. Finally, the names of the respondents, univocally Pema / Padma, reveal an at least formal belonging to the *nyingmapa* school.

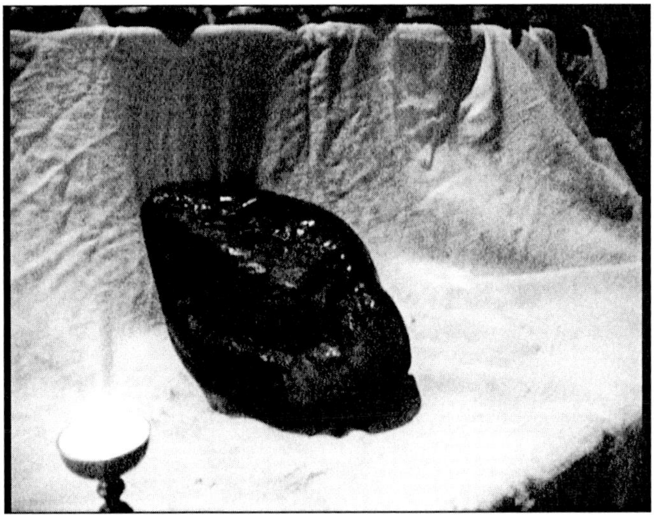

Fig. 1: The heart of a demon, Dirang Dtzong, photograph Stefano Beggiora, 2004.

A first conclusion is that both of these last characters (the *phrami* and the doctor), though not at the same level as the *bonpos*, clearly manifested shamanic traits, such as witnessing a dreamlike apprenticeship and some sort of subtle contact with the world of the spirits. Moreover the worship of *smen ma* is widespread and shared in similar forms across the different religious traditions of the place. Moreover, a strong attachment to the geography of the area seems to reveal as quite plausible a shamanic – even earlier than Buddhist – origin. After all it should be noted that there is a great process of change taking place in this region. It is not possible to know at this point whether Buddhism will be able to incorporate, absorb or homologate the cultures of indigenous peoples, but this seems to be the trend. In this process, the future evolution of the shamanic figures present in the valleys is not clear; conversely it is interesting to note that prominent religious figures, such as those of the *kutens*, despite being historically recognized by the major Buddhist religious authorities, have somewhat vague and hazy origins. As far as we can reconstruct many of the aspects that these phenomena manifested are overall, once again, shamanic in origin. These are rooted in the heritage of indigenous peoples of the frontier and in the local religions and folklore. This shamanic element – although perhaps more subdued and less ostentatious than the zeal of those who follow the word of the Lotus Born – continues to form a fervent and lively common substrate in these regions.

Fig. 2: Chetang Ropu, Jerigao, photograph Stefano Beggiora, 2004.

Fig. 3: Wang Di – Salari, photograph Stefano Beggiora, 2004.

Fig. 4: Nafra Circle – near Salari, photograph Stefano Beggiora, 2004

References

Athwal, Amardeep (2008): *China-India Relations – Contemporary Dynamics.* London & New York: Routledge.

Basilov, V. N. (1999): "Cosmos as Everyday Reality in Shamanism: an Attempt to Formulate a more Precise Definition of Shamanism", in A. Rigopoulos, R. Mastromattei (eds.): *Shamanic Cosmos. From India to the North Pole Star.* New Delhi: D.K. Printworld, 17-40.

Bellezza, J. V. (2005): *Calling Down the Gods. Spirit-Mediums, Sacred Mountains and Related Bon Textual Traditions in Upper Tibet.* Leiden/ Boston: Brill.

Bernier, R. M. (1997): *Himalayan Architecture.* Cranbury (NJ): Fairleigh Dickinson University Press.

Biswal, A. (2000): *Mystic Monpas of Himalaya.* New Delhi: Indus Publishing Company.

Chakravarty, S., Rai S. (1997): *The People of Himalayas, Bio-Cultural and Ecological Aspects.* Kolkata: Anthropological Survey of India.

Chand, R. (2009): "Monpas of Bhutan: A Study of Tribal Survival and Development Responses", *Bulletin of the Hiroshima University Museum* 1, 25-37.

Chaudhuri, S. (ed.) (2013): *Statistical Profile of Scheduled Tribes in India 2013.* Noida: Ministry of Tribal Affairs, Government of India.

Chutia, A. (2010): "Studies on Hunting and the Conservation of Wildlife Species in Arunachal Pradesh", *Sibcoltejo* 5, 56-67.

Dalton, J. (2004): "The Early Development of the Padmasambhava Legend in Tibet: A Study of IOL Tib J 644 and Pelliot tibétain 307", *Journal of the American Oriental Society* 124 (4), 759-772.

Drema, T. (2004): "Sacred Places of Monpas of Arunachal Pradesh", in Mibang T. Chaudhury S.K. (eds.): *Understanding Tribal Religion.* New Delhi: Mittal Publications, 209-222.

Dutta, S., B. Tripathy (2008): "Bon Cult among the Monpas of Arunachal Pradesh", in Tripathy B. (ed.): *Religious History of Arunachal Pradesh.* New Delhi: Gyan Publishing House, 274-286.

Filippi, G. G. (2008): "Oracles and Shamans in Arunachal Pradesh", *Central Asiatic Journal* 51 (1), 11 35.

Germano, D., K. Trainor (eds.)(2004): *Embodying the Dharma. Buddhist Relic Veneration in Asia.* Albany: State University of New York Press.

Goldstein, M. C. (1991): *A History of Modern Tibet, 1913–1951: The Demise of the Lamaist State.* Berkeley, Los Angeles: University of California Press.

Hyslop, G. (2009): "Preliminary Notes on Dakpa (Tawang Monpa)", in S. Morey, M. Post (eds.): *North East Indian Linguistic*, Vol. 2. New Delhi: Cambridge University Press, 3-21.

Hoppál, M. (1992): "Shamanism: An Archaic and/or Recent System of Beliefs", in A.-L. Siikala, M. Hoppál, *Studies on Shamanism.* Budapest: Akadémiai Kiadó, 117–131.

Hultkrantz, Å. (1996): "Ecological and Phenomenological Aspects of Shamanism", in V. Diószegi, M. Hoppál (eds.): *Shamanism in Siberia*, Vol. 2. Budapest: Akadémiai Kiadó, 1–31.

Ibata, A. (2004): "Bon Medicine among Monpas in Western Arunachal Pradesh", in A. K. Kalla, P. C. Joshi: *Tribal Health and Medicines.* New Delhi: Concept Publishing Company, 318-340.

Lecomte-Tilouine, M. (1987): "Hommes/divinités de la forêt: A travers le miroir au Népal central", *Études rurales* 107/108, 55-69.

Mizuno, K., L. Tenpa (2015): *Himalayan Nature and Tibetan Buddhist Culture in Arunachal Pradesh, India. A Study of Monpa.* Tokyo: Springer Japan.

Namsa et al. (2011): "Ethnobotany of the Monpa Ethnic Group at Arunachal Pradesh, India" *Journal of Ethnobiology and Ethnomedicine* 7 (1), 7-31.

Nébesky-Wojkowitz, R.de (1993): *Oracles and Demons of Tibet: the Cult and Iconography of the Tibetan Protective Deities.* Kathmandu: Tiwari's Pilgrims Book House.

Pommaret, F. (1994): "Entrance-keepers of a hidden country: Preliminary notes on the Monpa of south-central Bhutan", *Tibet Journal* 19 (3), 46-62.

Rinpoche, Tulku Thondup (1986): *Hidden Teachings of Tibet: An Explanation of the Terma Tradition of the Nyingma School of Buddhism.* London: Wisdom.

Sanders, F. (2006): "Sulla Invocazione e Invito del Signore Dharmapāla e della sua Corte", in M. Marchetto (ed.): *L'Ira degli Déi Venetian Academy of Indian Studies* (4), Venezia: Cafoscarina, 381-403.

Sanders, F. (2013): "Ancient Rituals in a Twilight World", *Journal of the International Association for Bon Research* 1. New Horizon in Bon Studies 3 – Inaugural issue (1), 333-43.

Savada, M. A. (ed.)(1993): *Nepal and Bhutan: Country Studies.* Washington DC: Library of Congress, Federal Research Division.

Sen, G. (2005): "The Road to Tawang", *India International Centre Quarterly* 32, 2/3 Where the Sun Rises When Shadows Fall: The North-East, 149-152.

Sidky, H. (2011): "The State Oracle of Tibet, Spirit Possession and Shamanism", *Numen* 58, 71-99.

Sidky, H. (2010): "Ethnographic Perspectives on Differentiating Shamans from other Ritual Intercessors", *Asian Ethnology* 69 (2), 213-240.

Singh, G. P. (2009): *Historical Researches into some Aspects of the Culture and Civilization of North-East India.* New Delhi: Gyan Publishing House.

Singh, K. R. et al. (2007): "Traditional Foods of *Monpa* tribe of West Kameng, Arunachal Pradesh", *Indian Journal of Traditional Knowledge* 6 (1), 25-36.

Singh, K. S. (1995): *People of Arunachal Pradesh* Vol. XIV. Calcutta: Seagull Books.

Singh, K. S. (2001): *The Scheduled Tribes.* New Delhi: Oxford University Press.

Sontheimer, G. D. (1994): "The *Vana* and the *Kṣetra*: The Tribal Background of Some Famous Cults", in G. C. Tripathi, H. Kulke (eds.): *Religion and Society in Eastern India.* New Delhi: Manohar, 117-64.

Subba, T. B., C. G. Ghosh (eds.) (2003): *The Anthropology of North-East India.* Anthropological Survey of India, North Eastern Hill University, New Delhi: Orient Blackswan.

Daily Headline – Dangerous Macumba: Afro-Brazilian religions in a popular newspaper during the 1950s Considerations regarding the marginalisation of Macumba in Rio de Janeiro city

Marcelo Vidaurre Archanjo

In this article I present and analyze periodical publications, news articles and columns regarding Afro-Brazilian religions published in "O DIA" newspaper between 1951 and 1959. During this period, it was mainly with reference to the term "macumba" that the majority of the news regarding Afro-Brazilian religions was constructed. In a general and stereotypic way "macumba" is perceived by the majoritarian urban middle class of Brazilian society as a criminal activity and synonymous with "decline" (non-progress) and "degeneration". In this way the construction of the category of "macumba" was instrumental in the marginalisation of the "black" population and their religiosity in Brazil. As a support to my analysis, I will also introduce some of the meanings attributed to the term "macumba" by some researchers of Afro-Brazilian religions (anthropologists, sociologists, folklorists and physicians) during the 20th century.

A good starting point to understand the meanings of the term "macumba" in Rio de Janeiro city is to link it with the creation and the bureaucratic organization of "Umbanda", *the* "Brazilian religion" according to its believers. It is recognized that the first "Umbanda" place of worship[1] was established by Zelio de Moraes (1891 – 1975) in Niteroi city during the 1920's. In 1938, this "Centro de Umbanda" was moved to Rio de Janeiro city center. According to Diana Brown (1985) its associates were mainly middle class people: trades people, government officials, military, self-employed, teachers, solicitors, reporters and some working class people. Brown also thinks that "Umbanda" was a way for the Brazilian middle class to express its values, its social ideals and, last but not least, its social class interests.

In 1939 Zelio de Moraes and several Umbandist leaders created the first Umbanda bureaucratic organization (União Espírita Umbandista do Brasil –

---

1 "Centro de Umbanda" in Portuguese language.

UEUB)[2]. Its main goal, according to their own words, was to "protect" the affiliated worship places. In 1941 the UEUB promoted the first Umbanda Congress in Rio de Janeiro city. In 1949 the UEUB launched a newspaper ("Jornal da Umbanda") to cover regional and national Umbanda meetings, to publish articles regarding the Umbanda doctrine and ritual and also to distribute Umbanda books and journals. During the 1950's and 1960's this newspaper was the main Umbanda periodical.

It was also during the 1950's that six other Umbanda bureaucratic organizations were created in Rio de Janeiro city, then the Federal Capital of Brazil. Under the guidance of Tancredo da Silva Pinto (1904–1979), the Umbandist Espiritist Federation ("Federação Espírita Umbandista") proposed a "kind of African oriented Umbanda". Its administrative staff was mainly composed of those with black skin color and mixed people, the so-called "mulatos".

In the first edition, from 1954, of the *Dictionary of Brazilian Folklore* (1984), Câmara Cascudo (1898–1986), a well-known Brazilian folklorist, defines the term "macumba" as an African musical percussion instrument, which produces the sound of scraping. This particular sound is produced by a small iron stick against an irregular surface. Câmara Cascudo also says that the term "macumba" is used to designate a similar religion that is called "Candomble" in Bahia and "Xango" in Pernambuco. Popularly "macumba" means witchcraft, "ebó" or "muamba", and also a witchcraft meeting as opposed to a religious meeting, the best example of this being "Candomble". Another meaning of "macumba" is that of something "artificial", "false", "simulated", and "not natural" or "the object that contains witchcraft and that transmits evil by contact". In this sense, the term "Macumba" is used to designate a "protector amulet", a "fetish", a ritually constructed object that protects the user.

João do Rio (1881-1921), the nickname of Paulo Barreto, a well-known Brazilian journalist, in his classic book first edited in 1904 – "*Religions of The Rio de Janeiro*"[3] – relates his visits to the worship places of different religions and also the interviews that he conducted with religious practitioners. According to João do Rio, everybody in Rio de Janeiro believes and fears the witchcraft (the "feitiço") of black people. He said that it was possible to pay for witchcraft for all sorts of aims: love, life, money or death.

The central João do Rio proposition was that in Rio de Janeiro city all the social strata were related to what he calls "black people witchcraft". However, João do Rio did not use the term "macumba" in his texts; he preferred to use the Brazilian synonym term for "witchcraft" ("feitiço").

---

2 Umbandista Spiritualist Union of Brazil

3 "*As Religiões do Rio*"

Arthur Ramos (1903-1949), a Brazilian psychiatrist and anthropologist, indicated that there was little data with regard to Afro-Brazilian worship of Bantu origins. Ramos proposed that in Rio de Janeiro city only the musician and composer Luciano Gallet (1893–1931), in his book "Black people in Brazilian music" (1928), related something regarding Bantu religiosity. To Gallet, the term "macumba" means the witchcraft in which the Bantu invoke their "saints".

According to Arthus Ramos (1988), some of the Bantu deities were used at Afro-Brazilian "macumbas", but to him these Bantu deities were "transformed" and "degraded". Ramos also understood that the "macumbas" was a "mix" of Gege-Nago, Kardecist spiritism and Catholic elements, a result of a broad syncretism. For him, Brazilian witchcraft has its origin in this syncretism and its practices were considered as "secret", "dangerous" and were forbidden by the "white" man. Some researchers understand that this sort of preconception was progressively internalized by the Afro-Brazilian population and became the way they understand their own religious practices. Arthur Ramos also considers that this is the origin of the Afro-Brazilian "sorcerer" or "wizard" that over time lost his social function but preserved the ritualistic aspects of his practice. As a consequence of this perspective, the Afro-Brazilian "sorcerer" is understood as responsible for many of the crimes that occur amongst the lower urban classes.

The French sociologist Roger Bastide (1898-1974) who lived and taught in Brazil between 1938 and 1958, thinks that the "macumba" can be better understood in the context of Brazilian industrialization (1971). He considers that the black population was not able to climb the social ladder during Brazilian industrialization. Bastide defines "macumba" as the expression of an Afro-Brazilian religiosity after having lost its traditional values. According to his perspective, "macumba" is opposed to "Umbanda", considered as the "new" and "authentic" Brazilian religion. "Umbanda" could be seen as the expression of a new Brazilian moment of the reorganization of social and cultural values. This was defined as a period in which the black population was introduced into the class system. Bastide considers that the big city had a deconstructive effect on the "black" population. To him (1971), "macumba" is the Brazilian Afro-descendent population's answer to the problems of facing a world that brought them nothing but "insecurity", "disorder" and "mobility".

Bastide also thinks that the main feature of "macumba" was its fluidity and its individualized aspects – and that it is these characteristics that are opposed to those of the Afro-Brazilian "traditional" religions: Candomble (in Bahia) and Xango (in Pernambuco). In "macumba", the priest would be able to invent different ways to perform their rituals and could create new deities to worship. To Bastide this characteristic of "macumba" characteristic was a consequence of the "devaluation" and "degradation" of Afro-Brazilian religiosity.

The spread of "Umbanda" religion pushed "macumba" to the Rio de Janeiro suburbs. Losing its religious characteristics, "macumba" became the Brazilian "black magic" or witchcraft and the "macumbeiro" the "insulated, sinister, and fearsome as a great sorcerer" (Bastide 1971: 417). From collective to individual form, from religion to magic, this is how Bastide understood the development of Afro-Brazilian religions.

In accordance with Bastide and with the mainstream Brazilian worldview, "macumba" is considered to be the main cause of all "evils" and ills that take place in Brazilian society. But the "macumba" practice can be seen to be the result of the social disaggregation, in Bastide's words: "the result of the social parasitism, the shameless exploitation of the lower classes credulity, and the loosening of the immoral tendencies, from rape to murder".[4]

The common preconception is that the places of worship of Afro-Brazilian religions are "dangerous", and are inhabited by all sorts of social misfits and "degenerate" people.

The phenomenon of social disorganization, caused by transformations in the social structure and caused in the final analysis by Brazilian industrialization, would have affected all social strata. According to Bastide this would have decreased the degree of solidarity and weakened community ties, atomizing the individual. In "macumba" a great number of people search for solutions to all sorts of life problems that affect them. It is also in "macumba" that the social dramas present themselves.

At the beginning of the 1970's, Marco Aurelio Luz and George Lapassade (1972) had a singular approach to the "macumba" phenomenon. These authors understood "macumba" as a ritual of liberation based on the theories of Marx, Freud and Wilhelm Reich in the context of religious institutions. They also considered that the most important aspect of "macumba" is the expression of repressed desire for freedom. Luz and Lapassade think that "macumba" ritual symbolizes that the human is not free, and must act to achieve their "full liberation".

It was also during the 1970s that Yvonne Maggie (1977) conducted ethnographic research in a single "Terreiro", demonstrating how the terms "macumba", "umbanda", "quimbanda" and "spiritism" were used. According to her observations the term "macumba" could be used in two different ways: 1) to designate the Afro-Brazilian religion of possession; 2) to accuse someone who supposedly uses witchcraft or "black magic" ("magia negra"), someone who "works for evil" – in this sense "quimbanda" is another term that also could be used as synonym for "macumba".

---

4 "O resultado do parasitismo social, a exploração desavergonhada da credulidade das classes baixas, e a perda nas tendências imorais, do estupro ao assassinato" (1971: 57)

Marcia Contins and Marcio Goldman (1983), in a case study involving murder and spirit possession,[5] discuss the terms "macumba" and "macumbeiro" as accusatory categories. The "Pomba-Gira" case is a murder committed by a medium while she was possessed by a female "Exu" – the "Pomba-Gira". This case was in the news for several months, mobilizing public opinion and the specialists (priests, lawyers, physicians, psychiatrists, commissioner of police, reporters and last but not least, anthropologists). The accusations against the medium were from two different points of view. On one side, internally within Afro-Brazilian religious belief systems, it was said that the medium was not "developed", meaning that she was not fully initiated. From the other side, from outsiders to Afro-Brazilian religious belief, the medium's religious practices were said to be "black magic", "witchcraft". Internally the accusations were related to individual issues: mediumship is an ability that has to be "developed" by the medium during his/her initiation process. Externally the accusations were collective and aimed at Afro-Brazilian religious groups as a whole – they were all accused as "misfits", "marginal" and "criminals".

Marcia Contins also points out that Brazilian society's ambivalence concerning "umbanda" religion, and all Afro-Brazilian religions, originates with the identification with "criminality" and with the belief in the reality of the possession of special powers. It is a common belief that is possible to use "macumba" to kill or to cure someone.

Contrasting with Bastide's ideas regarding "macumba", Reginaldo Prandi (1990) thinks that "macumba" was the name of the Rio de Janeiro Afro-Brazilian worship that preexisted to the creation of the "umbanda" religion. Prandi disagrees with Bastide that "macumba" was a "candomble" disaggregation. Prandi indicates that Arthur Ramos talked about Bantu worship in Rio de Janeiro at the beginning of the 20th century, similar to Nago's Orixas worship, with its own organization and characterized by the phenomenon of possession by the spirits of the dead. This latter feature is similar to the Bantu tradition of ancestor worship.

Liana Trindade (1991) defines "macumba" as a syncretic religion, the first effort at the systematization and codification of the Bantu belief system in a new society. The emergence of "umbanda" is indebted to the systematization of "macumba", recognized by Liana Trindade as the first centralization movement of Afro-Brazilian religiosities in Brazil. Many middle-class individuals, with their middle-class values, had an important role in this religious restructuring.

Ismael Pordeus (1993) thinks that both "macumba" and "umbanda" are reactions to modern Brazilian society's lifestyle. Pordeus understands that these religions emphasize the notion of "magic manipulation" through the reframing of

5 "*The Pomba-Gira Case*" is also the title of her (Marcia Contins' or Marcio Goldman's dissertation? Not clear here) Master Dissertation (1983): "*The Pomba-Gira Case: reflections regarding crime, possession and female image*".

the category "work" ("trabalho", "despacho", "feitiço"). Analysing how the category "work" ("trabalho") was reframed in Umbanda Spiritism, Pordeus understood that at the same time as Umbanda's creation – during the 1930s – Brazilian society was consolidating as an urban and industrial society, as well as establishing a rational and secular worldview with the valorisation of urban labour.

The main deity or "entity" – in both "Umbanda" and "Macumba" – through magical manipulation (the witchcraft – "feitiço" or "trabalho") is Exu. In reality, there are a large number of different Exus, both males and females (Pomba-Giras). All of them are ambiguous elements if we observe that on the one hand, they are strictly necessary to the magical manipulation ("trabalho", "feitiço" or "witchcraft") and on the other hand, they refuse to accept the value of "work" – to labor – in the modern society. In everyday life, all Exus are classified as marginal individuals: streetwise, criminals, murderers and prostitutes. The streets of the city are their main place of existence and, in Brazil, the streets are opposed to the home and family values (DaMatta 1997).

According Maria Lina Leão Teixeira (1994), the term "macumba" can have at least two meanings in accordance with its user: from an outsider perspective, "macumba" has a negative value and takes the form of an accusation; from an insider perspective, "macumba" can designate the several Afro-Brazilian religions or can also designate the "power", the "magical efficacy" of Afro-Brazilian religions.

Lísias Negrao (1996) highlights the secular character of the accusations against the Afro-Brazilian population and their religions. In accordance with Negrao, all the social stigmas that affect the Brazilian Afro-descendant population culminated with an attitude of hostility and fear that continues up to the present time. The links between the terms "macumba" and "umbanda", in their many senses, express the social dynamic of the Afro-descendant population in a society that was trying to become "modern" and "industrialized", according to its own ideas about what that might mean.

What is important to understand is the fact that in Brazil, "macumba" is linked with the practice of "witchcraft", or "black magic" – as the "magic of the black people" – the practice of causing harm to someone at a distance through magical means and with the support of spiritual beings. If "macumba" is linked with "magic", we have to keep in mind that it is also opposed to what is considered as *the* Brazilian religion itself, "umbanda". "Umbanda" writers, its ideologists, were successful in establishing it as *the* Brazilian religion. "Umbanda" is characterized as an ancient and traditional "African religion", and at the same time as a modern, a nationalistic – Brazilian religion. Some Brazilian national myths such as "racial democracy" and the supposed Brazilian "spiritual superiority" were adopted by the "Umbanda" ideology.

However, despite all the efforts of ideologists of the "Umbanda" religion to establish a distinction between "macumba" and "umbanda", in a common sense way for most of the population, the "Umbanda" religion and its adepts, in generic and derogatory terms are still denominated as "macumba" and "macumbeiros".

Despite the fact that most researchers – Brazilian sociologists, anthropologists and historians – indicate the lack of organisation of "macumba" as its main characteristic, and oppose it to the organizing and institutionalizing features of "Umbanda", there are some researchers (Ismael Pordeus, Reginaldo Prandi and Liana Trindade amongst them) that are trying to recreate the history of the Bantu in Rio de Janeiro with a view to reconstruct "macumba" origins. They demonstrate that there were some well-organized "macumba terreiros" (worship places) in Rio de Janeiro, and that internal conflicts within the Afro-Brazilian religious field were the cause of the damage to the term "macumba".

In order to establish an Afro-Brazilian religiosity in accordance with their own interests, the "Umbanda" leaders acted with the aim of creating a well delimited border separating them from "macumba". It is possible to support the notion that Umbanda, as an Afro-Brazilian religion created in Rio de Janeiro during the 1920s by an ascending urban middle class, is a reframing of Afro-Brazilian religious practices that already existed. The main goal of Umbanda is disciplinary and to standardize a large number of religious practices and beliefs. It was also its goal to blend all religious aspects that could be related with "the things of the black people" ("coisas de negros"), specially the use of drums, the animal sacrifices, and the use of "cachaça" (sugar cane rum).

The following on from this summary of the various ways that scholars have approached the problem of the relationship between Umbanda and macumba, I will now give some examples of how Brazilian society understands and classifies Afro-Brazilian religions based on my own research on newspapers. The main aim of this research was to collect and analyze "*O DIA*" newspapers published during the 1950's. My initial hypothesis was that the newspapers mainly reproduced the usual stereotypes linked with afro-Brazilian religions as "primitive" and "disordered".

The Rio de Janeiro morning daily newspaper "*O DIA*" was first published on July 5th 1951. With an affordable cost to the working class of Cr$0,50 (the Brazilian minimal wage was Cr$380,00), a typical "*O DIA*" edition was composed of 8 pages, with 24 pages in Sunday editions. Its owner was Chagas Freitas (1914 – 1991), a well-known Brazilian populist politician who was the Rio de Janeiro Governor during 1979 – 1983 (at the end of the last dictatorship period from 1964 to 1985). The characteristic features of the "*O DIA*" editorial were its criminal news that described, with unexpected details, bloody crimes and its informative articles that described the Rio de Janeiro suburban population's daily life. The "*O DIA*" was popularly recognized as a newspaper that "dripped blood".

The main "*O DIA*" content were the so called "fait divers", the "features", that usually fascinated people so much. The "features" essence was its capacity to generate astonishment, to cause disturbance. It is a fact that converting a police report into news requires a trained perception, a specific way of dealing with images and the ability to create stories that are able to stimulate in the reader a desired reaction. With this ability, everyday life events, even the most violent crimes, are transformed into spectacles.

The *O DIA* newspaper's main target population was the Rio de Janeiro working class, characterized as a "cheated" taxpayer that suffered a tough life, "without a health system, without public transport and with bad quality food", as was written in the first "O DIA" editorial.

During the period 1951 – 1959, a typical "O DIA" edition was composed as follows:

- Cover page – Headlines with sensationalistic approach
- Page 2 – newspaper editorial, national politics and national news
- Page 3 – Rio de Janeiro daily life news
- Page 4 – leisure and public utility
- Page 5 – Crime news
- Page 6 – Crime news
- Page 7 – Sports (horse racing mainly)
- Page 8 – Sports (soccer)

The collected data from "*O DIA*" regarding Afro-Brazilian religions are composed of 624 items: 178 news items, 40 informative reports and 406 editorials. These data were published as follows:

YEAR	NEWS and REPORTS	EDITORIALS	TOTAL
1951	7	14	21
1952	53 = 13 + 40 ("Aguerê")	4	57
1953	21	14	35
1954	20	50	70
1955	26	51	77
1956	26	53	79
1957	26	57	83
1958	13	69	82
1959	26	94	120
	218	406	624

We can also follow these data by month and year (**N** news and reports \ **E** editorials):

	Jan N\E	Feb N\E	Mar N\E	Apr N\E	May N\E	Jun N\E
1951	-	-	-	-	-	2\1
1952	1\-	2\-	-\1	4\2	1\-	-
1953	-	-	-	1\-	2\-	-
1954	-\5	3\4	1\4	3\4	1\5	3\4
1955	3\5	-\4	3\4	-\4	-\5	2\4
1956	4\5	6\4	1\4	1\5	3\4	1\4
1957	3\4	-\4	4\5	4\3	3\5	2\5
1958	2\8	-\8	1\10	1\8	1\9	-\9
1959	1\8	3\8	2\8	2\8	1\8	3\8
	Jul N\E	Aug N\E	Sep N\E	Oct N\E	Nov N\E	Dec N\E
1951	-\1	1\1	2\4	1\2	1\2	-\3
1952	3\-	2\1	3\-	24\-	12\-	-
1953	11\-	2\-	2\1	1\4	2\5	-\4
1954	1\3	1\5	1\4	1\5	4\3	2\4
1955	4\5	1\4	3\4	4\5	2\4	4\3
1956	5\5	1\4	2\5	1\4	1\4	-\5
1957	2\4	-\2	1\5	1\4	2\7	4\9
1958	1\8	1\10	5\9	-\8	1\10	1\9
1959	2\7	3\8	1\7	3\8	3\8	2\8

Some categories of accusation ("macumba", "macumbeiro") were (and continue to be) usual among newspapers, police, justice systems, intellectuals and Afro-Brazilian religions organizations and practitioners. The terms "macumba" and "macumbeiro" can be used to accuse someone who supposedly practices "witchcraft", someone who "works for evil". Those that are accused of practicing the so-called "lower spiritism" are usually linked with "sexuality", "crime", "witchcraft", "madness" and "quackery". I use similar categories to organize the "*O DIA*" data into four categories and fourteen sub-categories:

Group I	Death	Murder Suicide
Group II	Sexuality	Sex Abuse Homosexuality
Group III	Disorder	Violence Conflicts \ Turmoil Quackery Madness
Group IV	Religion	Witchcraft \ Magic Religious Festivals News \ reports regarding Umbanda or Candomblé Aguerê Contest (contest \ conflict)

GROUP I (Death):

Murder: 1952 January 23th – “THE MACUMBEIRO PLANNED THE CRIME” the accused nurse defended herself against a charge of premeditative poisoning of a patient

Murder: 1952 February 17th – “THE MACUMBA WAS THE MOTIVE FOR TWO CRIMES” the criminal, after attacking the médium (the so called “horse”), stabbed and killed the municipal guard and wounded a fisherman

Suicide: 1954 December 10th – “DRAGGED BY MACUMBA” suicide with an enchantment in his pocket ... A workman, Almir de Lima, Brazilian, black, single, 25 years old, committed suicide by drinking poison ... his father said that he “was a good worker and a communicative person until the moment that he joined the macumba, after that he left employment and avoided speaking with his father

Suicide: 1956 October 24th – “SUICIDE INFLUENCED BY THE MACUMBEIRO” A salesman, a naive and healthy man, believed in the lies of the sorcerer – two children orphaned – He suffered severe sinusitis.

GROUP II (Sexuality):

Sex Abuse: 1957 March 24th – “THE MACUMBEIRO MUDERED TEENAGERS AFTER HE SEDUCED THEM” He raped girls with the support of his wife – He strangled the babies.

Homosexuality: 1954 November 4th – “BARBARIC AND REVOLTING” the “pai-de-santo”, after cutting the homosexual with a razor, satisfied his “low appetites” on the miserable creature. The Police went to the “Terreiro” and arrested everybody

GROUP III (Disorder):

Violence: 1955 January 20th – “HE VOWED TO KILL THE PAI-DE-SANTO” his wife was bewitched after the “terreiro” worship

Conflicts\Turmoil: 1954 November 13th – “I AM Eshu” the man shouted and the spiritist worship finished... an armed group of people broke everything at the “Terreiro”. Only the altar was protected. Caboclo Sete Flechas (Seven Arrow Caboclo) cast out the heretic

Quackery: 1957 December 3rd – “the witchdoctor deluded the ignorant people for at least half a century” the old witch (‘macumbeira’) was arrested and sent to the gaol ... a large number of drugs and recipes were found at her home ... this is proof that she is acting as a physician without a license

Madness: 1955 January 14: “He was bewitched by his concubine and went crazy”

GROUP IV (Religion)

Witchcraft\Magic: 1958 April 10th – “(HE) RAPED THE TEENAGER THREATENING HER WITH WITCHCRAFT” the man says that He is a “macumbeiro”, perpetrator of several witchcrafts for all sorts of aims, from weddings to murders. He is a fake

Witchcraft\Magic: 1958 September 10th – “THE WITCH STABBED THE WOMAN WITH A SCISSORS”

Religious Festival: 1958 January 01/02 – "IEMANJA PARTY AT ARPOADOR BEACH" a truly Umbanda ritual… several Spiritist Organizations were at the beach

Religious Festival: 1958 January 3rd – "THE CARIOCA WELCOMED THE NEW YEAR WITH A CARNIVAL AND WORSHIP TO THE QUEEN OF THE SEA"

News and Reports Regarding Umbanda and Candomble: 1953 May 21st – "THE SANTE MISTERYS"… Umbanda baptism, a beautiful and exotic rite… the drums were played by true masters

News and Reports Regarding Umbanda and Candomble: 1957 December 6th – "IANSAN PARTY AT TERREIROS" good people attended the big party at Joãozinho da Gomeia "Iabassa"

There were also texts published in "*O DIA*" that did not talk about crime or death. These weekly editorials were written by the leaders of Umbandist Organizations concerning the Umbandist festivals, rituals and cosmology. In their editorials they delimited the borders between Umbanda and the other Afro-Brazilian religious groups, legitimating some practices, marginalizing other practices and establishing "a right way" to practice Umbanda (which was their own way).

An Umbandist editorial called "notas espiritas" ("spirit notes") started to be published in July 1951. It was not linked with any Umbandist Organization and its author signed with the initials C.R. This editorial was not published regularly. Some weeks it was published every day and on other weeks it was not published. According to the author, its goal was to answer the question "What is Umbanda?"

The relations between the Umbandist Organizations and the huge amount of local worship places (the so called "Terreiros") were mediated through the Umbandist Organizations leaders. In this sense, the writings (newspaper editorials and books) were an effective tool to add "wisdom" – a supposed "wisdom" – to its writers and at the same time to subtract the "wisdom" and the "power" – from those who "simply" live the doctrine. However, in accordance with Umbanda religious characteristics, the Umbandist Organizations never managed to impose themselves – their worldview – unconditionally over the worship places (the "Terreiros") and adepts. The relation with the Umbanda deities ("entidades de Umbanda") is personal and happens inside the "Terreiros", and it is this characteristic that gives a unique power to each Umbandist priest and priestesses ("pai-de-santo" and "mae-de-santo"). The main explicit function of the Umbandist Organizations was to provide juridical assistance to the "Terreiros", in order to help them organize their official activities and fulfil their bureaucratic responsibilities.

A new weekly editorial started on September 27th 1953 with the title "From the Umbandist Priestess" ("Dos Sacerdotes de Umbanda"). Its authors were Tancredo da Silva Pinto (Spiritist Umbandist Confederation President) and Byron Torres de Freitas (Spiritist Umbandist Federation of Rio de Janeiro President) and they regularly invited other Umbandist ideologists to write and publish in their column.

Under the guidance of Tancredo da Silva Pinto (1904 – 1979), the Umbandist Espiritist Federation (Federação Espírita Umbandista) proposed a "kind of African oriented Umbanda" as described by Tancredo ("O DIA" September 27th 1953). Its administrative staff was mainly composed of those with black skin color and mixed people, the so-called "mulatos".

From November 1957, this Umbandist editorial was published twice a week, on Saturdays and Sundays. The Sunday edition also went to the streets on Monday. Two other Umbandist leaders and ideologists also published in "From the Umbandist Priestess": Sandoval Batista dos Santos (Spiritist Umbandist of Rio de Janeiro Solicitor) and Ernesto Lourenço da Silva (Spiritist Umbandist Confederation Secretary). They also authored several books concerning Umbandist doctrine, cosmology and rituals.

The links between the Umbandist Organizations in the mass media and the political parties made possible their influence on Umbandist practices. The ritual manuals published by the Umbandist Organizations, although not always followed by the Umbanda practitioners at the worship places ("Terreiros"), had an important influence on the standardization of Umbanda ritual practices and contributed to the creation of a shared identity among Umbandists. The content of this Umbandist editorial column was as follows:

1. Regular visits to the places of worship (the so called "Terreiros");
2. The history of Umbanda in accordance with the Umbadist Organizations' point of view and interests;
3. The meaning of Umbanda rituals and cosmology;
4. How to do specific Umbandist rituals;
5. How to behave in accordance with the Umbandist doctrine.

The editorials titles and their content demonstrate that the Umbandist organizations goal was to codify and to standardize the Afro-Brazilian religious practices in accordance with their singular perspective. In doing so they also established boundaries between what they considered as the "true" and the "false" Umbanda, the so called "Macumba".

At the same time that the Umbandist Organizations were opposed to everybody that practiced legal and moral transgressions under the label of Afro-Brazilian religion, they also reinforced some stereotypes usually attributed to Afro-Brazilian religions by the non-adepts.

The Umbandist organizations purported to get away from the accusations of "impurity" and "primitivism" usually imputed to the so-called "Umbanda of the worship places" ("Umbanda dos Terreiros"). The Umbanda ritual practices that were – and still are – seen as signs of "primitivism", "barbarism" and "blackness" ("negritude"), show us how the notions of "purity" and "pollution" can express social conflicts and inequalities.

The Umbandist editorials were intended to elaborate representations in order to organize and to modernize Afro-Brazilian religiosity. On the other hand, the front-page "macumbeiros", as represented in the "*O DIA*" newspaper and in the discourse of Umbandist organizations, presented the "crime", the "disorder" and the "regressive aspects" of Brazilian culture and society.

It is at the intersection of these several aspects where the tense and ambiguous borders between the "allowed" and the "forbidden"; between the "true" and the "false"; between the "authentic" and the "inauthentic" in the Afro-Brazilian religious landscape are outlined. In "*O DIA*" the working class was characterized as "regressed" and immersed in "death", "sensuality" and "disorder". According to the newspaper's perspective, only a political project designed for these classes and conducted by the owner of "*O DIA*" and his political allies would be able to "develop" the values and ideals of modernity amongst them.

The "*O DIA*" discourse was mainly built on three positions: stories of crime and "disorder"; articles regarding cultural events usually characterized as "exotic" and "primitive"; editorials that expressed the Umbandist Organizations opinions, the "expertize" that aimed to teach behavior in accordance with "order" and "progress" (the slogans of the Brazilian national flag). Through its sensationalist daily headlines and its two pages of crime news a singular representation regarding the everyday life of a distinct Rio de Janeiro area – the "favelas"- was developed and the Rio de Janeiro periphery (the so called "Grande Rio"), and the people that lived in this areas, were imagined, represented and classified as "black people". A whole range of social deviances occupied the pages of "*O DIA*" newspaper in an effort to symbolically and politically order them.

As concluding remarks, I would like to point out that "Macumba" is a very popular term in Brazil, used to indicate the "witchcraft of the black people" (João do Rio, 1904). A term that works together with witchcraft belief, shared through all Brazilian social strata. Usually, "Macumba" is a term linked to the "evils" and ills that take place in Brazilian society and in this way is a term mainly used as an accusatory category – to accuse someone who is supposed practice the "witchcraft of the black people", someone who "works for evil", and someone who practices "black witchcraft".

Initially, researchers understood "Macumba" as a degradation of the Bantu religious beliefs mixed with Gege-Nago, Kardecist Spiritism and Catholic religious aspects. According to Roger Bastide, for example, "Macumba" is a degraded expression of the Afro-Brazilian religiosity. Some characteristics such as "fluidity" and "individualism" were attributed to "Macumba" as a negative sign, and opposed to the systematised/systematisers and collective aspects of Umbanda. Only recently, some researchers of the Afro-Brazilian religiosity understood "Macumba" as an initial attempt at the systematization of the multiple religious beliefs of the black slaves from different ethnicities brought to Brazil between 1533 and 1850. Unfortunately, this more recent research is not well known by Brazilian society.

What prevails, as I have demonstrated through my research on newspapers, is the notion that "Macumba", the "black witchcraft", is opposed to "Umbanda" – the "Brazilian religion". However, in a broad sense, the "Umbanda" strategy of denigrating and denouncing "Macumba" had as a side effect the reinforcement of the negative stereotypes that are applied to all Afro-Brazilian religious beliefs and believers.

References

Archanjo, Marcelo Vidaurre (1997): *Se Torcer sai Sangue: Uma Análise das Representações sobre Religiosidade Afro-Brasileira no Jornal O Dia* (If you Ring, it Bleeds: an Analysis of Representations on Afro-Brazilian Religiosity in the O Dia Newspaper). Master Dissertation in Sociology, UFRJ Federal University of Rio de Janeiro.

Brown, Diana (1985): *Uma Historia da Umbanda no Rio* (A History of Umbanda in Rio de Janeiro). Cadernos do ISER 18 Umbanda e Politica. Rio de Janeiro: Marco Zero Press, 9-42.

Bastide, Roger (1971): *As Religiões Africanas no Brasil* (The African Religions in Brazil). São Paulo: EDUSP Press.

Cascudo, Câmara (1984): *Dicionário do Folclore Brasileiro* (Brazilian Folklore Dictionary). Belo Horizonte: Itatiaia Press.

Contins, Marcia and Marcio Goldman (1984): "O Caso da Pomba-Gira: Religião e Violência. Uma Análise do Jogo Discursivo entre Umbanda e Sociedade" (The Pomba-Gira Case: Religion and Violence. An Analyse of the Discursive Game Between Umbanda and Society), *Revista Religiao e Sociedade* 11 (1), 103-132.

DaMatta, Roberto (1997): *A Casa e a Rua: espaço, cidadania, mulher e a morte no Brasil* (The House and the Street: social space, citizenship, woman and death in Brazil). Rio de Janeiro: Rocco Press.

Luz, Marco Aurelio, George Lapassade (1972): *O Segredo da Macumba* (The Macumba's Secret). Rio de Janeiro: Paz e Terra Press.

Negrão, Lisias Nogueira (1996): *Entre a Cruz e a Encruzilhada* (Between the Cross and the Crossroad). São Paulo: EDUSP Press.

Pordeus, Ismael (1993): *A Magia do Trabalho – Macumba Cearense e Festas de Possessão* (The Work of Magic – The Macumba from Ceara and the Possession Festivals). Fortaleza: Secretaria da Cultura e Desporto do Estado do Ceara Publisher.

Prandi, Reginaldo (1990): "Modernidade com Feitiçaria: Candomblé e Umbanda no Brasil no Século XX" (Modernity with Witchcraft: Candomble and Umbanda in Brasil during 20th Century), *Revista Tempo Social* 2 (1), 49-79.

Ramos, Arthur (1988): *O Negro Brasileiro* (The Brazilian Black People). Recife: Fundação Joaquim Nabuco, Massangana Press.

Rio, João do (1951): *As Religiões do Rio* (The Rio de Janeiro Religions). Rio de Janeiro: Garnier Press.

Teixeira, Maria Lina Leão (1994): "A Encruzilhada do Ser: Representações da [Lou]Cura em Terreiros de Candomblé" (The Being Crossroad: The representations of Madness on Candomble Worship Places), PhD Thesis in Social Anthropology, USP São Paulo University.

Trindade, Liana Maria Salvia (1993): *Construções Miticas e Históricas: Estudos sobre as representações e relações raciais em São Paulo do Século XVIII a atualidade* (Mythical and Historical Constructions: Study cases regarding the racial relations and representations in São Paulo from 18 Century to actuality), Livre-Docência in Social Anthropology Thesis, USP São Paulo University.

Velho, Yvonne Maggie Alves (1977): *Guerra de Orixa: Um Estudo de Ritual e Conflito* (Orixa's War: a Case Study of Ritual and Conflict). Rio de Janeiro: Zahar Press.

Reconfigurations of Indigenous Personhood in Western Siberia

Eva Toulouze

Institut National des Langues et Civilisations Orientales (INALCO), Paris

Abstract

The topic of this article is indigenous personhood as seen from a Western Siberian point of view. Often research about indigenous personhood focuses on what appears, from a Western point of view, to be the most distinctive aspect of indigenous personhood: "Data on personhood in animistic societies (...) invariably demonstrate that non-human entities may be regarded as social persons" (Brightman, Grotti, Ulturgasheva 2012: 2). Although this has been the main interest in previous scholarship, I shall not focus here on human-non human relations. The point of view chosen here is historical: it focuses on how colonisation has put pressure on configurations of human personhood in Western Siberia. The result of this pressure is a shift in the way human beings see themselves in their relations with the rest of their environment and has led to a simultaneous duality of perception with which indigenous people have had to cope. This has come about in different ways. I shall introduce an example of one of them, in analysing the conscious endeavours by a Nenets intellectual to work on his personhood in order to achieve indigenous 'wholeness'.

An attempt to a theoretical framework

The notion of personhood, which underlies this article, is neither a neutral nor a simple one. It is not within the scope of this article to explore all its philosophical implications; this would be a research it its own right. While the understanding of "personhood" as a common feature of humans, being rational and having moral status (Ikäheimo, Laitinen 2007: 8-9), is too wide for my scope, I am interested in more particular features of personhood: how persons in concrete communities situated in a concrete historical position see their place in relation to oneself, to the environment, to other existing "awarenesses". I am interested in analysing how for the indigenous peoples of Western Siberia this understanding has changed in the course of history, more precisely how it has been subject to ruptures.

Two main questions cannot be ignored while exploring this issue. One is the appropriateness of talking about personhood, which implies the existence of a subject: as Humphrey emphasises, because it is not possible to dissert the "subject" as a philosophical entity ignoring the fact it has been thoroughly deconstructed at the end of the 20th century (2008: 235). The second question concerns the contents of the notion "personhood" and its allegedly Western focus, as my aim is to reflect on non-Western understandings of personhood whilst taking into account the "Western pressure" it has experienced and its influence. In this introduction, I shall attempt to delineate some of the borders of my subject and to define what I shall and what I shall not develop.

In the article referenced above, which treats a similar topic, Caroline Humphrey develops at length different authors' views about how to cope with the "death of the subject". She pinpoints the contradiction between what philosophers have been arguing and both the ethnographic experience and the needs of anthropology, which cannot be satisfied with general issues, and need to delve into details that may not fit with universal categories and the "peculiarities" not covered or explained by them (see Humphrey 2008: 235). One of the ways to overcome the difficulties is to explore, as Humphrey does, different philosophers' responses to the deconstructive pattern, what can be called "subject two", which presents, depending on the philosopher, different features of the "subject" (Humphrey 2008: 259-60). Among the different new versions of the subject, the one she insists on as the most productive for her material is Alain Badiou's understanding of personhood emerging with the occurrence of an Event (Humphrey 2008: 260-280). Badiou, in Humphreys' words, "acknowledges the social and historical conditions of the formation of a subject" (2008: 360).[1] Moreover, Badiou, for whom the search for truth is the core of philosophy, insists that "there could be no truths without the subject" (Vihalem 2011: 74), thus justifying the necessity of the subject. For Badiou, "there is an indiscernible and incalculable event, completed by a finite subject aiming at understanding the infinite truth of the event and determined to be faithful to its implications" (Vihalem 2011: 78). As this impressive resume of this central tangle in Badiou's thought shows, in Badiou's vocabulary, these three notions – truth, subject and event – are impossible to separate from one another. Another conclusion one may draw is that all these notions are quite dissociated with the common use of the words used by Badiou and depict abstract phenomena. One has, therefore, to try to understand what meaning Badiou gives each one of them. The "event" may be seen as "a turning point from which truths

1 Not being a philosopher, I use here secondary literature in order to comment on the basis of a reliable interpretation.

can be affirmed" (Vihalem 2011: 70). As far as the subject is concerned, it "is far from being a substantial entity" (Vihalem 2011: 75). What is interesting for us is a series of processes: "There is something that can be thought as an event, so one considers the event having taken place. One thus accepts the implications (at least some of them) of this event and re-composes oneself (one's thoughts, one's actions, one's being) as the subject related or event allied to the event concerned, entering, as Badiou puts it, into the composition of the subject" (Vihalem 2011: 76). The understanding of "event", something "that maddens our ordinary knowledge" (Meillassoux 2008), is for Badiou a subjective turning point that changes a person and thus, "enables the emergence of subject two" and, through change, reveals his or her new personhood. I find this sequence quite inspiring, even if we take the words in their ordinary meaning. Neither Badiou nor Vihalem use the word personhood in connection with subject. But the way Vihalem explains how Badiou understands the recomposition of self allows the connection between the two notions.

This question has also been discussed within the framework of the anthropology of Christianity. Here, while the focus is directly connected with the individual/dividual opposition according to Strathern (see below), it is also linked to Badiou's understanding through Joel Robbins' argument on rupture, which comes forth in his debate with Mosko[2] which debates questions of continuity or rupture in conversion to Christianity (Mosko 2010; Robbins 2010; see also, on this debate Bialecki, Daswani 2015: 272). As far as my material is concerned, Robbins' case is most convincing, though he applies it to religion, while I deal mostly with history. But it is not to be doubted that the "event" which is at the basis of the changes I emphasise in personhood is a rupture, thus confirming the usefulness of Badiou's model for my reflections here.

The second question has been seriously discussed by Strathern, who argues that the individual is a Western understanding and may not be a proper conceptual tool to analyse non-European ethnic groups; in "The Gender of the Gift" (1988) she proposes the concept of the Melanesian "dividual", who may "ignore ideas about unitary individuals" (Humphrey 2008: 369): dividuals are "frequently constructed as the plural and composite site of the relationships that produce them. The singular person can be imagined as a social microcosm" (Strathern 1988 : 13), or, as described elsewhere, the Melanesian dividual person may "be in a state of division with respect to others" (Strathern 1992: 125). As Spiro sums up (relying on Markus and Kitayama's thoughts): "Thus, as a Westerner, I use

2 Joel Robbins insists on the importance of taking into account that conversion to Christianity has been lived by Melanesians as a fundamental rupture with the past, a fact that has been either neglected or underestimated by others anthropologists, among whom Mark Mosko. While anthropologists tend to insist on continuity, Robbins emphasises turning points, and this idea is relevant to my argument.

the word "I" exclusively, to denote only my own person (or my own self), alternatively to denote some psychic structure (an ego, a soul, whatever) within my person or self, but if I were a non-Westerner I would use the word "I" inclusively, to include other persons as well" (Spiro 1993: 108). While many authors have discussed this question, often presenting it as an "in/dividualism binary" (Bialecki, Daswani 2015: 274), but also discussing this opposition, I am still unsure, on the basis of my fieldwork, how to appreciate the Siberian case. One of the reasons is probably that Western Siberian indigenous peoples have been exposed to Russian contacts and later domination and influence for a very long time, from first contacts allegedly between the 9th to the 11th century (true, as far as the European Nenets are concerned), then with the conquest of the areas beyond the Urals since the middle of the 16th century. Thus, they are the first of Russia's peoples of the North to be integrated into the Russian world, and they have been exposed to the intrusive burden of Evangelisation from as early as the 18th century. Moreover, the first "event" I shall comment upon, the Bolshevik Revolution and its aftermath, more than 90 years ago, has set Russia' indigenous ethnic groups in even closer interaction with "Western" culture, in this case in its Russian form. It has been not only shaping their environment, but has also been forced upon them through powerful collective structures such as schools, the army or collective farms. One may argue that Russians carried with them one of the Western varieties of individuality. During the last 80 years, Russian natives have absorbed part of it, achieving thus yet another variety of hybrid culture, with definitely Western features, but with a strong different substrate. So, not without previous reflection or scruples, I shall analyse "indigenous personhood" among Siberian ethic groups according to a Western understanding. This is particularly justified in my last example, when the starting point of the awareness of self, in the case I shall develop, is a typically Western understanding (see also Dumont 1986).

My reflection is based on my fieldwork with the Forest Nenets poet, activist and reindeer herder Yuri Vella from 1998 until his death in September 2013. But in order to understand the "decision-event" (as Humphrey calls it) that changed his life between 1986 and 1990, we have to go back in history and to analyse the consequences of the previous event that changed the native peoples of the North's awareness in Russia. It would be proper to start the analysis from the very beginning, the state of this awareness before the Revolution, but alas materials are scarce: indigenous discourse has not come to us directly, for native societies were not literate and did not record themselves. The only records we have are reports from outsiders (for more details on this point, see Leete 2014), who seldom communicated directly with the natives and whose data, while precious on many other subjects, cannot be relied upon as far as native worldview and perception of the self is concerned.

I shall therefore start by commenting on the deeper changes undergone by the peoples of the North with the advent of Soviet rule, and only afterwards try to develop what peculiarities I can find in their worldview after this event. The changes occurred in two phases, which troubled the indigenous peoples as a whole and every person was involved deeply and traumatically. This may be seen as an event in Badiou's meaning of the word, which compelled the people to adapt just in order to survive. Collectively and openly, they submitted. Privately, "informally"[3] they tried to retain as many of the features that made sense to them as they could. Individually, they had to cope with different competing images of self, and each individual did it in his or her own way. I will then switch to one example of conscious work on personhood accomplished by a Nenets intellectual. He is not the only person that has undergone a critical change in the post-soviet period, but as I have been working with him for fifteen years, I had the opportunity to follow his endeavours and the inner pressure he was subjected to.

His example is not representative of how northern people adapted, on the contrary his model is quite a rare case – if not unique (for a more detailed analysis on the different adaptation models of intellectuals, see Toulouze 2000). But it is undoubtedly interesting because of the rare awareness of its subject and the explicit reflexion on these issues from his point of view. Other models might and should be studied in order to draw a typology of adaptation patterns that will show incredible resilience and readiness to shape the self in different ways in order to allow them to survive.

The Soviet reconstruction of the indigenous world

The peculiarities of the native world were totally unfamiliar to the Bolsheviks, who had most support in Russian populated areas (Fitzpatrick 1985: 61). There was no pre-defined Marxist theory about it, no predefined goals or strategies. They were not amongst the priorities in the first years of Soviet rule, when power was far from consolidated and urgent problems – military amongst others – were impending. In the civil war, during which many events took place in the North, the indigenous world withdrew from contacts with the Russians: deliveries were interrupted and they turned towards autarchy (Onishchuk 1986: 108; Gorodkov 1926: 59-60). Soviet policy toward the North was thus a mix of answering urgent questions and postponing a more encompassing approach of the problem. Answering urgent questions: if the Bolsheviks wanted to keep hold of power, they had to rule over all the territory of the Russian Empire. While they struggled to cope with the consequences of the civil war and to reconstruct the country, they had to consolidate their power in the Northern borders – with international

3 With the meaning given by Lyarskaya, Dudeck 2012: 62-64.

waters haunted by the British (as their landing in Arkhangelsk showed) and the Norwegians, and unfamiliar ethnic groups wandering in the tundra. But there were people among the Bolsheviks themselves or among the opposition to the tsarist regime who had some knowledge of Northern peoples: these were the exiles, Bolsheviks or populists, some of them scientists of international fame (Budarin 1952: 127; Slezkine 1994: 151). The new authorities turned to them for immediate policies, for urgent answers.

The first stage was thus a provisional policy conceived by competent well-wishers, gathered in a committee, the Committee of the North (Slezkine 1994: 150–152). In the first years of the Committee of the North they suffered from no interference. They were even able to elaborate a theory that allowed the native ethnic groups to find a position within the Soviet strategy: they were assimilated to the proletariat; class struggle was supposed to be unknown among them, for they were collectively victims of tsarist exploitation (Slezkine 1994: 152–156). The backbone of this first policy was to enhance the importance of education and to free them from external interference, which could be fatal to very frail communities. Such, at least, was the understanding of the policy-makers.

But their means were limited, their financial support shallow (Forsyth 1992: 244–246; Slezkine 1994: 136–141). Their policy's main tool was the so-called "red missionaries", a group of young people, mostly students, who volunteered to bring the Soviet "gospel" to those populations along with education. They also attempted to establish their position within Soviet power by relying on indigenous pre-existing structures, thus creating a syncretic system in the Provisional Statute of 1926, respectful of indigenous agency (Onishchuk 1986: 118–119). On the other hand, local power was not always, indeed not usually, in compliance with this spirit. Often local powers were either not aware of the indigenous peoples or had been officials or merchants formerly and were thus not directly interested in their welfare. Why spend energy and money for miserable backward populations, far from Soviet power's main goals such as industrialisation? (Slezkine 1994: 167, 170–171; a good example of resistance is given in the specialist press: Marin 1931). There was thus a double policy, engaged on the behalf of those peoples on the one hand, indifferent to them or even hindering them on the other.

How did the populations react to these changes? Yuri Vella writes, still in the Soviet period, with a slight sense of humour, that his grandfather, "through lack of political awareness and training", fled both from the Whites and from the Reds (Vella 1991: 53). Very probably this was a most widespread position: why would they support the one over the others? They fought over issues they were not concerned with. The expressions "White tsar" and "Red tsar" just illustrate their indifference to what was at stake. They were not likely to be concerned by the outcome of the war.

An Orthodox missionary, Irinarkh Shemanovski (see Toulouze 2005), who was the head of the Obdorsk mission[4] between 1898 and 1911, was impressed by the native's mistrust of the Russians and he reflected on the reason for the mistrust and the Russians' behaviour that brought it about. Things had hardly changed in so short a time. Still, all through the 1920s, the signals they received from the new power were mostly friendly: in the forest or the tundra, people were mainly in touch with the "red missionaries" who were devoted to their interests and had started to gain some trust from the local populations. The other representatives of the Soviet power hardly went so deep into their everyday life.

Certainly native populations were not as homogeneous as one could think. Local differences were relevant: in regions where Nenets reindeer herders were massively pauperised and subjected to richer masters – Russians, Komi, of even other Nenets –, as in the North-Eastern part of Europe, the Soviet message was often welcomed and could be understood.[5] The Yamal peninsula remained quite remote from the presence of Soviet power and Evladov, in his survey expedition in 1928, discovered that people knew very little of the new "Red tsar" (Evladov 1992). In general, the native population, with few exceptions, remained cautious, in an observatory position, but expecting more than before friendly behaviour from the representatives of the new power.

For the native population, the event that triggered a restructuring of their whole life, including personhood, is actually connected with the implementation of the second stage of Soviet policy. By the end of the twenties, the situation in the country had stabilised and the Bolsheviks started to implement their overall programme of collectivisation and standardisation. Exceptions were no longer welcome: everyone was supposed to become a Soviet citizen with equal rights and duties. That's why, as early as 1927, the doctrine that had been elaborated within the Committee of the North and according to which the Northern people, *in corpora*, were not concerned with class struggle became suspect (Slezkine 1994: 188-190). The well-wishing policy of the Committee of the North was rejected at the central level (Sergeyev 1964: 103). In spite of desperate attempts by its members and leaders to protect the communities (Slezkine 1994: 193), the Soviet machine ran over their protests and applied to them the same harsh treatment as to all other Soviet citizens. Sovietisation was forced at a very quick pace. Who did not or could not follow, was squeezed.

The so-called Kazym war, in the heart of Western Siberia, is a very good example of the implementation of these harsh policies, which were in stark contrast

4 Nowadays Salekhard, on the lower Ob.

5 We have an interesting testimony in an autobiographic novel by one of the first Nenets intellectuals, scholar and writer Anton Pyrerka (written in 1940 but published later), who was a poor Nenets and was happy of the freedom the Reds brought him from his master, who did not pay him and with whom he had no perspective of ever having a life of his own (Pyrerka 1949).

to the previous sympathetic approach, thus confounding the indigenous communities. In this tragic episode, the final confrontation between the indigenous groups and the Soviet authorities was the outcome of a long process that can be seen from the natives' point of view as a series of provocations: first children were forcibly brought to school, in a centre called *Kultbasa* (Cultural base, cf. Toulouze, Leete, Vallikivi 2015), while *kul*, for the natives, is a dangerous divinity. Then four shamans were arrested. Then the same shamans were prohibited from voting. Later a fishing brigade was sent to work on the shores of a sacred lake, where fishing is prohibited. Finally, a group of party and state representatives with a woman communist violated a sacred island, where women are not supposed to step. The natives, Khanty and Nenets, with their own agency responded: they took their children back from school, they fled into the wild, and finally they detained an official delegation and executed its members in a ritual way. The discovery of this fact lead to brutal repression that deprived the families of the Kazym river of their men, who were arrested and brought to court and then to prison, and the women of all means of subsistence (Leete 2002).[6]

In some ways this represents the last burst of native resistance to sovietisation. After this explosion, native resilience moves to underground tactics. Actually this expression suggests something more organised than it was in fact. We are speaking now of resilience, not of resistance. Resistance was broken. The communities attempted to keep what makes sense to them far from the gaze of the authorities and of the Russians. Their intimate, personal sphere became the stronghold where Khanty values and behaviours persisted (Lyarskaya, Dudeck 2012).

The constitutive elements of indigenous personhood after the event

Indigenous groups had to find out which were the elements of their culture that were so crucial to them that they had to be preserved in the new forceful conditions.[7] I do not argue that this process was undergone with full awareness: probably it was driven by necessity in tragic conditions. But those elements that were deliberately protected were certainly those that were considered the most important.

6 This episode has been differently treated. Khanty writer Eremei Aipin presents it as an episode of the Khanty fight for freedom from the Russians (2002). Tatiana Moldanova (1994), another Khanty writer, focuses on the suffering of the women after the repression. Cinema has also taken over: on the basis of Aipin's book a love story has been shot with Hollywood kitsch techniques (2009, *Red Ice. A saga about the Khanty*, by Oleg Fesenko) while Aleksej Fedorchenko's recent treatment, using a laconic cinematographic language, is much more sensitive (2014, *The Angels of the Revolution*).

7 In this part I rely mostly on my fieldwork made in Siberia since 1991.

The question of one's position in the world is central to animistic worldviews: the human is not the only subject and the only awareness, all their surroundings have an awareness of their own, all are entitled to subjectivity. As Graham Harvey puts it: "Animists are people who recognize that the world is full of persons, only some of whom are human" (Harvey 2006). It is in relation to them that the self has been defined. Relations with others are fundamentally part of the ontology of animistic groups: relations with ancestors, with animals, with plants, with spirits. Man must negotiate his/her position in regard to them and the understanding of self depends on it. This dimension of the animistic worldview, with all its consequences for an understanding of personhood, probably did not suffer much because of the abovementioned events. They were not directly contested. Relations with animals were not so much of concern to the state authorities. If on the one hand the materialistic worldview certainly does not accept the idea that animals or other natural elements have personhood and agency, this idea did not directly interfere, in ordinary life situations, with what was essential for the state.

I shall hereafter attempt to identify, on the basis of fieldwork carried out in Western Siberia between 1992 and 2013, some peculiar features of this modern Siberian animistic worldview, in order to try to understand the deep contradiction that indigenous groups and individuals have been confronted with for at least sixty years, the pressure of which has not entirely disappeared with the collapse of the Soviet Union.

I will not attempt to reconstruct, as often Soviet and Russian ethnography attempts to do, the state of the natives' culture "before the arrival of modernity", i.e. before the 1917 revolution. Neither am I interested in picking out animistic features and constructing upon them an ideal model. What I am interested in are the original characteristics of indigenous thinking we may identify nowadays, in all their hybridity and their contradictions. Those which reveal the tension this part of the population has gone through and may give a hint of what, in the traditional ontological system, makes sense for them at the end of the 20th century and at the beginning of the 21st.

"People who have reindeer and gods"

Once, in 1996, a Tundra Nenets woman in a reindeer herding brigade, formulated to my colleague, the Estonian anthropologist Liivo Niglas, what the Nenets are: "people who have reindeer and gods."[8] With this beautiful sentence, she summarises the core of what is important in the self for a simple Nenets reindeer herder: reindeer and gods. On the basis of this assertion as well as of his extensive fieldwork, Niglas concluded about the fundamental place that reindeer occupy

8 Oral information (1996).

not only in guaranteeing the Nenets reindeer herders' material well-being, but also their spiritual wholeness (Niglas 1997, 1997a, 1998, 1999, 2000, 2001).

Special relations with animals are central to animistic worldviews. In this we can identify the difference between different kinds of reindeer herding systems: the Nenets' system, deeply integrated in their worldview, in which reindeer are the core of the spiritual life and are herded not for economic profit but as an asset in itself, and for example the economically successful Izhma komi (*Iz'vatas*)[9], for whom "rational" reindeer-herding means relating to the reindeer as to capital (Kuratov 1925). For the latter, the herd is a commodity, for the Nenets, it is identity. That's probably why they have been able to retain, throughout the Soviet period, a strong particular identity, which distinguishes them from other herders in Soviet Russia. While the taiga "became a giant open-air meat factory", to quote Piers Vitebsky's words (Vitebsky 2005: 43), in Western Siberia Nenets reindeer herders were able to retain the core of their relations to the reindeer, in succeeding gradually to reproduce within the Soviet brigade, the main features of the traditional migrating kin group (Vitebsky 2005: 48). This means that the efforts of the Yamal Nenets were oriented towards preserving this essential dimension in their lives.

Even more interesting is the understanding of reindeer of the Forest Nenets, who live in a very different environment and whose herds are notably smaller than those of the Tundra Nenets, and do not provide the core of their life resources. Again: I am not attempting any reconstruction. As far as my knowledge of Forest Nenets culture goes, and according to the first extensive information about it (Verbov 1936), their herds were already then relatively small. Still, at least nowadays, reindeer are felt as the most pervasive identity factor. In 1999, I recorded a Forest Nenets elder woman's (Atiny Sobol'eva Kazamkina, Varyogan, probably born in 1934)[10] recollections of a longer migration from the Pur region to the Agan basin that seems to recall images of a Tundra Nenets migration, with long caravans and huge herds. Either my information about history is inaccurate (which is possible, for data are not abundant from so early a period), or Atiny Kazamkina remembers, with a young girl's sense of proportion, things bigger than they were. But it is also possible that reindeer occupy nowadays such a place in the Forest Nenets' awareness, that it throws a particular light on all that concerns this animal and influences even memory.

In the last part of this article I shall focus on this woman's son, one particular individual, an intellectual who was at the same time a reindeer herder, Yuri Vella.

---

9 About the Izhma Komi see Shabaev, Sharapov 2011; about Izhma Komi reindeer herders see Istomin 2004, Dwyer, Istomin 2009, 2010.

10 She does not know it herself. But she thinks she was about 14 years old when she gave birth to her first son (and the only one from her first husband), who was to become the Forest Nenets writer and reindeer herder Yuri Vella (see below).

On the qualitative level, I am impressed by the link Yuri Vella always stressed between reindeer and children. It was not the link emphasised by Willerslev and Ulturgasheva (2012: 53-58), of the child as a substitute in hunt or the child as having a guardian-reindeer. For Vella, the link between children and reindeer was very much rooted in the actual relationships between the children and the herd. Every grand-child has his or her reindeer and Yuri emphasised that not the parents but the reindeer raised the children. This understanding was well rooted in the animistic perception of the reindeer as having agency and personhood, the reindeer as wise and having a deeper understanding of the world than the limited human.[11] Contact with the reindeer teaches, educates the child, I would even say civilises him or her and makes a person of him or her.

The Tundra Nenets woman who summed up the core of the Nenets identity did not focus only on reindeer; the gods were also part of it. This woman has undergone the entire Soviet school atheist brainwashing, and still gods were a central part of the way she saw herself and her community. My interpretation of this sentence is that the Nenets are characterised by their environment, both visible and invisible. Their identity is merged with it and with its agents. I do not interpret the verb "have" as a sign for possession, but as a connector: they have reindeer and gods in the sense that they belong to a world in which there are reindeer and gods. I shall come back later to the Soviet fight against god (and gods).

The awareness of self, as it has been developed in Western culture, seems to be replaced here by a wider understanding. Its borders are blurred at different levels. Is it a particular form of what Strathern calls the dividual, characterised by multiplicity and fractionality?

An extended understanding of the self: person, family, clan, ethnic group and beyond

The self tends to be inclusive and encompasses the different levels of kinship: in the case of Yuri Vella we see how family coherence becomes part of the identity of the patriarch (for more details, see Toulouze, Niglas 2006). In the last years of his life, dealing with the authorities, he presented himself as the head of a family of 24 members: a mother, a wife, a brother, four daughters, four sons-in-law, and her daughters' children as well as one grand-daughter's husband and children. Often outsiders would ask why he should take under his responsibility his sons-in law, who are adult healthy men and might have themselves borne the burden

[11] This very short text from Yuri Vella illustrates this understanding: "A reindeer herder hides in the bush, he looks at his reindeer and thinks "How well did I fool the reindeer. He doesn't see me!" Indifferent, the reindeer sucks lichen and thinks: "Let him believe it if he wants to" (Vella 2005: 6).

of supporting their wives and children. But this question comes from another worldview. In Yuri's, it did not exist: mentally, morally, he was the one to support the burden of his whole clan.

The importance of clan in the Forest Nenets' everyday life in remote times is only to be imagined. We know that in the first period of the Soviet era, as it was traditional already in tsarist Russia, the clan was generally taken over by the authorities as the basic institution regulating the Siberian native's life. There was even a word for that: "clan system" (rodovoy story). The reality beyond this generalising institution is difficult to grasp: the kinship system worked differently in each region, and generalisations did not take into account very particular realities: while in the Yamal peninsula the clan was still at the end of the 20th century an institution with real impact on everyday life (exogamy rules, mutual assistance, moiety exogamy, see Niglas 2001: 59), on the European side of the Urals we know that as early as the end of the 19th century its relevance for the life of the Nenets was not comparable.

Albeit that in the case of the Forest Nenets at the end of the 20th century, the "clan system" seems to have become quite inoperative in everyday life, it is retained in the people's awareness by becoming a surname[12] and, oddly enough, by a general respect for exogamy rules (Verbov 1936).[13] Yuri Vella on the other hand, claims responsibility for the whole of his clan. Once, in the winter of 1999, as I was living in Yuri's and his wife's log hut, we had some visitors. A Russian filmmaker who had made a film about him brought him the film and she was accompanied by several friends. They brought as a present a bottle of vodka. Yuri, who did not drink at all, invited the whole company into the hut, and rather formally, made a "native chief" speech in which he recalled rather poignantly how he was the head of his clan, despite being too young, because spirits had killed all his male kin (except him and a small three-years old child).

My fieldwork also leads me to another remark about identity, in this case about ethnic identity. I have the impression (Toulouze 2012) that awareness of ethnic belonging is fading. I had this feeling during my fieldwork, by noticing that the women – Yuri's wife is a Khanty, some daughters have registered as Khanty, others as Nenets – looked for handicraft patterns in journals and took over patterns they liked, whatever their ethnic origin (for example Mansi); by listening to

---

12 This is a general rule, but there are exceptions and more complicated personal or group histories that explain anomalies: for example Ajvaseda Varjogan.

13 In his 1936 ethnography, Verbov reveals the exogamy rules of the Forest Nenets. They are more complicated than for others because they include Khanty clans. In Varyogan, I have met only one case of " improper " marriage in which the spouses were both Nenets (and it was a case of marriage between two elder people, who did not have children together), although nowadays the marriages are decided by the spouses themselves and without the initiative or interference of parents.

Yuri telling folk tales in the evening, but without mentioning their ethnic origin; or by talking to the children who, as a lesson about indigenous languages, did not know to which of the local languages a word belonged. But it became very clear in Liivo Niglas' film "Yuri Vella's world" (2001): at some moment he develops the idea that every person has a measure allocated to him or to her. He must recognise when he must stop. Then he says: "Many in my kin did not recognise it. My father, Aleksandr Aipin, both died young". Anyone who knows the region is well aware that Aipin is a Khanty clan. So Vella considers this particular Khanty man as somebody of his kin[14] (Toulouze, Niglas 2012).

A geographic projection of this extended self

The blurring of the borders defining the self is also felt on another level. The indigenous self is also deeply integrated into landscape, into surrounding nature. As people are part of the identity of nature, and nature, particularly places, are part of the identity of the people. I have spent several months at Yuri Vella's place in the Western Siberian taiga and his favourite way of speaking about the people who were relevant to his life, especially of ancestors and kin, was to tell stories about them and about places connected with them. He would drive his car and stop and tell a story that happened to one or another person. People had geography as well as history. His last monologue, filmed by Olga Kornienko some weeks before his demise, illustrates eloquently this peculiarity – Yuri reflects on heritage: when leaving this world, people leave behind something, and this something are places. They leave their memory connected with the places and his thoughts, while preparing to quit this world, were focused on the places he would leave behind.

Thus, indigenous personhood, at least in Western Siberia, seems, on the basis of my fieldwork, to be an extended personhood, in which the self is a complex concept whose borders are blurred and may encompass both kin, past and present, as well as the environment.

Soviet changes and outputs

This understanding of personhood has lived through difficult historical times. While native ontology was challenged before the 20th century, for example with the Orthodox missionaries' evangelisation attempts, it had never been as fundamentally under attack as in the Soviet period. The former penetration attempts

14 I thank Laur Vallikivi for his comment on this point: According to his fieldwork, the relative indifference to indigenous ethnicity seems to be characteristic of multi-ethnic regions. He noticed that for Yukaghirs (with the exception of ethnic activists) to be registered as Evens was not considered as a problem.

into native life were superficial. They were integrated in tax systems and legal systems (Forsyth 1992; Slezkine 1994), but these institutional enterprises were aimed at changing behaviours, but not thinking.[15] Christianisation was more ambitious, but much less than later Protestant evangelisation of some communities of reindeer herders (see Vallikivi 2005): Orthodoxy is very much a ritualised religion, in which the proposition of adherence is much less demanding of core change. This does not mean that Orthodox missionaries were not concerned by the superficial and pragmatic religiosity they identified in their neophytes, but their ambition was limited by their means: few men in charge of huge alien, unknown territories with limited resources and not backed by the State authority. But with the new Bolshevik regime, things changed thoroughly.

The Soviets were borne by a demanding ideology that encompassed every field of human action. They were moved by a project, which was totalitarian, and as such, did not take into account differences in ontologies. This project was holistic and had universal ambitions.

The Soviet project for the North

Behind the changes in society that the Bolsheviks wanted to achieve – to have a society without class exploitation, based on collective ownership – there was also an ontological project whose aim was to change both the society and the human being within it.

Society was to be built on rational rules that would structure the whole system, based on general work. As far as the human being is concerned, the aim of the soviet "construction" has been summed up as an attempt to create a "Soviet person,"[16] supposed to be free of the individualism and egoism developed by capitalism, and the bearer of several qualities – social involvement, activity, devotion to the Party, and characterised by a deep equality, which in the Bolsheviks' understanding was equal to standardisation. In this system, all cultural differences, all particularities, seen as results of centuries' long exploitation and oppression, were to be eliminated. The Northern people, who had been granted by the former regime particular privileges, were to become similar to all other Soviet citizens.

This endeavour included the fight against what were called the relics of the past (perezhitki proshlogo) that were to be systematically uprooted. Religion, in all its possible forms, was one of them; social consensus was another one. Since the beginning of the thirties, the fight against shamanism was very resolute in the North (Suslov 1931; Bogoraz-Tan 1932; X plenum 1934: 154–155; Slezkine

[15] This does not mean that we can dismiss as insignificant the possible Russian influence on indigenous communities: On the long term, even superficial contacts my lead to self-evidences.

[16] For a critique of the result, see Zinovyev 1986

1994: 226–227; Leete 1996: 394). Materialism was to be generally promoted, and the new person to be devoid of any irrationality in his or her way of thinking. All that was connected to older beliefs was considered to be superstition and had to be uprooted. Powerful instruments of change were supposed to act on both levels – the social and the individual (on all these questions see also Dudeck 2013: 72).

The instruments of change

We may list three main instruments used to give new shape to society. These were all collective institutions that operated throughout the whole society and in which all Soviet citizens were at some moment of their life, to be integrated.

Chronologically, in the life of an individual, the first one was the school. It was also the most powerful, because it exercised authority over the children; it was also the most problematic. In spite of serious endeavours, at the beginning of the Soviet period (and until today), to find proper ways to develop education within nomadic population, no better form was found than the boarding school (Lunacharski 1927). It was also the fittest model to instil new values in a totally Soviet environment. This usually meant alienation both from the family (at a very young age) and from the indigenous environment, the indigenous skills. Children reacted to school in different ways (as it is everywhere, but certainly with more extreme consequences).[17] Some of them – mostly girls – adapted and enjoyed their stay. Usually, those who graduated later from University, who became intellectuals, writers, are among those who adapted not too painfully to school. But they were not the majority. For some children, the rupture with the familiar environment was unbearable, and they fled. Some were caught, others escaped for a while, and others were lost. The majority however, survived. But the difficulties they had to face were often misinterpreted and many children, because of their silences and their laborious expression, were considered as intellectually limited and sent to other institutions. Teachers, Russians as a rule, were not able to cope with children suffering from trauma brought about by a different environment, emotional uprooting and unfamiliar language.[18]

School and especially boarding schools were the means for rooting hygiene[19] (as understood in Western culture), physical habits (Russian versus native diet)

---

17 See Heimo Lappalainen's documentary about the Evenk experience in the nineties (*Taiga Nomads* part III 1992). See also Valentin Kuik's documentary *Flight* (Lend 1995) about Khanty children and school.

18 Nenets filmmaker Anastasia Lapsui draws on her own experience as a child when in her *Seven songs from the tundra* (2000) she shows a Nenets girl coming to school and having her hair cut. It is also the inspiration for her film *Pudana* (*The last of her clan* 2010).

19 One of the main arguments of Soviet propaganda was that the children learnt to brush their teeth. That's how Anastasia Lapsui and Markku Lehmuskallio found the main character for the film Anna (1997), that tells what happened to a Nganassan girl filmed at the beginning of the

as well as fundamental values based on materialism. The various school subjects allowed them to shape the children's understanding of the world according to materialistic and evolutionary principles. These were in explicit contradiction with the traditional worldview of the indigenous peoples. But the latter learnt to live in the Russian way and adapted to all the necessary contexts.

However, when they went back to life in nature, they were helpless. While on the one hand they lacked the indispensable techniques to survive, on the other hand they couldn't make sense of their environment. This new challenge led to different answers, from total denial (total integration into town/village environment and adherence to its values) to a kind of double standards – the town/village acquired standard and the nature traditional one, each of which was actualised depending on the situational environment.

Other institutions, while not meant to teach, were nevertheless useful tools to nurture the values learnt at school. The army was an important moment in young men's life: for two years they were immersed in a standardised environment, with other young men coming from all over the Soviet Union. The army is always a powerful standardising tool: people from different origins need a common language to communicate, while strong experiences shared with other young people rooted through the emotionality of the life they led fed into their personhood. While boys, as a rule, adapted less willingly to school, the army provided the necessary integration within the Soviet system.

In the experience of work, the kolkhoz and the sovkhoz were also institutions that carried the Soviet spirit. Still this spirit was probably less totally present than in the abovementioned frameworks. Often, the bosses were from the same nationality (unlike at school or in the army). If the activities were traditional, contact both with nature and with other natives sharing the same values were unavoidable. At the same time, the collective work units were the way to integrate into Soviet life the indigenous peoples' traditional husbandry activities. So they were the core form of implementation of the Soviet project in the North, but at the same time they were actually the weakest link. Depending on the place, the implementation could present conspicuous peculiarities: the brigade in Yamal Nenets reindeer herding could be a thoroughly Nenets framework, composed by kin, and where all the rituals necessary to keep good balance with the gods could be performed; on the other hand, in the Western tundras, shift herding kept herders and their families under control.

---

fifties brushing her teeth.

The deceptive force of discourse

As usual in any kind of conversion attempt, discourse is one of the ways to influence both children and adults and to change their worldview (Vallikivi 2009). Soviet discourse was permanently present in the indigenous peoples' life, especially through the aforementioned institutions.

In regards to the Soviet ideological shaping of indigenous personhood, discourse was certainly a tool, but a blunt one. In cultures of silence such as (at least) Western Siberian ones, it was very difficult to engage with natives in dialogue. Discourse was not challenged, it was accepted, but the level of discourse interiorisation was diverse. Some were able to reproduce it, and could progress in the Party's hierarchy. Some did not even try. Some just replied through silence. Some interpreted quite freely what they heard: Yuri Vella liked to tell the story of a Nenets Party secretary in Varyogan, who was asked what communism was and answered after having thought for a little while, that it was eaten with bread. This anecdote shows one of the possible ways, probably the most extreme, in which words may function: being deprived of any meaning and having just a phatic effect. In other cases, the Soviet colonial discourse was properly interiorised: one Varyogan Nenets explained to me seriously once in 1999: "the Nenets were a primitive people, the Russians have civilised them".

So words and their repetition might have an influence on how singular persons saw themselves and the world around, but it is not safe to take it for granted that discourse would have the desired effect. Individual agency has to do with the reception of discourse.

The importance of the environment

Still, while analysing the outcome of all this indoctrination work, we cannot omit the situative dimension: behaviour and discourse, which are the signs that we have at our disposal to appreciate our informants' worldview and thoughts on themselves, may change depending on the environment: the village or the "wild". There are rules to be respected while in the forest, which are not relevant while living in the village: all makes sense with nature around, and each element of the environment is alive. So, every step, even a trivial one, made by a person, for example where to pee in the forest, required the making of choices that have to do with the understanding of space and rules.

While the village is an environment conceived by Russians, and thus carries their world, the taiga and the tundra were originally an indigenous environment. Over centuries indigenous groups wandered in these environments according to their needs and covered the space in their own way. Hunters moved looking for game, herders followed their reindeer, and families lived either moving with their herds throughout the year or changed camps each season on smaller areas. But the 20th century has induced a two-folded change: sedentarisation, a programme of sovietisation largely achieved by the 1950s, emptied the taiga of its indigenous and human inhabitants; at the same time, oil drilling has led to the invasion of this peculiar space by hordes of oil workers for whom the environment is considered an enemy to crush and to annihilate. The clash of worldviews and values is closer, it becomes explicit. But for the indigenous peoples, most of whom at least partly remain connected to the taiga, it is still the space where their traditional understandings reflect a meaningful truth and where central aspects of their personhood are actualised, while, on the other hand, they remain latent in the village.

The forest (or the tundra) is a place where reindeer are pastured and where the presence of gods is felt. On a more practical level, the forest is a place where you can move around with your knife, as traditionally, and not be accused of carrying a weapon; it is a place where it is natural to wear traditional clothing, which is comfortable and adapted to the needs. It is also a place where all Russian rules are not permanently implemented: it is possible to ride a car without an official driving license, for there are usually no officials to implement the rules. But the problem in recent decades is that while indigenous peoples have their own rules by which to live in this void, now the taiga is inhabited also by others, for whom the void means total impunity. In this void, they may perpetrate acts they would not dream of in a context ruled by law: most of them wouldn't think of stealing a cow or desecrating a grave-yard. But it is what they do when they chase reindeer by helicopter (in 1990, the spreading of this practice provoked a demonstration by the Varyogan villagers) or when they dig graves (see a poetic text by Yuri Vella on this topic).[20] Thus, the peace of the indigenous world, where natives could live according to their particular rules is disturbed by the presence of people for whom the absence of one set of laws is not replaced by another but by total absence of any behavioural rules.

One could recount several examples of different ways that have been chosen by Western Siberian natives to cope with the abovementioned contradictions. One

---

20 "For what reason? Yesterday I was passing by the clan cemetery of Aipins. What I saw beats any reasonable explanation. The majority of graves have been dug up. These are not the traces of animal claws, they are traces of spades, used by the human beings. What were they looking for here? Why? The hidden treasures they didn't find in the labases at the sacred grove? (...) Here lies the thrown aside rotten boot of the singer Shchimka. One can see the piece of bone – perhaps, the former foot? Is it the one he mangled once when in his youth, he was bringing the fish train to Surgut, after the war? And at the neighbouring grave of Àyzer, plundered as well? Here are the traces of the fireplace, somebody had arranged. Two sticks and a kettle with a hole, put on a horizontal stick, swinging like a pendulum. And inside, a white skull. What on earth does this mean, oh you people?! By instinct, I close my eyes imagining. Here I lie, at the end of the cemetery, dug out by some hooligan. And a curious and gnarled unfinished thought scratches into the weather-beaten skull: What have I done to you? (Vella 2008: 36-37).

example I will not develop, but which is undoubtedly relevant is Anna Nerkagi's, a tundra Nenets writer. In one of her first novels, Aniko of the Noho's clan, she presents the autobiographical example of a young girl who in boarding school dreams about the taiga, but returning back there she discovers that she is not able to stand the life of her people and that she has no place in either of her two worlds (Nerkagi 1977). Anna Nerkagi's quest is still on: first, like Vella, she went back to the tundra, she tried to be useful to her people by managing a trading post in the tundra, she renounced writing, then she converted to Orthodoxy... But this is the topic for a more detailed study (see for the first period of her life and work Samson Normand de Chambourg 1998).

Yuri Vella's experience: the "event"

Much has been written about Yuri Vella,[21] but what I want to emphasize in this article is the work on himself he made in the last 15 years of his life[22] in order to recover a whole personhood after an event that had for him consequences comparable to a Pauline revelation (see Badiou 2003).

In the first four decades of his life, Yuri did not explicitly question the truths he had grown up with. He had a settled life in the village, with proper contact with nature (he was a hunter), with a native wife and four daughters who attended the village boarding school, with a hobby – he wrote poetry in Russian – and a repressed regret not to have reindeer to live with.

The event he experienced was not shared by his closest relatives, nor by his wife or by his daughters. He decided to attend the Moscow Literary Institute and, while continuing to work as a hunter, he spent one week per month in Moscow attending lectures and reading. This was his turning point. This "event" has two faces: on the one hand it changed deeply his relationship to authority, on the other his relation to the concept of culture. And it led to his personal struggle to reshape his own personhood.

The relationship to authority: as I said, Yuri did not question the truths taught by the Party and he even applied twice for membership. Curiously, he was not accepted, which shows certain clear-sightedness from the Party local organisation. His application to the Party shows that he was totally sincere in his adhesion to what he had been taught to consider as the truth. So when he discovered at the Institute that things were not as they were presented in the official version of Soviet history – he had been told that in the civil war the Whites were bandits, and he discovered that there were eminent intellectuals and poets among them –, this

21 About Yuri Vella and his work, as well as for scans of his works, see jurivella.ru.

22 I have been a witness myself of these 15 years. I have spent as a whole 6 months in his camp and have met him often outside Siberia. So this part relies on my fieldwork and on material that Estonian anthropologist and filmmaker Liivo Niglas has shot about him in the same period.

triggered a trust crisis in regard to all that he had been told only on the strength of authority and he started to sieve all kind of information critically. Nevermore was he to accept any assertion on mere authority.

The second point is the concept of culture. The Russian word "kultura" (about the meaning in Russian use of this word see Grant 1995: 15-16), as well as the equivalent to "civilisation", "tsivilizatsia", are used as an absolute, but are in fact synonymous with the dominant, i.e. Russian culture or civilisation, versus the indigenous peoples' absence of culture and civilisation. These notions have been so generally repeated that they have widely been interiorised by the natives; living in nature is "not civilised"; going to the village is "to go back to civilisation". Yuri certainly accepted these categories before becoming a student in Moscow. But then he discovered that Russian culture was not the only one existing in the world. That the ancient Roman model, the ancient Greek model, were all different kind of cultures, and he understood that the Nenets have also their culture, which is a culture in its own right, different from the Russian one, but not fundamentally inferior.

He came back from Moscow with a new boldness. This "event" triggered a general awareness. He understood what they had been submitted to and he tried to cleanse himself of the former indoctrination and to find a new personhood made of authentic Nenets materials. Moreover, times were complicated: it was 1990, it was clear that the Soviet world could not go on in the same way.

He allowed himself his old dream of living with reindeer and made a very courageous and original choice: he bought reindeer and went with his wife to life in the forest. It was a big jump into the unknown, but it was an unknown he wished to domesticate, to make his own. He had no skills with reindeer, so he had to learn all from scratch. He had to build a living in the forest, log huts in different places depending on the season, several dozens of kilometres of fences, to keep his reindeer within. So he did, with the help of his wife, who was not happy at all, but who followed her husband's lead (although she recognised later it threatened their relationship). It was an entirely new life.

A new personhood

It is easy to follow the innovations in the couple's life but not so comfortable to attempt to follow the inner changes Yuri worked on himself. It was not a proclaimed goal. I was a permanent work, to put his personhood in compliance with his new life. It was not a work he talked about: he had no interlocutor. His wife was struggling to adapt to a life that was not of her choice. He tried to reconquer the wisdom of a native chief, to rediscover peculiarities of native life, to start thinking as a Nenets.

For this he could draw on different sources: his native identity had strongly relied on his grand-mother Nengi's teachings, and she remained perhaps the only undiscussed authority, on whom he wrote and whom he mentioned until his last days. Then he had his neighbours. These were older Forest Nenets men, from whom he learned to be a reindeer herder – Oysya Yusi, who had left the kolkhoz in 1953 and had never more gone to the village, Auli Yussi, Pavel Aivaseda, Vahalyuma Aivaseda, all closer friends, whom he recognised as his teachers, whom he listened to. They were also the ones with whom he could speak Nenets and who could tell him Nenets tales or songs. They became his network.

As a private person, he had a real sorrow he could not solve: he had no son to carry on the name and his clan. He tried to solve this problem in a very traditional indigenous way. He envisaged taking a second wife, a "younger wife", of course in agreement with his wife. She even looked for possible candidates. But finally she was emotionally unprepared and the plan was abandoned. But I think it is a good example of this period in which Yuri Vella tries to fit himself in the mould of a traditional head of family.

I do not know whether he prayed before, or whether he was the one to lead a sacrifice of reindeer. Usually it is the elder of the clan who does it, but he had none other around him. He certainly learnt from the older men, who were "real", lifelong reindeer-herders. They transmitted to him their spirituality. The rituals he knew from childhood, but without practical experience (he was five years old when he lost his father) he had now to perform them as the older male in his family and in his clan.

Actually both these points – fathering a son and praying – have much to do with male identity. This part of his personhood was very relevant for Yuri Vella and he attempted to develop it in an indigenous way, i.e. in a patriarchal way. He was also very impatient with public women, even elder women, when they took a too important role in religious ceremonies. I suppose that the character and the choices of the females surrounding him could have influenced the form this particular aspect took with Vella. Here, the distinction was very clear between the Vella at his camp, and the Vella in alien territory. At his camp Yuri did not dialogue with his wife or his daughters. He could monologue (at least when we were present), but he did not expect any answer or comment. And the women of his household did not pay attention to his words. Actually when I was at his camp, I was treated as one of them (which was flattering but also very frustrating). And the difference was noticeable in other contexts, for outside "his" world, Yuri dialogued very much with me. But this form of communication was impossible in his territory, because it did not fit with Yuri's camp personhood.

As a public person Yuri developed and liked to demonstrate some skills that are directly connected with indigenous knowledge: he always liked to do what I call "play Sherlock Holmes": he showed his ability to read nature or reindeer, and to deduce from a very small clue lots of information about the people living in the forest. He liked also to fight oil drillers with tools taken from the indigenous way of seeing the world: that's how he used a tepee in the regional capital or he pursued until the end of his life the story of the president's reindeer (much has been written on this topic: Novikova 2000; Butenschön 2003; Khanzerova 2009; Leete 2013). He intended to be seen as a native and thus he fought as a native.

As a public person, was Yuri Vella, as he sometimes said, the leader of the Forest Nenets? He was a socially very active character, but his actions were deeply individual; although they were supposed to be to the advantage of all the Khanty and the Nenets living in the forest, they were decided and carried out by Yuri completely alone. So one could say he was a self-appointed spokesman, for he had the ability to speak to the people of the other culture. But I dare argue that he was not recognised by the other Forest Nenets as their leader. He was too uncomfortable a character to be widely popular. Firstly, he did not drink, which set him apart from the other men. Then his choice to live in the forest was seen by many village dwellers as too extreme and his opposition to oil drillers too bold. People were in awe and respected him, recognised his superiority in many domains. But they also criticised him mercilessly, refusing his quest for indigeneity.

The question of authenticity

One question we cannot avoid is the authenticity of Yuri's behaviour and discourse. While looking at the films made about him, we often have the impression that Yuri acts. But I know through experience that, while he was indeed stimulated by the camera, actually his behaviour did not differ substantially from what it was when the camera was not around.

On the other hand I can safely say that yes, Yuri acted, but he acted his own character. This impression is given by the rationalised dimension of his behaviour. His behaviour is rational, he does exactly what he wants to do, not because of a deep impulse of doing so (we cannot exclude that the impulse existed), but because such behaviour is in compliance with the image of himself he wanted to give, not only to others, but also, and mainly himself. What distinguishes his comportment from that of the other Khanty or Nenets is the utmost awareness. He is as he is because of an intellectual need of being so, not because he has no choice. Actually he has a choice: he knows how to behave in different ways in other contexts. His awareness has destroyed spontaneity.

But Yuri's awareness did not allow him to ignore how much was not achieved in his endeavour. He was aware the he had started too late to fulfil his dream and he was particularly aware that he was alone. He did not speak of it. But he alluded to it when he spoke of his goal. He did not put the mark too high. He did not pretend to have built a life in the forest. He considered his enterprise as a "museum": what he wanted to do, was to show how it is possible to live a decent and dignified life in the forest in the 21st century. He wanted to show it both to the "newcomers", Russian and foreigners alike, and to his kin, the local Khanty and Nenets, who were afraid of regaining what had been theirs and who had adopted the Russian way of thinking.

Yuri was always thinking of planting seeds for the future: what was important for him was to build foundations for an unforeseeable future, when oil resources would be extinguished and the indigenous peoples would remain with an injured land and landscape and perhaps unable to live on it. It was important for him to prepare conditions for people to go back to long forgotten nature if they desire it.

Conclusion

As with all other natives, two worldviews and subsequently two understandings of self were competing in Yuri Vella: the traditional one, transmitted by the elder generation and inspired by the natural environment and the new, inspired by Soviet values, and transmitted by different Soviet institutions. As is the case with most natives, at the beginning of his life, while being familiar with the indigenous world, Yuri grew up as a village dweller and a "modern" Soviet person, embracing all the dominating principles of his society. In this dichotomy, he faced the problem all acculturated indigenous people are confronted with. His way of solving the inner pressure before the "event" was very ordinary: he ignored the contradictions and tried to live fully both lives and to shape his personhood into adaptability. Still he had a tool in that period, which certainly allowed him to relieve the pressure: he wrote.

The event, the awakening of an awareness of the colonial pressure put on him and on his kin led to a conscious work on himself in order to retrieve original features that had been buried under the "modern" village self. Very few Northern intellectuals have lived something similar: most have remained in the mould and tried to represent publicly a world which has become alien to them. Vella has attempted to delve into this world and to make it his own. From this point of view he has produced a sample of original thinking and lived a very rich experience.

This experience confirms the relevance of the notion of Event in the changes concerning indigenous personhood. Unlike many accounts of indigenous personhood, I have decided to focus mostly on hybridity, on how the intruding Western thinking patterns have profoundly influenced the way Western Siberian indigenous peoples have been used to see themselves in their different environments. I have tried to retrace this hybridity in a general way and to analyse one example of the response to the contradictions induced. This quest for authenticity within one's personhood is also, in itself, a consequence of this hybridity: it presupposes the awareness of the existence of one whole personhood to reshape according to some fundamental principles. It presupposes the awareness of something that has been lost and that is perceived as a whole, and the attempt to isolate different parts in it and to put them in compliance with what they were supposed to be originally, before the brain-washing of the last 70 years.

I consider this article a first attempt to disentangle a complex issue: as Spiro emphasises, "it is not inaccurate to say that the person or self has been studied in only a small fraction of human societies" (1993: 107). This topic would need further studies and, particularly, further ethnography with other, different examples of possible responses in order to be able to draw a typology of the deeper effects of colonisation on the minds of indigenous peoples.

References

X plenum (1934): Резолюция X расширенного пленума Комитета Севера при Президиуме ВЦИК (17-26 апреля 1934), [Resolution of the 10th enlarged plenum of the Comittee of the North of all-Russia Central Executive Committee] *Советский Север*, 138-156.

Aipin (2002): Айпин, Еремей, *Божья Матерь в кровавых снегах* [The Mother of God in bloody snow], Издательский дом "ПАКРУС".

Badiou, Alain (2003): *Saint Paul: The Foundation of Universalism*, translated by Ray Brassier. Stanford: Stanford University Press.

Bialecki, Jon, Daswani Girish (2015): "What is an individual? The view from Christianity", *HAU: Journal of Ethnographic Theory* 5 (1), 271-294.

Bogoraz-Tan (1932): Богораз-Тан, Владимир, "Религия, как тормоз строительства среди малых народностей Севера" [Religion as a bracket to the construction among the small peoples of the North], *Советский Север*, 142-157.

Brightman, Marc, Vanessa Elisa Grotti, Olga Ulturgasheva (2012): *Animism in rainforest and tundra/ personhood, animals, plants and things in contemporary Amazonia and Siberia*. London: Berghahn books.

Budarin (1952): Бударин, Михаил, *Прошлое и натоящее народов Северо-Западной Сибири* [The past and the present of the Western-Siberian peoples]. Омск.

Butenschön, Marianna (2003): "Jelzin, Putin und die Präsidentenkuh: Vom einsamen Kampf des Rentierzüchters Jurij Wella gegen den Ölkonzern LUKoil", *Freitag* 03.10.2003, http://www.freitag.de/politik/0341-russland.

Dudeck, Stephan (2013): "Oral History of Empires by Elders in the Arctic (ORHELIA): A Common History, a Common Economy, Common Language Roots, and Different Practices among Four Arctic Indigenous Peoples" in Oral History: Dialogue With Society / Mutvārdu vēsture: dialogsar sabiedrību, 56-76.

Dwyer, Mark J., Kirill V. Istomin (2009): "Komi reindeer herding: the effects of socialist and post-socialist change on mobility and land use", *Polar Research* 28, 282-297.

Dwyer, Mark J., Kirill V. Istomin (2010): "Dynamic Mutual Adaptation: Human-Animal Interaction in Reindeer Herding Pastoralism", *Hum Ecol* 38, 613-623.

Evladov (1992): Евладов, Владимир, *По тундрам Ямала к Белому Острову. Экспедиция на Крайний Север полуострова Ямала в 1928-1929 гг.*

[Through the tundras of Yamal towards the White Island. An expedition in the Far North of the Yamal Peninsula in 1928-29], Тюмень.

Fitzpatrick, Sheila (1985): "The Civil War as a Formative Experience", *Bolshevik Culture: Experiment and Order in the Russia Revolution*, Ed. Abbott Gleason et al., Bloomington, 57-76.

Forsyth, James (1992): *A History of the Peoples of Siberia, Russia's North-Asian Colony 1581-1990*, Cambridge U.P.

Gorodkov (1926): Городков Б.Н., *Краткий очерк населения Крайнего северо-востока Западной Сибири* [Short essay on the population of the far North-Est of Western Siberia], Москва, 50-76.

Grant, Bruce (1995): *In the Soviet House of Culture. A Century of Perestroikas.* Priceton: Princeton University Press.

Harvey, Graham (2006): *Animism: Respecting the Living World*, Columbia: Columbia University Press.

Humphrey, Caroline (2008): "Reassembling individual subjects, events and decisions in troubled times", *Anthropological Theory* SAGE Publications. Los Angeles, London, New Delhi and Singapore, http://ant.sagepub.com, Vol. 8 (4), 357–380.

Ikäheimo, Heikki, Arto Laitinen (2007): Dimensions of Personhood, Imprint Academic.

Istomin, Kirill (2004): Истомин Кирилл, *Этноэкологическая характеристика коми-ижемского оленеводства* [Ethno-ecological characterisation of the Izhma Komi reindeer herding], кандидатская диссертация, Сыктывкар.

Khanzerova (2009): Ханзерова Ирина, "История президентских оленей" [The story of the President's reindeer], *Наръяна Вындер* 01.08.09, http://www.jurivella.ru/index.php/2009-07-30-13-15-45/81-2003.

Kuratov (1925): Куратов А., "Состояние оленеводства в Большеземельской и Малоземельских тундрах и на Новой Земле" [The state of reindeer herding in the Tundras of the Big Land and of the Small Land as well as in Novaya Zemlya], Коми му, Вып 1, 5-9.

Leete, Art (1996): "Märkmeid Kazõmi sõjast", *Akadeemia 2/1996*, Tartu, 392-405.

Leete, Art (2002): *Kazõmi sõda. Šamanistliku kultuuri allakäik Lääne-Siberis*, Tartu Ülikooli kirjastus.

Leete, Art (2013): "Sacrifices de rennes et pétrole: dialogue entre rituel et droits des peuples autochtones", *Études finno-ougriennes* n°46, Paris: L'Harmattan/ADEFO, 57-88.

Leete, Art (2014): *Guileless Indigenes and Hidden Passion: Descriptions of Ob-Ugrians and Samoyeds through the Centuries*, Helsinki: Suomalainen Tiedeakatemia Academia Scientiarum Fennica.

Liarskaya, Elena, Stephan Dudeck (2012): "Multiple privacies in Western Siberian indigenous lifestyles" in Margherita Carucci (ed.), *Revealing privacy. Debating the Understandings of Privacy,* Peter Lang, 60-74.

Lunacharski (1927): Луначарский А. В., "Задачи Наркомпроса на Крайнем Севере" [The tasks of the People's Commissariat for Education in the Far North], *Северная Азия*, 1927/3, 18-22.

Meillassoux Quentin (2008): "Histoire et événement chez Alain Badiou", *Intervention au séminaire "Marx au XXI*e *siècle: l'esprit et la lettre* (Paris, 2 février 2008), http://www.marxau21.fr/index.php?option=com_content&view=article&id=83:histoire-et-evenement-chez-alain-badiou&catid=39:badiou-alain&Itemid=62.

Moldanova (1994): Молданова Татьяна, “В гнездышке одиноком: отр. из повести” [In the solitary small nest: excerpt of a short novel], *Современная литература народов Севера и Дальнего Востока* Ч. 1, Москва 1994, 166-181.

Mosko Mark (2010): “Partible penitents: Dividual personhood and Christian practice in Melanesia and the West.” *Journal of the Royal Anthropological Institute* 16 (2), 215-40.

Nerkagi (1977): Неркаги, Анна Павловна, *Анико из рода Ного* [Anna of the Noho clan], Москва: Молодая гвардия.

Niglas, Liivo (1997a): “La femme chez les éleveurs de rennes nenets”, *Études finno-ougriennes* 29, 85-104.

Niglas, Liivo (1997b): “Reindeer in the Nenets Worldview”, *Pro Ethnologia* 5, 7-33.

Niglas, Liivo (1998): “Le renne dans l’univers mental des Nenets” *Boréales: revue du Centre de recherches inter-nordiques* 74/77, 169-187.

Niglas, Liivo (2000): “Reindeer as the Moulder of the Ethnic Identity of the Yamal Nenets”, *Arctic Studies*, Tartu: Eesti Rahva Muuseum, 87-92.

Niglas, Liivo (2001): “Jamali neenetsite eluviis ja maailmapilt” in A. Leete, L. Niglas. A. Barkalaja, Tartu (Eds.): *Põhjapõder arktilises kultuuris*. Eesti Rahva Muuseum, 26-78.

Novikova Natalya (2000): “You need to have rights to be free, or “An oath on a bear’s claw””. English translation from the official periodical of *RAIPON Mir korennykh narodov zhivaia arktika* [Indigenous Peoples’ World Living Arctic.] No. 3 http://www.npolar.no/ansipra/english/MKN/MKN03-16.html (last accessed on 10 June 2010).

Onishchuk (1986): Онищук, Николай Тимофеевич, *Создание советской национальной государственности народностей Севера* [The constitution of Soviet national statehood for the peoples of the North], Томск.

Pyrerka (1940): Пыреркa Антон, *Младший сын Вэдо* [Vedo’s younger son], Архангельск 1949.

Robbins Joel (2010): “Melanesia, Christianity, and cultural change: A comment on Mosko’s ‘partible penitents’”*Journal of the Royal Anthropological Institute* 16 (2), 241-43.

Samson Normand de Chambourg Dominique (1989): *Ilir d’Anna Nerkagui, une page de vie autochtone dans le Grand Nord sibérien 1917-1997*, Paris: L’Harmattan.

Sergeyev (1964): Сергеев, М. А., *Некапиталистический путь развития малых народов Севера* [The noncapitalist way for the development of the small peoples of the North], Ленинград 1955.

Shabaev, Yuri, Valeri Sharapov (2011): “Izhma Komis and Pomors: Two Models of Cultural Transformation” *Journal of Ethnology and Folkloristics*, Vol. 5 (1), 97-122.

Slezkine, Yuri (1994): *Arctic Mirrors. Russia and the Small Peoples of the North.* Ithaca (New York): Cornell.

Spiro, Melford E. (1993): “Is the Western conception of the Self ‘Peculiar’ within the Context of the World Cultures?” *Ethos*, Vol. 21 (2), 107-153.

Strathern, Marilyn (1988): *The gender of the gift: Problems with women and problems with society in Melanesia*. Berkeley: University of California Press.

Strathern, Marilyn (1992): *Reproducing the Future: Essays on Anthropology, Kinship and the New reproductive technologies*. Manchester.

Suslov (1931): Суслов И.М., “Шаманство и борьба с ним” [Shamanism and the fight against it], *Советский Север*, 1931/3-4, 89-152.

Toulouze, Eva (2000): “Adaptational models of Intellectuals among the Northern peoples” *Cultural identity of Arctic peoples. Arctic Studies 4 Pro ethnologia 10*, Tartu, 7-15.

Toulouze, Eva (2005): "Irinarh Šemanovskij et la mission d'Obdorsk: une page de l'évangélisation des Khantys et des Nenets" *Études Finno-ougriennes*, Vol. 37, 29-63.

Toulouze, Eva (2012): "Forest Nenets Folklore and Identity" in Cornelius Hasselblatt, Adriaan van der Hoeven (Eds.): *Finno-Ugric Folklore, Myth and Cultural Identity*, Studia Fenno-Ugrica Groningana 7, Maastricht: Shaker Publishing BV 2012, 227-240.

Toulouze, Åva, Art Leete, Laur Vallikivi (2015): "The cultural bases in the North: Sovietisation and indigenous resistance" in Andrej Kotljarchuk, Olle Sundstrom (Eds.): *Minorities in the Stalin's Soviet Union: New Dimensions of Research.* Umea: Umeå University.

Toulouze, Eva, Liivo Niglas (2006): "Parler de soi pour changer le monde", *Sign Systems Studies* 34 (2), 509-525.

Toulouze, Eva, Liivo Niglas (2012): "Native spirituality in (re)constructed personhood: observing and filming Yuri Vella", *Folklore. Electronic Journal of Folklore*, 133-170.

Vallikivi, Laur (2005): *Arktika nomaadid šamanismi ja kristluse vahel: Jamb-to neenetsite pöördumine baptismi* [The Arctic nomads between shamanhood and Christianity; the conversion of the Yamb-to Nenets to Baptism], Tartu: Tartu Ülikooli Kirjastus.

Vallikivi, Laur (2009): "Christianisation of words and selves: Nenets reindeer herders joining the state through conversion" in Pelkmans, M. (Ed.): *Conversion After Socialism: Disruptions, Modernities and the Technologies of Faith.* Oxford, New York: Berghahn, 59-83.

Vella (1991): Вэлла, Юрий, *Вести из стойбища* [News from my camp], Свердловск 1991.

Vella (2005): Вэлла, Юрий, *Азбука оленевода* [The reindeer herder's ABC], Нижневартовск – Санкт-Петербург 2005.

Vella (2008): Вэлла, Юрий, *Ветерок с озера (7x7)* [Youri Vaella *Breeze from the Lake (7x7)*], Khanty-Mansiisk, Poligrafist 2008.

Verbov (1936): Вербов, Г. Д., "Лесные ненцы" [The Forest Nenets], *Советская этнография*, № 2, 57-70.

Vihalem, Margus (2011): "What is 'the subject' the name for? The conceptual structure of Alain Badiou's theory of the subject", *Sign System Studies* 39 (1), 60-80.

Vitebsky, Piers (2005): *Reindeer people, Living with animals and spirits in Siberia*, Happer Perennial.

Willerslev, Rane (2007): *Soul Hunters: Hunting, Animism and Personhood among the Siberian Yukaghirs*, University of California Press.

Willerslev, Rane, Olga Ulturgasheva (2012): "Revisiting the Animism versus Totemism Debate: Fabricating Persons among the Eveny and Chukchi of North-eastern Siberia", in M. Brightman, V. E. Grotti, O. Ulturgasheva (eds.): *Shamanism in Rainforest and Tundra: Personhood in the Shamanic Ecologies of Contemporary Amazonia and Siberia.* New York and London: Berghahn Books, 48-68.

Zinovyev, Aleksandr (1986): *Homo sovieticus*, Grove/Atlantic.

Ethnicity in a Moldavian Csángó Settlement – Minority Identity as Hybrid Identity[1]

Lehel Peti

A general presentation of the Moldavian Csángós

The Moldavian Catholics living in the counties of Bacău, Neamţ, Iaşi, Vaslui, Vrancea, Galaţi, and Botoşani in Romania are referred to as *Moldavian Csángós* in the relevant scholarly literature (see Tánczos 2010: 62). Hungarian and international research, along with a part of Romanian research, considers them as an ethnic group of Hungarian origin, whose linguistic assimilation has been uninterrupted since the 16th century (see Tánczos 2011a: 9, 20). As a result of this assimilation process, only a small proportion of this ethnic group, primarily of the middle and older generation, still speak Hungarian today,[2] and even in their case, the use of Hungarian is restricted to certain situations within the private sphere. Besides their Hungarian dialect, the main criterion employed by the Moldavian Csángós to differentiate themselves from Orthodox Romanians is Catholicism, which thoroughly shapes their mentality, worldview, and value system. The Romanian state regards the Moldavian Csángós only as a religious and not as an ethnic minority group. On the other hand, "Hungarians living in Hungary and Transylvania, as well as the Csángó intellectuals with a Hungarian identity, view the Csángós not as an autonomous minority but as a part of the Hungarian nation" (Peti 2015a: 51).

---

1 The present analysis was prepared within the framework of the research project entitled "Manifestations of Ethnicity within Minority Communities (2011–2012)", financed by the Romanian Institute for Research on National Minorities (*Institutul pentru Studierea Problemelor Minorităţilor Naţionale* [ISPMN]). The co-director of the research project was Dénes Kiss. During the research we have conducted fieldwork based upon a uniform criteria system in localities inhabited by national minorities (Greek, Armenian, Ukrainian, Swabian, and Turkish villages). I would like to thank all the participants of the project (Dénes Kiss, Tamás Kiss, Ilka Veress, Attila Deák, Melinda Kardos), and also László Fosztó, Vilmos Tánczos, Heltai János Imre, József Lőrincz, James Kapaló and Lidia Guzy for their remarks on previous versions on this analysis.

2 For the generational distribution of the Hungarian language proficiency levels of the Csángós, see the data published by Vilmos Tánczos, as well as their graphic representation (Tánczos 2010, 2012).

In 2001, the European Council accepted recommendation nr. 1521 which made it compulsory for Romania to protect the traditional Csángó culture and language.[3] Although the Recommendation of the European Council is not clear whether it considers the Moldavian Csángós as an ethnic minority separate from Hungarians and their language as a separate one, or as a Hungarian minority and one of the Hungarian dialects (see Laihonen 2017), European Council reporter Mrs. Tytti Isohookana Asunmaa (responsible for the acceptance of Recommendation 1521) sees the best way to promote the interests of the Csángós in their definition as an independent ethnic minority (separate from Hungarians) and interprets the Recommendation of the European Council in this manner (see Isohookana, Asunmaa, Tánczos 2015: 29, Laihonen, Kovács, Snellman 2015: 16). However on the basis of this document, the Moldavian Csángós represent a separate ethnic minority group, with a specific culture and language, from the perspective of European political policy.

The 1989 regime change in Romania brought about intense globalisation processes for Moldavian Csángós. The opening of the western labor market has led to an increase in migration to foreign countries for this ethnic group, and has also contributed to a radical change in its way of life. The results of the 2011 Population and Housing Census in Romania indicate that the exodus of the Moldavian Csángós to western countries has increased enormously during the last decade due to labor migration. According to the data, the number of Roman Catholics has decreased by 46 139 people since 2002, that is, 19.66%, in the seven Moldavian counties inhabited by Moldavian Csángós. Compared to the 1992 census, the number of Moldavian Catholics in these seven Moldavian counties had declined by 7 993 people by 2002 (see Tánczos 2010: 62-63). The significant decrease in the Moldavian Catholic population can be explained by international migration. This excessive migration has led to a radical change in the lifestyle of the source communities and has also caused the reorganisation of the lifestyle of the persons involved in labor migration in a transnational framework.

The Moldavian Csángós have lived until recently within the framework of a traditionally organised rural society. In the socialist era, a part of the population migrated to work in the industrial complexes of the neighboring metropolitan areas. The population that stayed in the villages was employed on the collective farms.

3 Recommendation 2001 [2011].

Fig. 1: The religious composition of the counties inhabited by Moldavian Csángós according to the 2002 and 2011 census data

	2002		2011			
		%		%	Difference in absolute numbers	Difference in percentage
Orthodox	3669387	91.89	3074073	91.36	-595314	-16.22
Roman Catholic	235144	5.88	188865	5.61	-46279	-19.68
Small churches	46281	1.15	55314	1.64	9033	0.49
Other	42308	1.05	44997	1.33	2689	0.28
Total population	3993120		3364608		-628512	-15.73

The pathway to becoming an intellectual led through the priesthood. Agrarian employment was especially high among the Moldavian Csángós even in the early 2000s, as attested by the database of the Integrated Public Use Microdata Series, International (IPUMS-International).[4] The analysis of the occupational groups of the seven counties inhabited by Moldavian Csángós according to their affiliation to larger religious groups reveals that the percentage of Roman Catholics working in agriculture was 43.06%. The percentage of Roman Catholics working as craftsmen and artisans was also high: 21.64%.

According to the information supplied by the same database, the educational level of Roman Catholics in Bacău County is significantly lower than that of the Orthodox population. Within the rural population, the percentage of highly educated people is double amongst those of the Orthodox faith compared to amongst Roman Catholics. The highest educational level reached by the great majority of Roman Catholics is offered by vocational and apprentice schools that train skilled laborers. Since the bulk of the Roman Catholic population of Bacău County consists of labor migrants working in industrial complexes, who came from the rural areas to the urban centers, the uneven distribution of educational levels was also "imported" to the cities. The percentage of the highly educated among the Orthodox population is more than two and a half times greater than that of the Catholics. It can be assumed on the basis of this data that the Catholic population is in a more disadvantaged situation with regard to social stratification than the Orthodox population.

4 The data related to Romania were provided by the Romanian National Institute of Statistics.

Fig. 2: The occupational groups of the seven counties inhabited by Moldavian Csángós according to their affiliation to larger religious groups in 2002 (%) (IPUMS-International)

	Legislators, leaders	Intellectuals, scientific occupations	Technicians, artisans	Office workers	Services, commerce	Agriculture	Craftsmen, artisans	Machine operators, factory workers, mechanics	Elementary occupations	Military	No response	Unknown	Total
Roman Catholic	1,83	3,06	4,38	1,74	5,90	43,06	21,64	8,82	8,69	0,59	0,02	0,25	100
Orthodox	3,00	6,35	8,07	3,51	7,21	38,35	16,24	9,77	6,44	0,44	0,05	0,57	100
Pentecostal	1,97	1,12	3,79	2,53	5,76	56,46	10,67	7,30	9,13	0,42		0,84	100
Adventist \ Seventhday Adventist	2,73	4,69	6,45	0,59	7,03	56,45	10,16	3,91	7,03	0,20		0,78	100
Baptist	2,88	11,51	14,39	2,88	10,07	27,34	14,39	9,35	5,76	0,72		0,72	100
Old-Rite Orthodox	2,32	6,03	4,41	1,62	3,71	57,77	14,62	5,34	3,48	0,46		0,23	100
Evangelical Christian	2,86	2,39	7,88	2,63	7,88	39,86	16,95	9,31	7,40	0,24		2,63	100

Fig. 3: The educational attainment of people affiliated to the larger religious groups of Bacău County 2002 (%) (IPUMS-International)

	No response	Without school education	Elementary education (grades V - IIV)	Lower secondary education (grades V - VIII)	Special education (2002)	Vocational or apprentice school	Special education	High school (grades IX - XII)	Vocational high school	Technical high school	Postgraduate school \ craftsman training	Short-term higher education	Long-term higher education	Unspecified education level	Total %
Roman Catholic	14.0	3.3	0.2	21.2	0.0	32.5	0.2	2.1	6.3	15.8	1.0	0.1	1.3	2.1	100
Orthodox	11.7	3.3	0.1	19.0	0.1	26.1	0.1	4.3	11.5	14.6	2.6	0.3	4.9	1.5	100
Pentecostal	31.3	6.3	0.3	19.3		21.3		0.9	6.0	10.3			1.4	2.9	100
Adventist \ Seventhday Adventist	6.2	1.9		23.3		39.5		2.9	7.6	11.4	1.9		2.9	2.4	100
Baptist	23.1	1.9		17.3		30.8		1.9	5.8	3.8	3.8		7.7	3.8	100
Old-Rite Orthodox	9.2	5.8	0.8	24.2		21.7		1.7	18.3	11.7	1.7		2.5	2.5	100
Evangelical Christian	11.3	3.5		19.1		24.8		6.4	7.1	20.6	4.3		2.1	0.7	100

The disadvantaged situation of the Moldavian Csángós within the social stratification of the counties which they inhabit and their employment in occupational categories with lower income levels has without a doubt influenced the massive labor migration of this ethnic group towards the West during the last decade.

The quantitative research of Vilmos Tánczos, which includes the totality of Moldavian Catholic settlements, numerically demonstrates that the linguistic assimilation of Moldavian Csángós has accelerated during the last decade, and this population has now come to the point of complete language change (Tánczos 2010). According to his researches, the number of Csángós still speaking Hungarian has decreased from 62 265 to 44 269 within 15 years, which means a decrease by 28,9% (see Tánczos 2010: 145).

According to the collected data of the Population and Housing Census at county level, the regional distribution of Moldavian Roman Catholics is the following: Bacău County – 16.32%, Neamţ County – 10.53%, Iaşi County – 4.8%, Vrancea County – 1.34%, Vaslui County – 1.31%, Galaţi County – 0.3%, Botoşani County – 0.16%.

Research issue and methodology

My study focuses on ethnicity processes of a Moldavian Csángó village, Valea Seacă (Bogdánfalva), with particular emphasis on language use. In my analysis, I attempt to understand the role played by ethnicity in the language use of this community, which has reached the stage of radical social transformation and language shift. Furthermore, I try to determine the patterns that shape the identity of the Csángós, a minority group stigmatised in multiple ways for its Csángó minority language use, but also differentiated from the Romanian majority when speaking Romanian, and further stigmatised because of its cultural and religious otherness and special position occupied within the social stratification. The migration practice established after the 1989 Romanian regime change and aimed at Hungary, followed by the western migration with the 2007 enlargement of the European Union, when Romania joined the EU, has led to the adoption of transnational models of life-conduct by large groups of Csángó society,[5] which established new social contact points, rewrote the rules of relating to communities of different ethnicity, and created new models of adaptation. In my analysis, I reflect upon the effects of the major economic and social changes within the Moldavian Csángó communities on their ethnicity, upon the new identity attitudes which have emerged, and also upon the ways in which these processes have amplified the hybridisation processes associated with Moldavian Csángó ethnicity.

5 On the effects of migration on the Csángós way of life, see: Lajos 2010.

I have conducted ethnographic field research in this settlement on several occasions. However, the ethnographic material which serves as the basis for my present analysis and is more narrowly focused on the subject was collected in 2011 and 2012. The main research method consisted in semi-structured interviews concentrating on individual life paths, in which I asked the informants about life situations and experiences thought to be relevant from the perspective of experiencing their ethnicity in everyday life. The interviews were conducted mainly in Romanian. I spoke in Hungarian only with elderly informants and even among them only with those who could express themselves without difficulty in Hungarian.

A questionnaire-based survey related to ethnicity was also conducted by interviewers within the same settlement in January 2012. The questionnaire was written in Romanian, and we stratified the sample of 100 informants according to gender and age.[6]

During my analysis I will also rely upon observations relevant to the subject which I have made in other Moldavian Csángó settlements, therewith alluding to the wider context of the region inhabited by Csángós and the social historical processes in which Valea Seacă (Bogdánfalva) is firmly rooted. As in the other studies, my starting point in presenting the relevant contexts for the manifestation of ethnicity has been the model of Richard Jenkins for defining the contexts for social and ethnic categorisation.[7] Among the contexts of ethnic categorisation – as defined by Jenkins and adapted to our different fields of research – we have been focusing on the following: *kinship and informal relations* (*marriage*, *family*, *neighborhood*, *collegiality and friendship*), *religion*, *institutions and ethno-politics*, *economic life*.[8] Additionally, we have studied the functions of *language use* and *folklore* within the expression of ethnicity as autonomous contexts. In this article I will analyze issues related to the language use.

According to the methodology of my research, the analysis will also contain short case studies on representative personalities belonging to different social groups. Caroline Brettel emphasizes the importance of personal narratives for migration studies, stating that through these "we can come to know the patterns of the migration process and its subjective experience" (Brettel 2003: 43). At the end

6 I have analysed the database built on the basis of the questionnaire-based survey in a separate study (see Peti 2015b).

7 Jenkins 2002: 255-261, see also Jenkins 2008: 65-74. These are the following: routine public interaction, sexual relationships, community relationships, informal relationships, marriage and kinship, market relationships, employment, administrative distribution, institutionalised politics, official categorisation (see Jenkins 2002: 256, figure 2). The author also mentions among the further aspects of ethnic categorisation the following factors: child-rearing, friendship relations, education, religion, and institutionalised social regulation (see Jenkins 2002: 261).

8 The Methodological guidelines of the project were elaborated by Dénes Kiss.

of my analysis I will explore the way in which migration influences ethnicity in specific cases, based on the life experiences of two migrants.

Scientific discourses focusing on Moldavian Csángó identity often refer to the traditional structure of the identity of this ethnic group. The basic characteristic of this identity structure is the lack of what is often considered the most important components of ethnic identity relating to the formation of nations. This is due to the fact that the Moldavian Csángós were left out of the processes that led to the formation of civic nations. These components are: the consciousness of common origins, common historical experience and memory, an emotional and symbolic relationship to specific cultural traits and to language and so on (see Tánczos 2011b: 266; Tánczos 2011a: 28). In the absence of these components, the most important element of community in the case of the Moldavian Csángós consists of a sense of belonging to the Roman Catholic faith. The scholarly literature on the Moldavian Csángós uses the terms *prenational form of identity* (Arens 2005: 345) and *prenational identity* (Tánczos 2011b: 256) for designating this type of identity, which is primarily defined by religious affiliation. The preservation of this identity structure is explained within the same scholarly literature by the considerable isolation of this ethnic group, its limited contacts with communities of a different culture and religion, and the traditional character of its way of life and mentality.

The Village

Valea Seacă (Bogdánfalva) is a Moldavian Csángó settlement of average size and institutional infrastructure. According to the official census statistics of 2002, its population was 2135, of which 1880 people are of Roman Catholic and 255 of Orthodox faith. Although the statistics do not reflect this, there are also a few people who are Adventists. Administratively, the village belongs to the much larger Nicolae Bălcescu (Ferdinándújfalu). Valea Seacă's streets and buildings vividly reflect the social changes of the more distant and recent past. Its houses built of mud and covered with tin roofs, the crosses and statues of saints in front of them, and the entire structure of the village made up of narrow dead-end streets, all reflect a lifestyle built on peasant farming, the peasant value system, and on the kinship of blood relations.[9] The more recent buildings, ostentatious in their size and color, which have also already formed their separate streets, are symbols of the labor migrant culture. They are more secular and transnational in character and have been established after the regime change and have begun to replace the traditional peasant structures.[10]

9 For more details about Valea Seacă (Bogdánfalva), see: Kós 1981.

10 For a more detailed presentation of the village, see: Peti 2015b: 972-973.

In the interviews conducted in Valea Seacă (Bogdánfalva), which contain biographical episodes, one often encounters the clear differentiation of Csángós and Romanians on the basis of their spoken language (but without any ideological implications of ethnicity[11]):

[Translator's note (TN): The informant speaks in Hungarian dialect.] In my grandmother's times... they didn't say "kucsma", they said "bundasapka" [TN: fur hat]. "Bundasapka". And then in our parts the Romanians said: "Măi, căciula" [TN: Hey, remove your hat!]. Which is "kucsma". And they also said: "gyufa" [TN: matches]. But then they began to call it: "chibric" [TN: from the Romanian word "chibrit"]. They have heard that the Romanians call it "chibrit", so our people, the Csángós, began to call it "chibric".[12]

According to the scholarly literature dedicated to the language use of the Csángós, even in those villages where the minority Hungarian dialect is still spoken on some level of proficiency beside the dominant Romanian language, it is only used in informal situations. One of the reasons for this fact is that the Csángós consider their own dialect shameful, "neither Romanian nor Hungarian", a kind of "bastard", mixed language.[13]

[TN: The informant speaks in Hungarian dialect.] It's a mixed language: neither Hungarian nor Vlach [TN: Romanian]. Like I always say: "We are like Hungarian Gypsies, man!" Why do I say this? Because when we don't know the word in Romanian, we say it in Hungarian. And when we don't know the word in Hungarian, we say it in Romanian. Just like the Gypsies. When the Gypsies can't find the right words, they say it in Romanian.[14]

The Moldavian Csángós are conscious of the fact that those Hungarians from Transylvania and Hungary who visit them regard the Csángó dialect as Hungarian. However, because they sharply differentiate themselves from Hungarians, if

11 The role of ideological and non-ideological contexts within the construction of Csángó ethnicity and the importance of language in creating identity, which is influenced by ideological contexts, is emphasised by Vilmos Tánczos: "Because the symbolic and ideological relationship to language is not yet formed in the case of ethnic communities which are on the prenational level, language is not nearly as important for them as it is for those communities which have constituted themselves as nations and relate to language not only pragmatically but also ideologically" [...] (Tánczos 2011b: 258-259).

12 *Az én öreganyám... nem mondták "kucsma", azt mondták "bundasapka". Bundasapka. Idefelé aztán ha mandták a ramányak: "Măi, căciula". Há kucsmát. Vaj mondták: "gyufa". De ezek azután mondták: "chibric". Hallatták, a romónyok mondják chibrit, ezek a mieink, a csángók, chibric.*

13 The scholarly literature dealing with the language use of the Moldavian Csángós has dealt extensively with this subject. I will only mention here some of the studies which address this issue critically: Tánczos 2011a, 2011b; Szilágyi 2002; Heltai 2004: 132.

14 *Sz így megvegyült: szem magyar, szem oláh. Jén úgy mondom örökké: "Mi ilyen magyar cigányak vagyunk, hejj, te!" Hogy mért? Azért, hol nem találjuk ki románul, mondjuk magyarul. Hol nem találjuk magyarul, mondjuk rományul. Mind a cigányok. Cigányok ha nem találja jól az ő nyelvét, kezdi rományul.*

asked whether they speak Hungarian, they find it important to stress that they speak Csángó, not "pure Hungarian". At the same time, they also know that they can make themselves more or less understood in Hungary in their Csángó dialect. Many of them have made this experience first as guest workers and visitors in Hungary, and later while transiting Hungary on the way to other countries. A middle-aged woman guest worker's response to my question whom she understands better, Transylvanian Hungarians or Hungarians living in Hungary, reflects this attitude very clearly. She told me that she does not understand them if they speak "pure Hungarian", because they speak Csángó here in their village, which is neither Hungarian nor Romanian, but a kind of mixture. Another characteristic linguistic behavior, especially of the middle generation, whose members still know the Csángó language, but predominantly use Romanian in everyday communication situations, is that they respond in Hungarian (viz. in Csángó language) if they are asked a question in Hungarian, but supply further explanations in Romanian.

[TN: The informant begins to speak in Hungarian dialect]. We do speak a little [TN: Hungarian]. A dialect of it. [TN: The informant uses here the Romanian word for 'dialect', but inflects it according to Hungarian grammar. Then, the informant shifts to Romanian.] A bit of dialect, some Csángó. Not pure Hungarian. If we go to Hungary, we understand a little. Yes. [And can you understand each other better with the Hungarians living in Transylvania? Or is it the same as with those living in Hungary?] [TN: The researcher asks this question in Romanian.] If they speak pure Hungarian, then we don't understand. Cause we speak Csángó. Neither Hungarian nor Romanian. It's a kind of mixture.[15]

Although the Moldavian Csángós are conscious of the fact of cross-linguistic mixing, they do not always know which of the words they use within their own language are Hungarian and which are Romanian (see Tánczos 2011b: 197). I have even met an informant who, during our conversation, substituted the Hungarian words usually used in his native language, considered by him Romanian, with words which he learned during his stay as a guest worker in Hungary, deemed by the informant "more Hungarian".

The sense of shame felt because of the stigmatisation of their minority dialect often comes to expression in interviews in which value judgments are made with respect to its status. The development of this sense of shame was also supported by the nationalist discourse disseminated by the Church and by the official school education, which explained the existence of the minority dialect spoken by the Moldavian Csángós (insofar as it recognised it at all) with the fact that the ancestors of the Csángós were Hungarianised Romanians. As Hungarian forms

---

15 *Beszélünk egy kicsit. Diálektot. Un dialect, un pic de ceangăiească. Ungureasca pură nu. Dacă mergem în Ungaria, ceva înţelegem. Da. [Şi vă înţelegeţi mai bine cu cei din Transilvania? Sau la fel ca şi cu cei din Ungaria?] Dacă au să vorbească aşa ungurească pură, atuncea nu. Că la noi e ceangăi. Nici ungur nu e, nici român nu e. Un fel de amestecătură.*

of education were introduced, the disseminators of this discourse threatened the parents by saying that their children will not learn to speak Romanian correctly if they are taught the local dialect.

The written language landscape of Valea Seacă (Bogdánfalva) is dominated exclusively by Romanian inscriptions, as is the case in all Moldavian Csángó settlements without exception. Inscriptions and books in Hungarian, satellite dishes with the inscription Duna TV [TN: a Hungarian public television channel], received as a gift from the Hungarian Public Television, can only be found in the "Hungarian houses" run by foundations, which serve as locations for Hungarian language education.

In addition to the already mentioned factors stemming from religious differences, Orthodox Moldavian Romanians also distinguish themselves from Moldavian Csángós, who have become linguistically assimilated almost completely and cannot speak the Csángó dialect well, or do not speak it at all, on the basis of their Romanian language use. They do not regard them as "true Romanians", in the same way they do not regard as "true Romanians" those Moldavian Csángós who still use the Csángó dialect in certain situations. If the Csángós speak in Romanian in front of Orthodox Romanians, they can recognize them immediately as being Csángó, no matter how high the level of their language proficiency. I have heard many stories about Romanians making fun of the Csángós at urban workplaces or during the mandatory military service not only because of the Csángós' unusual intonation or the faulty grammatical constructions which they used, but even on account of the literary grammatical constructions which the Csángós have learned in school, all being foreign to the speakers of the Romanian dialect prevalent in Moldova, who caricatured the Csángós' peculiar intonation and grammatical constructions. *[TN: The informant speaks in Romanian.] When I was working in Bacău, the Romanians mocked me*[16] – a middle-aged man, who is currently a guest worker, told me. Another man, also middle-aged, who lives in Bacău and only spends the weekends in his native village, told me that as a child he spoke in Hungarian with his parents, and he only learned Romanian in kindergarten. This man now does not use the Csángó dialect at all and only speaks in Romanian with his wife and children. He understands to a certain level the speakers of the standard Hungarian dialect and can even speak in the local Hungarian dialect, but he says he feels ridiculous when trying to communicate in Hungarian with a native speaker.[17] As for the social rootedness and the lifestyle of

---

16 *Când am lucrat în Bacău, românii făceau mişto de mine.*

17 *[TN: The informant speaks in Romanian.] Last week I went to Sovata [NT: a town in Mureş County, central Romania, part of the Székely Land region of the historical Transylvania province; also a popular health resort], because I am now on vacation. (...) Of course, I don't have a command of the Hungarian vocabulary. But I know some words, street names, "utca" [TN: street], "nemes" [TN: noble], words I can guess, or I have read somewhere, such as "Rigó-tó" [TN: Blackbird Lake]. It's a*

this informant, his Csángó identity was not exposed to his social environment. It only becomes "blatant" in the urban context, if he engages himself in conversation with Romanian speakers who are not Moldavian Csángós. According to his own impression, in such cases the Romanian speaker who is not of Moldavian Csángó origin can immediately feel that his mother tongue is not Romanian, in spite of his high level of linguistic assimilation.

One of the most important factors in the stigmatisation of the Csángó identity by the Orthodox Romanians, although not the only such factor, is the "mixed language" spoken by the Csángós. The stigmatisation of the Csángó identity is also due to their lower social status, determined by the Csángós' peasant social system and their lower education level than that of the Orthodox Romanians. The introverted Csángó villages, with their economy based predominantly on agriculture and livestock farming, mostly lacking any intellectuals, for a long time only had contact with the Romanian majority surrounding them, whose language they spoke incorrectly. The Csángós stereotypes of the Orthodox Romanians also refer to their air of superiority and derogatory attitude towards them. One of my informants, a middle-aged man working in Bacău County even expressed the opinion that, since the surrounding Romanians have treated the Csángós as "outcasts" and "pariahs" for such a long time, assimilation to the Romanians – the faster and more complete, the better – appears to the Csángó youth as an effective means of escaping stigmatisation. From the Romanian majority's point of view, the cultural otherness of the Csángós, their lower position in the social system, and their

---

lake in Sovata, where there was also some kind of Hungarian inscription, there were some inscriptions in three languages. Or at the station, it said "állomas" [TN: dialectal variation of the Hungarian word for (train or bus) station, "állomás"]. I didn't know the word, but we also say "megállsz" [TN: the Hungarian word for "to stop", first person singular form of the present indicative], which is "to stop". So, "állomas". A place for something to stop or, in other words, a station... it was also written in Romanian, which has helped me. Because I could make parallels. Other than that, fluent Hungarian speech is kind of a shock for me. For if I speak, a Hungarian can understand me. Not all the words, because I don't have a command of them all, but I can understand the language. So, if I speak with a Hungarian, he can understand me. But as for me, if he starts to speak, I kind of get lost. Because I can't understand all the things he says. He speaks in pure Hungarian and uses all the correct grammatical forms, which makes me...

Eu am fost la Sovata, săptămâna trecută, pentru că sunt în concediu. (...) Sigur că eu n-am o cunoştinţă a vocabularului unguresc. Dar străzi, "utca", "nemes", cuvinte care le aproximez, şi le-am citit, "Rigó-tó." Este la Sovata un lac, scria şi pe ungureşte pe acolo, pe trei limbi scria pe acolo. Sau la gară "állomas", eu nu ştiam, dar la noi se spune "megállsz", adica te opreşti. "Állomas." Chestie de oprit de stat ceva pe loc, este o gară, o... scria şi în româneşte, faptul că scria pe româneşte pe mine mă ajuta. Pentru că făceam paralele. Altfel un vorbit ungureşte foarte cursiv, adică aşa pentru mine e o lovitură de teatru. Pentru că eu dacă vorbesc, un maghiar mă înţelege. Nu toate cuvintele, pentru că eu nu stăpânesc pe toate, dar înţeleg. Înţelege ce spun. Eu când vorbeşte el, mă cam dă de pământ. Pentru că nu înţeleg toate lucrurile pe care le spune el. El spune curat ungureşte, şi foloseşte toate formele gramaticale corect, care pe mine mă...

distinct Roman Catholic religion has always called into question the possibility of their integration and their loyalty. As for the attitudes of the Csángós towards Romanians, the critical link in the chain of factors which makes their integration into the Romanian majority so problematic consists in the most obvious signifier of Csángó identity, the Hungarian dialect spoken by them, on account of which they had to repeatedly face the "accusation" of belonging to the Hungarians. These accusations can represent critical moments for those persons who consciously seek integration into the Romanian ethnic group, as the following quote from an interview illustrates:

[TN: The informant speaks in Romanian.] Young people don't give a squat about this spoken language, they are far removed from such issues. For them, only the Romanian language exists. They consider the Hungarian language as a kind of accident. [How?] As something accidental. Because we have come to experience embarrassing situations while living next to the Romanians... You're Csángó, you're Hungarian... I myself have experienced such things. Even now there are crazy people who think like this. But I put them in their place, and I do it in Hungarian. People are struggling with feelings of inferiority towards the majority, who view them exactly as we view the Gypsies.[18]

An often-used strategy for avoiding stigmatisation involves hiding their Csángó identity in alien environments. It is a recurring element in their narratives about how they spent their military service that they have kept it a secret that they speak Hungarian, even if there were other Hungarians, viz. Székelys[19] in their military unit. The punchline of these stories is almost always the moment when they unexpectedly reveal that they can also understand Hungarian, generally in situations when the Szeklers have behaved with an air of superiority towards the Csángós or the Romanians, or when they spoke arrogantly about them amongst each other.

The data collected by way of surveys indicate that the vast majority think that the Csángós speak the Romanian language differently than the Orthodox Romanians. Some of these respondents also feel that the Orthodox Romanians are bothered by the way in which the Csángós speak Romanian. More specifically, according to 50 respondents, in situations when the Csángós speak in Romanian in front of the Orthodox Romanians, the Romanians can sense that they speak the

18 *Cu cât a apărut tineretul, şi nu dă doi lei pe limba asta vorbită, este ruptă de aşa ceva. Pentru ei nu mai există decât limba română. Consideră limba maghiară un accident. [Adică?] Adică întâmplător. Am vorbit, şi datorită faptului, că în relaţia cu românii am fost puşi în situaţii stânjenitoare . . . , eşti ceangău, eşti ungur . . . , asta am simţit şi eu. şi acuma mai sunt "nebuni" de ăştia. Dar eu pun la punct pe ungureşte. Lumea se simţei în grad de inferioritate faţă de majoritate, care majoritate ne privea aşa exact cum privim noi ţiganii.*

19 A minority group of Hungarian identity and language, with a specific historical consciouness, living in a larger homogenous community in Romania, in the region west from the Carpathian Mountains.

language differently, but are not bothered by this, while 24 respondents stated that the Romanians not only note the difference, but are also bothered by it. 74% of the respondents think that the Orthodox Romanians speak Romanian differently than they do. This data indicates that, in spite of their high-level of linguistic assimilation, the Romanian-speaking Moldavian Csángós still feel different from the Orthodox Romanians.

Linguistic research conducted among the Moldavian Csángós has shown that "the members of the Romanian-Hungarian bilingual linguistic communities of Moldova consider their own minority dialect in some cases more or less, but in any case different from the other dialects spoken in the Carpathian Basin" (Heltai 2004: 132). At the same time, many researchers have noted that the Csángós make a distinction regarding the purity of the language as spoken by Hungarians from Transylvania and Hungary. Namely, they consider the dialect spoken by Hungarians living in Hungary as superior to the Hungarian dialect spoken in Transylvania (see Tánczos 1996: 165). According to Vilmos Tánczos, "the consciousness of the fact that the Csángó dialect of the Hungarian language spoken in Moldova is different from the "pure" Hungarian language spoken in Budapest causes a separation also on the ethnic level of communal identity" (Tánczos 2011b: 265). However, their ideas about the "linguistic contamination" of Transylvanian Hungarians do not constitute for them a basis for ethnic identification with Transylvanian Hungarians.

Valea Seacă (Bogdánfalva) is among those settlements in which the Csángó minority dialect is still being used in informal situations, although the data indicate a sharp decline in the use of this dialect and the acceleration of language change. According to the research of Vilmos Tánczos, encompassing all Csángó settlements, Valea Seacă (Bogdánfalva) is among the Csángó villages which are the fastest to go through language change (Tánczos 2010: 98). Our own research surveys also attest to the fact that the members of the younger generation "use the Csángó dialect beside Romanian only very rarely, when speaking with their grandparents, and even more sparsely when communicating with their parents" (Peti 2015b: 982).

The data supplied by the same research survey indicates that "the relevance of the Csángó language is almost exclusively restricted to the private sphere, to the communication with family members and neighbors, while the Romanian language is absolutely dominant within institutions and also in the domain of media consumption" (Peti 2015b: 984).

The labor migration of the Csángós within their home country, Romania, as well as to foreign countries, has generated mutually opposing processes in language use. On the one hand, it has increased the stigmatisation of the local dialect. On the other hand, it has contributed to the formation of a kind of pragmatic attitude towards language, as the knowledge of the Hungarian dialect also gave the

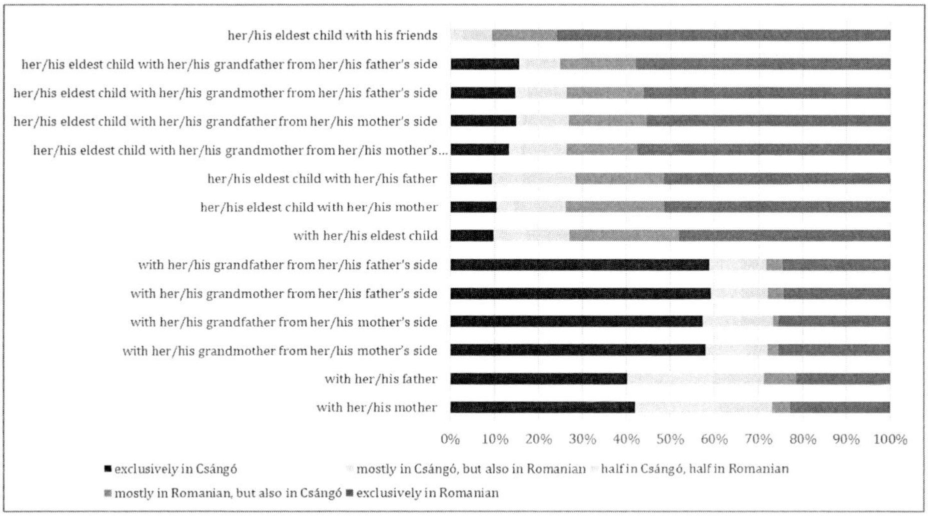

Fig 1: Linguistic code-switching of the surveyed population (%) (Peti 2015b: 982)

Csángós a communication advantage in many areas of life (for example, completing the compulsory military service in Transylvanian towns, keeping in touch with relatives who have moved to Transylvania, access to employment in Hungary, crossing the border, etc.) (see Peti 2015b: 978).

Gabi is a woman in her late thirties, who owns the general store of the village. Her husband has worked in Hungary for a couple of years. As for herself, she remained in the village with the children, and has paid only passing visits to her husband in Hungary. Currently, she sends all of her four children to the Hungarian language classes organised outside the normal school curriculum. In the summer of 2011, the children have even gone to a summer camp organised in Hungary. In 2012, Gabi and other parents have officially requested the introduction of Hungarian language lessons into the school curriculum. When I asked her why she considers it important for her children to learn Hungarian, her response was: *you don't even have to go to Hungary, just to Braşov (Brassó) or Sfântu Gheorghe (Sepsiszentgyörgy), and if you don't know how to ask for bread in Hungarian, they will not serve you in the grocery store*. Then she recounted a story about a journey she made to Braşov (Brassó) with the godparents of her older daughter. The occasion was her brother's taking the military oath of allegiance, a ceremony which she wished to attend. The godfather of her daughter wanted to buy bread in the grocery store, but because he asked for it in Romanian, they did not give him any. Then her husband asked for bread in Hungarian, and he was indeed served. To this, her relative remarked: *see, they take your side, not mine*. She also explained to me that the reason for the salespeople not serving them was not that they did not understand the request; they were just waiting for them to ask for the bread in Hungarian.

According to this narrative, it is important to know how to speak Hungarian in Romania because it can help you avoid situations of disadvantage due to the nationalism of Transylvanian Hungarians. She also illustrated the "practicality" of Hungarian linguistic knowledge with the "lessons learned" from other narratives. Most of these narratives were related to border crossings to Hungary, on the occasion of which, as soon as it came out that they can speak Hungarian, the customs officers treated them much differently and did not check their luggage as thoroughly as that of the other travelers, or they got help to solve their problems

Gabi's experience of ethnicity is connected to her encounter with outside attitudes towards the languages spoken by her, i.e. the Romanian and the Hungarian language. The more affected she feels within these narratives, the more authentic they feel for her (for instance, she herself was there in Braşov/Brassó when they did not serve them with any bread, her own luggage has not been checked as she crossed the Hungarian border when the customs officers found out that there were Csángós on the bus, etc.). However, the fact that she sent her four children to Hungarian language classes is not a matter of course even in Valea Seacă (Bogdánfalva). The introduction of the Hungarian language classes in Valea Seacă (Bogdánfalva) was an event which stirred up the whole community and called on everyone to make up their mind and take a stand. As in the case of the majority of Moldavian Csángó communities, the organisation of the "Hungarian school" has been an ideologically heavily burdened process which mobilised many different idcas, interests, and sentiments. Gabi's choice to send her children to Hungarian language classes meant a firm position taken on this issue. However, it also put her loyalty to the majority of her own community into question and opened the possibility of many different interpretations. For Gabi, the cooperation with her community and living according to community norms is exceptionally important, as attested by the way in which she spoke about how *many parents* send their children to Hungarian language classes and that *many people* have requested Hungarian language to be officially taught in school. Within Gabi's cooperation with her community, the option of sending her children to Hungarian language classes was a sensitive point. Through the narratives she recounted, Gabi also sought to legitimize herself and her choice. Her point was that by choosing to send her children to Hungarian language classes she has chosen the "practical route", on the basis of considerations that are accepted by her community as a whole. With the "morals" of the stories she recounted and with her arguments she has tried to prove that her attitude towards the Hungarian language classes was nothing else than her way of adapting to the relevant expectations of her community.

Conclusion

Hungarian labor migration has increased the prestige of the Csángó dialect with regard to its practical use, but the misunderstandings during communication, the bewilderment of Hungarians at the particularities of the Csángó language, etc., has also increased the consciousness of the separation of the Csángós from Hungarians. Paradoxically, from the perspective of the Csángós, the awareness of the linguistic differences further increases the stigmatised status of the Csángó dialect. At the same time, this phenomena also contributes to the strengthening of the local Csángó identity, which focuses upon the local value system of the Csángó villages and posits communities on this basis. This identity is further confirmed during the migration process directed at western countries. Tánczos Vilmos has also remarked on this phenomena, terming the novel "post-national"[20] identity attitudes, which revalue the traditional elements of Csángó culture, as the "new Csángó self-consciousness", observed by him primarily in the case of the Csángó intellectuals (see Tánczos 2011b: 265).

The status of the guest workers is also stigmatised in the target countries of the Csángó migrants, especially because Csángós are identified as Romanian guest workers. In the context of migration, the Csángó identity represents an "invisible identity" for the majority society, which functions similarly to the "safety net"[21] of ethnicity as discussed by Alejandro Portes in the case of migrant communities living under circumstances characterised by the aversion of the majority society (see Portes 1999: 465). The invisible Csángó ethnicity is capable to offer a basis for the construction of an identity with a new content, built on the sense of familiarity with the language, culture, and value system of the Moldavian Catholic villages, because it has a neutral status in the migration context. In this situation, the identification of the Csángós with the Romanian ethnicity by the inhabitants of the target country of the guest workers weights against their full acceptance the Orthodox Romanian ethnicity. Although migration directed at western countries intensifies the process of language shift, as opposed to migration directed at Hungary, the Csángós re-establish their awareness of the differences which are also important in their (Romanian) language use during their contacts with Orthodox Romanians. The awareness of the differences relating to culture, values, and standards produces meanings associated with ethnicity which are more important than the differences from Orthodox Romanians regarding Romanian language use.

As a result of the recommendation nr. 1521 of the European Council, the dismissive and obstructive attitude of the public institutions toward the activities of the Csángó foundations, organised along "Hungarian lines" and directed at the

[20] Concept introduced by Tánczos Vilmos.

[21] Concept introduced by Alajandro Portes.

protection of their interests and the preservation of their identity (e.g. Hungarian education in Csángó villages) has ceased. However, the same cannot be said of the Catholic Church functioning in Moldova (see Peti 2015a: 51-52). The manifestation/strengthening of Csángó identity elements based on the local Catholic values system and behavioral standards in the case of Moldavian Csángós involved in foreign labor migration is the result of processes independent from the activities of the foundations, directed at the preservation of the local (Moldavian) identity – on which the recommendation of the European Council had a beneficial effect – , although their general direction is aligned with the international expectations expressed in the recommendation of the European Council.

The transnational context which has come to determine the way of life of the Moldavian Csángó community, which in their autochthonous living environment is stigmatised due to social and linguistic reasons, has led to the hybridisation of Csángó identity. For Csángó guest workers who, as a reaction to the challenges of modernisation, have been flowing into Hungary, and then, after the 2007 accession of Romania to the EU, to western neo-Latin countries, mostly inhabited by Catholics, labor migration also carries the chance to overcome the stigmatised Csángó identity.

The social changes of the recent past have resulted in the strengthening of the hybridisation processes of Moldavian Csángó identity. While in their home environment the assumption of Romanian identity functions as a strategy for delimiting themselves from the stigmatised Csángó identity, labor migration dissolves for Csángó guest workers the stigma of Csángó ethnicity and carries the possibility for strengthening a Csángó identity constructed from local cultural elements and built on a revalued basis.

Bibliography

Arens, Meinolf (2005): "A moldvai magyarok/csángók kutatásának feladatai" (Research Assignments of the Moldavian Csángós), in István Kinda, Ferenc Pozsony (eds.): *Adaptáció és modernizáció a moldvai csángó falvakban* (Adaptation and Modernization in the Moldavian Csángó Villages) (Kolozsvár: Kriza János Néprajzi Társaság), 336-351.

Brettel, Caroline (2003): *Anthropology and Migration. Essays on Transnationalism, Ethnicity, and Identity.* Oxford: Altamira Press. Walnut Creek–Lanham–New York.

Heltai, János Imre (2004): "A magyar–román nyelvcserével kapcsolatos vélekedések moldvai kétnyelvű beszélőközösségekben" (Opinions Regarding the Hungarian-Romanian Language Exchange in Moldavian Bilingual Language Communities) in Jenő Kiss (ed.): *Nyelv és nyelvhasználat a moldvai csángók körében* (Language and Language Use at the Moldavian Csángós)- Budapest: Magyar Nyelvtudományi Társaság, 125-135. (A Magyar Nyelvtudományi Társaság Kiadványai. 221.)

Isohookana-Asunmaa, Tytti, Outi Tánczos (2015): "Endeavors for a Living Csángó Language: Role of the European Council Recommendation 1521 in Maintaining Csángó Language and Culture", *Uralica Helsingiensia* (8), 25–43.

Jenkins, Richard (2002): "Az etnicitás újragondolása: identitás, kategorizáció és hatalom" (Rethinking Ethnicity: Identity, Categorization and Power) *Magyar Kisebbség* VII (4), (26.), 243-268.

Jenkins, Richard (2008): *Rethinking Ethnicity. Arguments and Explorations* (Second Edition). Los Angeles, London, New Delhi, Singapore: Sage Publications.

Laihonen, Petteri (in press): "Cuvânt-introductiv: ce ar trebui să ştie lumea despre ceangăii din Moldova" (Foreword: What Everybody should Know about the Moldavian Csángós) in Vilmos Tánczos: *Vreau să fiu român!* (I want to be Romanian!). Cluj-Napoca: Editura ISPMN.

Laihonen, Petteri, Magdolna Kovács, Hanna Snellman (2015): "In Search of New Perspectives on the Moldavian Csángós" *Uralica Helsingiensia* (8), 7-24.

Lajos, Veronika (2010): "Modernizációs stratégiák és hagyományos kötődések. A társadalmi átmenet szimbolikus határhelyzetei egy moldvai csángó közösségben – egy lujzikalagori asszony példája" (Modernization Strategies and Traditional Bonding. Symbolic Crossroads of Social Transitions in a Moldavian Csángó Community – a Case of a Woman from Luizi-Călugăra) [doktori disszertáció] Dissertatiton, Debreceni Egyetem, Bölcsészettudományi Kar, Debrecen. https://dea.lib.unideb.hu/dea/bitstream/handle/2437/103477/Lajos%20Veronika%20ertekezes%20elektronikus-t.pdf?sequence (last accessed on 8 July 2016).

Portes, Alejandro (1999): "Conclusions: Towards a new world – the origins and effects of transnational activities", *Ethnic and Racial Studies* 22(2), March, 463-477.

Peti, Lehel (2015a): "Studies on Moldavian Csángós in Romania and Their Impact on the Local Communities", *Uralica Helsingiensia* 8, 47-70.

Peti, Lehel (2015b): "Etnicitás, nyelvhasználat és migráció egy moldvai csángó településen" (Ethnicity, Language Use and Migration in a Moldavian Csángó Settlement), in Albert Zsolt Jakab, István Kinda (eds.): *Aranykapu. Tanulmányok Pozsony Ferenc tiszteletére.* (Studies in the Honor of Ferenc Pozsony.) Kolozsvár: Kriza János Néprajzi Társaság – Szabadtéri Néprajzi Múzeum – Székely Nemzeti Múzeum, 971–992.

Szilágyi, N. Sándor (2002): "Despre dialectele ceangăieşti din Moldova" (About the Moldavian Csángó Dialects) *Altera* VIII (17-18), 81-89.

Tánczos, Vilmos (1996): "'Én román akarok lenni!' Csángók Erdélyben" ('I Want to Be Romanian!' Moldavian Csángós in Transylvania) in Vilmos Tánczos *Keletnek megnyílt kapuja.* Néprajzi esszék (Ethnographic Essays) Kolozsvár: KOM-PRESS Korunk Baráti Társaság, 160-174.

Tánczos, Vilmos (2006): "A moldvai csángók asszimilációja történeti perspektívában" (The Assimilation of the Moldavian Csángós in a Historical Perspective) *Székelyföld* X (11), 114-136.

Tánczos, Vilmos (2010): "A moldvai csángók magyar nyelvismerete 2008-2010-ben" (The Hungarian Language Command of the Moldavian Csángós in 2008–2010) *Magyar Kisebbség* XV (3-4), (57-58), 62-156.

Tánczos, Vilmos (2011a): "A moldvai csángók nyelvcseréje történeti perspektívában" (The Language Shift of the Moldavian Csángós in a Historical Perspective) in Vilmos Tánczos *Madárnyelven.* A moldvai csángók nyelvéről (About the Language of the Moldavian Csángós) Kolozsvár: Erdélyi Múzeum Egyesület, 9-28.

Tánczos, Vilmos (2011b): "'Hát mondja meg kend, hogy én mi vagyok!'" A csángó nyelvi identitás tényezői: helyzetjelentés a 2011-es népszámlálás kapcsán ('Well, You Tell Me what I Am!' The Factors of the Csángó Linguistic Identity: Situation Report on the 2011 Census), in Vilmos Tánczos *Madárnyelven. A moldvai csángók nyelvéről* (About the Language of the Moldavian Csángós) Kolozsvár: Erdélyi Múzeum Egyesület, 253-284.

Tánczos, Vilmos (2012): *Language Shift among the Moldavian Csángós* (Cluj-Napoca: The Romanian Institute for Research on National Minorities).

Databases, statistics, and other sources

IPUMS-International

Minnesota Population Center. *Integrated Public Use Microdata Series, International: Version 6.4* [Machine-readable database]. Minneapolis: University of Minnesota, 2015. *2011 Recensământul populaţiei şi al locuinţelor.* Institutul Naţional de Statistică. *Hivatalos Népszámlálási Statisztika.* Nemzeti Statisztikai Hivatal, Románia.

Recommendation 2001 [2011] = 1521. (2001) sz. ajánlás. A csángó kisebbségi kultúra Romániában. – Recomandarea 1521 (2001). Cultura minorităţii ceangăieşti din România. – Recomendation 1521 (2001) Csango Minority Culture in Romania. – Medgyesi Emese (ed.), *Mük szeretünk itt élni = Aici ne este drag să trăim = We like to live here.* Kolozsvár: Stúdium Kft. 371-373.

Wise Virgins and Mothers of God: Women, Possession and Sexuality in the Early Inochentist Movement[1]

James A. Kapaló
University College Cork, Cork

Abstract

Woman and young girls played an important role in the emergence and spread of the Inochentist movement in twentieth century Moldova. Inochentism had its origins amongst the politically and economically marginalized Moldovan ethnic communities on the edge of the Russian Empire. This chapter explores the implications of Inochentie's apocalyptic and charismatic ministry in relation to questions of gender, sexuality and reproduction situating Inochentism within the context of the upheavals that followed the Bolshevik revolution and the social and political transformation of the territories bordering Russia and Romania.

Inochentie's revival embraced a "peripheral possession" (Lewis 1989) cult of young martyrs, in which possessed women and girls took on privileged positions within the communities. A new parity was also established symbolically between 'sisters' and 'brothers' in the movement, the most striking evidence for this are the images in which men and women are shown commanding equal dignity and honour. Contemporary sources often refer to Inochentists as originating from "the most backward part of the population" (Alexandrov 1958, 20), the rural, uneducated peasant classes. Objectively this may appear to be the case, but Inochentists were also innovators as women began to 'act differently', rejecting some aspects of the institutional patriarchal religious and social order, in particular rejecting the civic duty to give birth, bring up, and offer to the state future citizens, soldiers and workers.

1 Special thanks to Dr Kevin Cawley for some inspiring discussions on the "dangerous" role of women during periods of religious change (see his "Dangerous Women in the Early Catholic Church in Korea". In: Religious Transformation in Modern Asia. Brill 2015) and to Dr Lidia Guzy for her comparative insights into women's possession cults. Thanks also to Dumitru Lisnic for Russian translations.

Introduction

This article explores the role of women and young girls in the Inochentist movement in early twentieth century Bessarabia and Ukraine. Inochentism is a movement that was founded in the opening decade of the twentieth century by the activities of the Orthodox monk Inochentie Levizor in the Russian province of Kherson and the neighboring province of Bessarabia, today's Republic of Moldova. The visions, miraculous deeds and apocalyptic message of Inochentie inspired a uniquely immanent form of Christian mysticism that intensified during long periods of fascist and Soviet repression throughout 20th century. Women came to play a particularly important role in the movement as the most effective proselytizers, as young virgin 'martyrs' possessed by demons in order to redeem the world, and also as leaders, breaking the established patterns of both rural Moldovan life and of emerging Soviet womanhood. Alongside the male leadership of the movement, some women were elevated to the status of co-divine regents entitled the 'Mother of God'. Giving up their former lives, families and possessions, many young women devotees disappeared into the 'sectarian underground', as it was referred to by Soviet authorities. The 'sisters' and 'Mothers of God' of the Inochentist underground performed gender in a radically changed religious and political landscape, establishing new religious roles and challenging the politics of gendered citizenship in the Romanian and Soviet states (Trimble Alliaume 2006: 94).

Despite its relative obscurity, Inochentism can tell us a lot about the religious transformations that took place in twentieth century Moldova and Eastern Europe. Henk de Roest, in discussing Western radical ecclesiologies, opts for the category of 'marginal' as a "non-judgmental" term to describe ecclesiologies "which have arisen out of, or are located on, the margins of mainstream (or 'traditional') churches" (Henk de Roest 2008: 251). As de Roest points out, narratives told by members of such groups "to articulate and justify their identity" are often excluded from discussions about the histories, identities and trajectories of their mainstream counterparts. Inochentism generally receives no more than a short footnote in the history of the Russian and Romanian Orthodox Churches. An appreciation of Inochentism's marginal character, and particularly the marginalized status of the women that joined the movement, enhances our understanding of vernacular Orthodoxy and the relationship between religion and politics in twentieth century Moldova. Social marginalisation and state-sponsored repression contributed to the transformation of religious communities and their worldviews. Studies have documented the various ways in which women's roles in religious life extended during communism as part of the general "domestification" of religion that took place in the absence of male clergy and functioning churches and in the face of state anti-religion campaigns (Dragadze 1993; Kononenko 2006: 48-50; see also

Douglas 2005; Hann 2010). In this chapter, I trace the expression of women's agency in popular Orthodoxy prior to and in the early years of Soviet power, focusing on the interrelated questions of ecstatic forms of practice, sexuality and motherhood.

This study, which has grown out of extended periods of ethnographic fieldwork in the Republic of Moldova from 2005 onwards, draws on some key Romanian language sources, particularly Nicolae Popovschi's early 1926 history of the Inochentist movement (Popovschi 1926) and the original 1924 hagiography, *Life and Deeds of Inochentie of Balta* (*În scurt viaţa* 1924), written by his followers, as well as later Soviet and Romanian press articles. The Romanian press (during the inter-war and wartime periods) and the Soviet press (from the late 1920s onwards) dedicated considerable attention to the question of religious sects and how to combat their 'pernicious' influence on society. The popular Soviet press publications, which included women's magazines such as *Femeia Moldovei* (The Moldovan Woman) and the youth newspaper *Tinerea Moldovei* (The Youth of Moldavia) made use of criminal cases against Inochentists in their articles to illustrate the social danger and the threat they represented to the Soviet state. They also offer us some striking visual images that inform our understanding of women's roles in the movement. The pioneer article on Inochentism in English by J. Eugene Clay (Clay 1998) gives a generally reliable outline of the origins and development of the movement but due to his limited selection of sources presents an argument that over emphasizes the ethno-national dimension of the origins and significance of the movement. The present study approaches the movement from the perspective of its gender dynamic, which is intimately related to Inochentism's central message of the approaching End of Days.

The Religious and Ethic Context

At the beginning of the twentieth century the Russian province of Bessarabia, as the territory of the present day Republic of Moldova was known for much of its history, was a rural agricultural backwater on the western border of the Russian Empire. It was ethnically and linguistically heterogeneous with no single group able to claim an absolute majority of the population. Much of the rural population of the province, however, was constituted of Romanian-speaking ethnic Moldavians with urban culture dominated by Russians and Jews (Livezeanu 1995: 89-90; King 2000). In this sense, society was structured along imperialist colonial lines, with Moldavians, who had seen their distinct political and cultural autonomy within the empire eroded (King 2000: 23) – together with some other rural minorities – representing a backward, largely illiterate, peasant strata. The neighboring territories of Russia, Kherson and Podolia, were also home to many ethnic Moldovans, alongside Ukrainians, German settlers and others. The narratives I recount in this article straddle the shifting borders and ethnic dividing lines in the region. The Russian province of Bessarabia became the Romanian province of Bessarabia in 1918, which in turn was incorporated into the Soviet Union as the *Moldovan Soviet Socialist Republic* 1940-41 when the territory was re-occupied by the Soviet forces following the Molotov-Ribbentrop pact, and again from 1944-1991, following the defeat of Romanian forces in the war. Parts of Kherson and Podolia in western Ukraine, where ethnic Moldavians constituted a sizeable minority (King 2000: 54), became in 1924 the *Moldovan Autonomous Soviet Socialist Republic* (MASSR), parts of which are later absorbed back into the new *Moldovan Soviet Socialist Republic* in 1940. Following Moldovan independence in 1991 these territories broke away to form the internationally unrecognized *Pridnestrovian Moldavian Republic*, or Transnistria as it is widely known. Inochentism unfolded on these disputed territories. The shifting boundaries described above required actors, whether in the political, economic or religious sphere, to engage in 'boundary work'. The religious leaders discussed in this article frequently crossed borders between states, between religious communities and between ethnic groups, displaying considerable ingenuity and creative spirit (see Kapaló 2017).

Bessarabian society in the first few decades of the 20th century passed through a period of unprecedented change. In terms of the religious landscape, the traditional dominance of Russian Orthodoxy was challenged by Tsar Nicholas's Edict of Religious Toleration of 1905. Introduced during the 1905 revolution as a concession to appease his opponents, it opened the way for diverse groups such as Baptists, Adventists and Evangelicals to gain legal recognition and at least nominal acceptability, adding significantly to religious diversity in the region (Baran 2014: 15). Rural Bessarabia in particular became especially diverse, having already received German protestant settlers in the 19th century as well as waves of Russian Orthodox dissenters, Old Believers, Molokans and Skoptsy (Zhuk 2004: 6-18).

In 1909, a religious revival sparked by a Moldovan monk, Ioan Levizor, set the Bessarabian countryside alight. Under the monastic name Inochentie, he drew many thousands of pilgrims seeking healing and spiritual nourishment to his monastery in Balta, close to the border with Bessarabia in today's Ukraine (see fig. 1), creating what one early foreign commentator referred to as a "Moldavian Lourdes" (Clark 1927: 108). The movement troubled the Russian Orthodox Church in the region to such an extent that the Church removed Inochentie to the Russian Far North and the Tsarist authorities and Church missionaries hounded his followers, soon labeled dangerous "sectarians" (see Clay 1999; King 2000: 74-75). These events gave birth to an outpouring of apocalyptic expectation that ignited the Moldovan and Ukrainian countryside with religious fervor. The emergence of a national movement amongst Bessarabian intellectuals at this time, calling for autonomy, self-government and Moldovan language rights, meant that Inochentie's

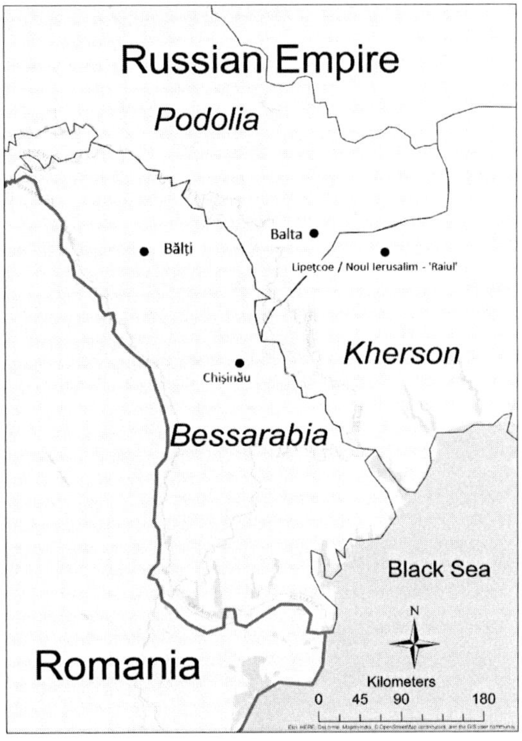

Fig. 1: Map showing the place of origin of the Inochentist movement, Balta and the Garden of Paradise in Lipețcoe, situated close to the border between the Russian provinces of Podolia, Kherson and Bessarabia.

fervent message preached in the local Moldovan dialect was interpreted in political as well as religious terms, and indeed this became the dominant interpretive frame (see Niculescu 1941; Nistor 1991; Clay 1998; Bâtcă 1999). The religious and spiritual aspects of the movement were rarely taken seriously at the time.

The explosion of Inochentism in Bessarabia was happening at the same time as St. Petersburg high society was gripped by the charismatic preaching and healing of another peasant holy man, Grigory Efimovich Rasputin. In many ways the contrast between the two men and their followers could not have been greater, the one at the heart of imperial power, adored by the Tsar and his family; the other an object of peasant devotion in a rural backwater of the empire. Both reflect, however, the attraction and power of traditional peasant mysticism at a time of uncertainty and rapid social change in Russian society. Inochentie, like Rasputin (although of course to a lesser extent), became an object of fascination for writers and intellectuals in Moscow and Bucharest who viewed this outpouring of peasant spirituality in romantic terms. Both men also attracted a wide following of women devotees, which inevitably led to questions about their moral standing and sexual ethics.

Following the revolution of 1917, Bessarabia first declared its autonomy within the Russian Empire and was then occupied and annexed by Romania (King 2000: 32-35). Inochentie's flock, that was very largely (but not exclusively) composed of ethnic Moldovans from Bessarabia was cut off from the sacred centre of the movement, which during Inochentie's imprisonment in the far North had been transferred to a new site in Ananiev district in Kherson province. There, Inochentie's followers, on land donated by local landowners, had founded a utopian community (Popovschi 1926: 229-233). Complete with gardens and orchards to sustain it, his followers had dug a vast underground monastic complex they named *Grădina Raiului*, the Garden of Paradise. Many hundreds, according to some accounts thousands, of Moldovan peasants sold their land and moved to join the community (Popovschi 1926: 229-252). Inochentie returned here briefly after he was released during the revolution before his death later that same year. Soon after, one or two days after the feast of Epiphany (January 6th) 1918, the site was ransacked by Bolshevik soldiers and local peasants who beat the leaders and murdered some of Inochentie's followers (Popovschi 1926: 247).

On 14th September 1920 (there is some uncertainty over this date as Popovschi gives the year as 1921) the community was violently repressed by the Bolsheviks for a second time (Clay 1998: 259), many followers were arrested or killed, and the land was transformed into a collective farm (King 2000: 74-75; Korchinsky 1934; Popovschi 1926). These events surrounding Inochentie gave birth to an outpouring of apocalyptic expectation and laid the grounds for the ongoing success of the movement. A series of later charismatic leaders that shared Inochentie's vision of the impending End of Days and who inherited his followers, ensured the continued popularity of the movement through the decades of the twentieth century.

Soon after the territory of Bessarabia passed to Greater Romania at the end of the First World War, the introduction of the Revised Julian Calendar by the Romanian Orthodox Church in 1924 provoked a religious crisis, especially in the eastern part of the country: in the western part of Moldavia (which had been part of the Romanian state since unification in 1862) and in Bessarabia, both of which had strong monastic institutions and traditions. Resistance to the new calendar resulted in violent confrontations between the Gendarmerie and *stilişti*, the term used to refer to those who continued to adhere to the old style calendar. In the 1930s, this led to mass 'revolts' with several killings reported in the national press (see for example *Universul*, 16th September 1936). For the Church and state authorities the calendar was a question of social, moral and religious order (Croitoru 1936) but for large portions of the Orthodox population it represented a sign of the impending end of times. Inochentists and Stilists, galvanized around the issue of the calendar, were together seen as having fallen prey to a fanatical brand of mysticism dangerous to the social order and to the new nation. These groups rejected Church reform and in so doing challenged the authority of the new state to order society according to its modernizing agenda.

> They exploit the animal feelings and use the religious hysteria that is so common amongst our peasants, and then, in an atmosphere of mysticism, it is easy to convert the naïve to sin and make them sick with various social ills that then spread them further. Here lies the social danger (Croitaru 1936: 121).

Inochentists and Stilists were seen as socially, religiously and politically destabilizing and the visible role that women played in both movements added to the moral hysteria in the rhetoric of the Orthodox Church and the popular press ("Tinere csi frumoase" in *Capitala*, September 21, 1926). These religious confrontations added to the general eschatological fervor of the time that had been heightened first by the millennium, then the loss of the Russo-Japanese war, the First World War, the collapse of the Russian empire and finally the rise of Bolshevism. The establishment of Greater Romania and the nation-building project that ensued in Bessarabia, including land reform and male suffrage, all contributed to the upheavals experienced by the rural classes.

By 1925, inspired by nationalist ideas, a whole range of new and foreign religious movements that had begun to expand amongst Romanians had been effectively outlawed and religious proselytism banned in Romania (Dobrincu 2007: 586-587). Across the porous border in neighboring Soviet Ukraine the work of building socialism was underway with the League of the Militant Godless preaching atheism and antireligious propaganda (Baran 2014: 17). By segments of the rural population, the Orthodox Church was considered to be hopelessly compromised, whether by its accommodation to communism in the Soviet Union or to Western influence, in particular the introduction of the new calendar, in Romania.

The colonial legacy of the Russian Empire and Church, the perceived backwardness, superstition and mystical predilections of the Moldovan peasants, are a more or less constant theme in contemporary Orthodox literature (see for example Croitoru 1936; Nica 1943) and are echoed in the psychiatrist Yakovenko's report (see below). The strength and authority of monasticism in Bessarabia and Moldavia, and the general political and social upheavals were also contributory factors in the success of Inochentism in Bessarabia and Romania in the 1920s. Women, both young and old, played an especially important role in the movement from its inception.

Women, the Church and the State

In the context of these dramatic religious, social and political changes, the traditional role of rural women was, of course, also challenged. In her discussion of traditional Romanian peasant society, Gail Kligman highlights the persistence of "'traditional' patriarchal values and behavioral norms" (1984: 167). This includes the sex-bound relations between "public and private domains of activity" and their relation to domestic and agricultural production (Kligman 1984: 167). Women's power in this traditional sense was confined to the private sphere and was tied to the rite of passage of the wedding, which defined women's status within families and extended families. The maintenance of these power relations between the sexes "require cultural reinforcements" to legitimize them (Worobec 1990: 229). An important dimension of these cultural controls related to the teachings of the Orthodox Church, which viewed women as both bodily impure and sexually dangerous. They were associated with sexual sin in particular (Kivelson 2006: 100-101). Women's bodily cycles and reproductive power inspired "fear and awe" in men and the Orthodox Church reinforced these ideas and regulated these powers by, for example, physically separating men and women in Church, banning women from the sanctuary of the Church and from approaching the high alter, and only allowing postmenstrual women to bake communion bread. In this religious cultural system, women were viewed as temptresses whose virginity before marriage was to be protected at all costs and after which she could become a "virtuous wife and mother" (Worobec 1990: 232).

In interwar Romania the imperative to consolidate the newly enlarged ethnic state and secure its future ensured that social policy, guided by the new science of eugenics (see Bucur 2002; Turda 2007), reinforced a traditional biologically determined role for women in the new state. The ideal of motherhood as a sacred ideal was also propagated by the fascist legionary movement (Clark 2013: 23-24). In harmony with Orthodox Christian assumptions women were to be controlled and marshaled for the benefit of the state and the nation.

> Women were generally viewed as weak and unstable, which also made them more dangerous, and thus required the protection and oversight of the state (and indirectly men). In this convoluted and contradictory view of women, is the obvious double standard, the attempt not only to control women's sexuality but also to mobilize it for the sake of the eugenic ideal: increasing the rate of "healthy births" (Bucur 2007: 338)

At the same time, over the new border between Romania and the Soviet Union formed by the river Dniester, the Soviet state made promises, based on Marxist-Leninist theory, to construct a new society, the basis of which would be the 'New Man' (Hall 2014: 159). Part of this endeavor entailed the dismantling of the patriarchal structures of the Tsarist state and, through the introduction of new laws and policies, the enhancement of the public role of women. When it came to human reproduction, however, this ideological task was to be subordinated to the broader interests of society and the state, "motherhood was not a private matter" (Goldman 1993: 256). Alongside pressure to enter the workforce, the state instigated a pronatalist campaign in 1936 and motherhood became the primary goal for all women in the official discourse (Olson, Adonyeva 2012: 75). The term "holiness" even entered official Soviet discourse in relation to motherhood (Iushkova cited in Olson, Adonyeva 2012: 75). Women in both the Soviet Union and in Greater Romania, therefore, were "claimed by the state to perform civic duties such as giving birth to, bringing up, and offering to the state future citizens, soldiers and workers" (Trimble Alliaume 2006: 94). The power of this claim on women's bodies, in both interwar Romania and during communism, can hardly be disputed. In the period from the 1920s through the 1950s, discourses on both religious sects and gender included doctrinal and theological arguments based on traditional patriarchal values as well as condemnations of the harm that reproductive choice, and particularly abstention on the grounds of religious belief, cause to the nation and society.

Against this backdrop of political upheaval, the new biopolitics of nationalist and socialist states and the fervent apocalypticism of the first decades of the twentieth century, the religious choices of women, and especially young women, offer us important insights into the transformation of gender relations. The choices made by women joining the Inochentist movement, who were overwhelmingly of rural and peasant background, were both radical and personally transformative. In particular, Inochentism offered ascetic and ecstatic forms of practice, positions of authority and a real alternative to married life.

The Women around Inochentie

Women were at the heart of Inochentie's revival from the beginning, one of the earliest reports to attest to the role of women and young girls was the 1911 report of the missionary council of Chişinău diocese which was penned with the aim of putting a stop to the enthusiastic revival. Perhaps unsurprisingly, the condemnatory report chose to focus on the unstable and emotional character of the women attracted to the movement.

> Those gathered (who always included some hysterical women (*Klikushi*) who were considered to be prophetesses) sang prayers and read akathists. One of the leaders asperged everyone with holy water and anointed the congregation with oil supposedly taken from the grave of Father Feodosie in Baltă [the holy man around whose relics the pilgrimage to Balta had first begun]. They peformed various spells over those present, and told the pilgrims that each person was possessed by a demon, or even several demons. As a result those who had weak nerves – especially women and girls – entered a neurotic frenzy, screamed,

hiccuped, jumped about, and beat themselves in convulsions. The leaders treated them as though they were possessed by sprinkling them with water, anointing them with oil, and blowing into thier faces to exorcise the demons (cited in Clay 1998: 255).

Nicolae Popovschi in his exhaustive account of the origins of the Inochentist movement published in 1926, also points to the important role that women played. He describes this in much more measured, and perhaps less partizan terms, instead focussing on the womens' role in "propaganda" and the collection of offerings for the movement. The significance of women seems to have intensified following the arrest and imprisonment of Inochentie in 1912 (Popovschi 1926: 109). According to early reports, women, wandered the villages spreading the news of the movement and seeking new adherents. In some villages "women appeared to be leading the whole movement: collecting money, gathering people together for prayer at night, helping to dig 'miraculous' wells, intervening with the local parish to conduct communal memorial liturgies" (Popovschi 1926: 110).

Another early account, first published in 1938 in the journal *Viaţa Basarabiei* but based on the author's personal experience of visiting Inochentie's monastery, describes how amongst the closest followers of Inochentie, those who "spread the fame of his holiness and his words to all Moldavians", were the sisters "Antonina Turcuman, Iuliţa Gorea, Glicheria from Mâzaci, Eufemia from Gârboveţ and many other "wise virgins" (Cazacu 2011: 33). They are described as collecting gifts from Inochentie's followers when they came to visit his cell (Cazacu 2011: 33). The gathering of offerings was an important practice that enabled the movement to grow and amass considerable wealth, one of the reasons that the neighboring bishops became suspicious, and perhaps envious, of the movement (Serafim 1913: 2). Botoşăneanu states that it was down to "the preaching of women, so-called sisters, that the movement spread over the river Prut" into the rest of Romania (Botoşăneanu 1929: 53). Amongst these women followers were also nuns, some from Răciula convent in Bessarabia (Popovschi 1926: 121). Certain other monastic centres, especially the male monastery of Hâncu in Lăpuşna county, sheltered Inochentist sympathizers for several decades after Inochentie's death.

One explanation for Women's attraction to the movement was Inochentie's preaching in the local Moldavian language at a time when the Orthodox Church only sanctioned and conducted the liturgy in Slavonic and when preaching was restricted to the Russian language. Illiteracy rates amongst Moldovan women were very high with only one in ten women able to read according to the 1926 census (King 2000: 74). Many women spoke no Russian and so when they

... heard a word of spiritual comfort in a language they could understand, they put everything aside and followed him, like they were following God. Women who to that day had not learned Russian adored him and venerated him, they were fanatics, lost and dizzy, all the more so because Inochentie was also very handsome and good looking (Rudiev 1942: 10).

Here Rudiev, one of the Orthodox missionaries sent to Tansnistria where Inchentie first preached in the 1940s, paints the women followers of Inochentie as not only ignorant of Russian, and therefore naturally attracted to Inochentie's preaching in Romanian, but he also implies their spiritual gullibility and sexual and moral weakness.

In the Inochentist hagiography *Life and Deeds* published in 1924, when describing life at *Grădina Raiului* the underground community, there is a section that refers to the role of young women that portrays these young women in quite different terms. Here they are pious and dedicated to a traditional form of monastic ascetic practice.

The cellars were composed of eight tunnels, and in each tunnel their were cells facing each other and in each cell lived two or three older girls, many of them stayed up all night reading the Psalter, Acathists and many other prayers. They led an ascetic life in fast and prayer (*În scurt viața* 1924: 62).

A special place within the movement was reserved to Inochentie's mother. Popovschi describes her as "having a sincere religiosity that nevertheless may have erred in some respects" (Popovschi 1926: 110) going on to describe the holy images in her room which included a "photograph of Inochentie surrounded by paintings, on which were painted the Ascension of the Savior with two angels in flight, which was stuck to the photograph" (Popovschi 1926: 110). This account provides evidence of the important role that visual representations played in the early movement in communicating the special identity of Inochentie (see Kapaló 2014). She is said to have been recognized by Inochentie's followers as having "superiority in religious questions and as having their deep respect: they kissed the ground near her house, received blessings from her and kissed her hand" and it was claimed that she was referred to by his followers as *măiculița Domnului*, "dear little mother of God", and *născătoare de Dumnezeu*, "Mother of God". His mother denied these controversial claims when interviewed by an Orthodox missionary priest later in 1913 (Popovschi 1926: 111) but the use of this title for important women in the movement continued throughout its history.

Another early account draws attention to a woman who appeared to be very close to Inochentie. A Bessarabian priest, father Zamă, in an interview with the famous Romanian sociologist Henri Stahl, gives his personal recollection of trip to meet Inochentie at the height of his influence at the monastery in Balta, probably around 1910 or 1911. Visiting Inochentie in his monastic cell the priest also encountered "the pious Glikeria, the prophetess – as she was named... She was dressed in black, her head covered with a white headscarf" (Stahl 1931: 178) –

she may well have been the same "Glicheria from Mâzaci" referred to by Cazacu. In the conversation that followed this woman was outspoken, admonishing father Zamă.

> ... you secular priests, you rob the world, take money, get rich, you are hypocrites, you smoke". She rebuked me and said "Stand with your hands in front of you before the Holy Icons", she spoke like this to me. I stood, listened and said nothing. After she had said this to me, I turned to father Inochentie and asked: "father Inochentie, what spirit lives inside sister Glikeria?" As I knew that she was a sister [nun]. But he said to me: "The Demon of the South lives inside her.

Father Zamă then explained to Stahl the belief that there is a Demon of the South and a Demon of the North. Inochentie then replied to Father Zamă: "Inside her lives the Demon of the South, Father, and I have blessed her many times and I have prayed a lot, and I expelled the demon from inside." Father Zamă then turned to Glikeria and asked the same question regarding Inochentie:

> "Sister Glikeria, what spirit lives inside father Inochentie?"
>
> And she said: "Inside him there are a legion of demons." (she said): "There are a legion of demons, father, there is a fornicator that is not of this world."

In Father Zamă's account, Glikeria then went on to explain that all of Inochentie's sins had been written by demons in blood on the hide of a buffalo. But when he was made a monk and everybody went "la, la, la, la" [reading] through the book, then the sins started to be erased from the hide" (Stahl 1931: 179). This account of one of the women close to Inochentie points to one of the major themes of debate surrounding the early movement, the significance of possession, especailly of young women, and Inochentie's powers of exorcism. Glikeria, standing as she did in this account next to Inochentie in his monastic quarters, is "allowed many liberties" (Lewis 1989: 27) through her status as one of the "possessed" women that flocked to his side.

When reading these early accounts it is important to consider the intent of their authors. The erratic, emotional and irrational behaviour of women as reported by the official Church missionary reports was part of a concerted effort to discredit Inochentie and prevent people from visiting his monastery. They draw on strong cultural and religious assumptions about the nature of women, their defenceless and their susceptability to the influence of harmful men, but also there inherent sinfulness. Those who later sought to discredit Inochentie, which included both the Orthodox Church and Bolshevik authorities, had good reason to exaggerate, something that later commentators who preferred to interpret the movement in the more positive frame as a national spiritual revival were also keen to point out (Niculescu 1941: 14). As we have seen above, Niculai Popovschi, the Bessarabian Church historian who gives the most thorough, balanced and well-researched account of events, in the short section of his book dedicated to women (Popovschi 1926: 109-11), chose to empahsize quite different aspects of their role. Instead he focuses on the organisational and practical importance of women as proselytizers and activists. Elsewhere, however, he too gives a detailed account of the phenomenon of communal possession, especially amongst teenagers and women (see below).

Demons and Possession

Contemporary commentators, who were mostly missionary priests or theologians, were of the view that Inochentism had no systematic or serious doctrines (Popovschi 1926: 135; Botoşăneanu 1929: 51; Nica 1943: 42). They identified, however, that its most characteristic belief was that the End of Days is very close indeed, a view later believed to have been "borrowed from Baptists and Adventists" (Botoşăneanu 1929: 51). In 1912 and 1913, followers of Inochentie calculated the time of the Final Judgement in a matter of weeks and months and when this failed to come to pass they considered that mankind was merely enjoying a reprieve thanks to the power of the prayers of Inochentie. According to reports gathered by Popovschi "Their belief remained unshaken, even more so, as they interpreted actual events in their lives as signs of proof of their beliefs", the outbreak of the World war being one such incontravertable proof (Popovschi 1926: 136). According to the testimony of Inochentie's followers, as human evil "becomes more terrible and the Devil entangles man in his nets, demons can enter people because of their sins and for this reason "sin reigns in the world", and all of this "can be perceived most clearly through the suffering of the sick" (Popovschi 1926: 137). The Inochentist conception of illness and possession has some unique characteristic elements described below that differ from the standard Orthodox view. Many of Inochentie's followers experienced an unusual condition of extreme spiritual distress. This "tension, for those of weak nervous disposition, easily became a state of illness" (Popovschi 1926: 124). This condition became so widespread that it warranted a special investigation commissioned by the Govenor of Kherson province and the local Bishop Dimitri, to investigate the religious "mass psychosis" taking place on their territory (Clay 1998: 261) according to which "the suffering of the 'possessed' were redeeming the world and prepariung the way for the Kingdom of God" (Clay 1998: 255). The psychiatrist who undertook to examine those who were falling victim to this strange sickness, V. S. Yakovenko, published his finding in two articles in the Russian Journal of Psychiatry in 1911 (Yakovenko 1911a, 1911b). In his report he quotes from another report prepared by Tiraspol region's Medical Officer, D. M. Taiga, who states that "a blind teenage girl is considered to be the leader [of people who are possessed]. It is believed that she lost her eyesight as a result of the sins of her parents" (Yakovenko 1911a:

192). Taiga also reports that the young possessed people are able to prophesy and that they do this on request of the local population. When asked by Yakovenko, the young people denied this was true. Upon arrival in the village of Cioburciu, Yakovenko was able to speak to a group of "possessed" young people, composed of a 10 year-old boy, three teenage girls aged between 15-17 years and one young man who was 18 years of age. Amongst this group the most intelligent was a blind girl who spoke only Romanian. She answered most of the questions Yakovenko asked and when the blind girl spoke the other two looked attentively to her. They all had, according to Yakovenko, slight symptoms of "possession" (Yakovlenko 1911a: 195-197).

Popovschi, drawing on this report and the accounts of several other witnesses, explains this distinctive brand of Inochentist possession and demonology in the following terms.

> Man, they believe, is spared the Devil if he leads a worldly life far from God.
>
> The burden of the Devil changes, however, when man starts to think of his sins. "When the sinner" – says Tărăţă [an important Inochentist preacher] – "discovers his sins in confession before Inochentie, he shows him the unclean spirit that rules him. Then the Devil, no longer able to make the man sin, tries as his legacy and through bouts of illness and anxiety not let him take communion bread, kiss the cross, or drink holy water. In this way, the unclean spirit retaliates for the man's repentance because it revealed its presence."
>
> That the sick have unclean spirits inside them, Inochentists use as proof of the fact that they remain unharmed in body despite throwing themselves to the ground, hitting themselves against walls and enduring other torments (Popovschi 1926: 137).

Popovschi closes his account of illness and ecstasy in the early Inochentist movement by identifying three distinct stages to possession:

> The ecstasy begins when the Inochentists, under the influence of certain stimulation – the preaching, the prayers, begin to become emotional, they lose their composure and fall into a state of weakness. Their primary thought in that moment was about their individual sinfulness which consumed their whole being provoking a terrible feeling in their spirit. Imbued with this feeling, the sick cried bitter tears, in loud voice they begin to repent their sins and forgetting all shame, in front of the crowds and for all to hear, they confess when and how they have sinned.
>
> After this comes the second stage. The agonising torment, with the confession of the most difficult and secret errors of life now revealed, leads the souls of the sick to great happiness and excitement. This state grows stronger and stronger, spreading throughout the body leading some into an ecstatic dance. At this point begins the third stage, the most tempestuous, ecstasy itself, when the sick person feels filled by the "Devil", by the "unclean spirit", and seems to have visions, sometimes able to reveal the secret thoughts of men, to foretell the future etc. This is the final moment of ecstasy, after which follows an unusual calm, but at the same time a great fatigue, exhausion, close to paralysis. Of course not all the sick exhibit these stages of ecstasy with these detailed characteristics.

Furthermore, in reality the stages described pass with great swiftness, such that even the most attentive observers amongst the investigators of Inochentism easily fail to notice many details of what happens to the sick (Popovschi 1926: 132).

The possession cult that emerges from these accounts bears one of the key hallmarks of I. M. Lewis's category of "peripheral possession" (Lewis 1989). Lewis regards certain forms of possession, those that are most often found amongst women and that are initially considered as a illness, as "thinly disguised protest movements", a kind of "clandestine ecstasy" that can be targeted against the dominant sex (Lewis 1989: 26). In outlining the charateristics of such cults, Lewis makes the point that the afflicted are morally innocent, "the women who succumb to these afflictions cannot help themselves" (Lewis 1989: 27). The young people that experience possession after visiting Inochentie and confessing their sins are not morally culpable but are instead shown to be pure of spirit because of their desire to approach God, and hence they suffer the attack of malign spirits. They are socially peripheral in Lewis's terms but through their experience of possession take on a privileged position (Lewis 1989: 27). The "young martyrs" of the village of Ciuburciu described in Yakovenko's account (Yakovenko 1911a; Clay 1998: 255) as well as the status enjoyed by the nun Glikeria (Stahl 1931: 178-179) point to this undestanding. The idea that the mass possessions and ecstatic frenzy witnessed amongst the pilgrims to Balta was a means to "express protest by the politically impotent" (Lewis 1989: 26) is plausible but should be weighed against other significant aspects of the movement. In the case of Inochentism, the marginal situation of the Moldovan ethnic minority and the peripheral role of women in traditional society and religion, needs to be complemented with a understanding of the implications of the intense apocalyptic character of the movement which also transformed women's lives in other ways.

Apocalypticism and Sexuality

The sick that attended Inochentie were not all suffering from this kind of demonic possesion illness, many also saught healing for more conventional medical conditions. In 1912, after Inochentie had been removed to Murmansk monastery in Olonets province in the Russian far north, of the many sick that followed him their the majority were women, around one hundread and fifty (*În scurt viaţa* 1924: 24). These women along with many others who responded to Inochentie's apocalyptic message abandoned normal family life. Men, women and children, the sick and the possessed embarked on long pilgrimages, initially to Balta, but later they followed Inochentie to Kam'yanets' monastery in Podolia, his first place of exile. From there they followed him to Murmansk monastery in Olonets and finally to Solovetsky prison monastery on the White Sea. According to his hagiography, the most devoted even followed him to his final place of imprisonment, the remote Anzersky hermitage (*În scurt viața* 1924: 46). The resulting abandonment of family life that was a consequence of these long pilgrimages became another main cause of concern on the part of the Orthodox Church hierarchy. Inochentie was accused of encouraging a complete rejection amongst his followers of their former lives as married peasant householders.

We have an indication of what Inochentie preached about marriage from some reliable sources. Cazacu (2011 [1938]: 36-37), who was not antagonistic towards Inochentie and his movement, quotes directly from Inochentie's preaching on this question of marriage as the End of Days approaches.

- The time for marriage and weddings is passed! The End is close; children are now disobedient, and those who will be born from now on, will fight and kill their parents, they will be like devils you will see.
- Therefore I say to you, time is short for all. Those that have a wife should be as though they have none.
- The unmarried man takes care of the affairs of the Lord, so as to please the Lord, but he who is married takes care of the things of the world, so as to please the woman; the unmarried woman takes care of the affairs of the Lord, to be holy in body and soul, but she who is married takes care of the world so as to please the man.
- Therefore I say to you, live as brothers and sisters, and women shave your hair so that it is not a temptation.

The conjugal norms and sexual relations of peasant society were certainly challenged by this message. In Inochentie's *Life and Deeds* there are also references to this aspect of his teaching. One of the main charges leveled at Inochentie in the account of his trial before the Holy Synod and Tsar Nicholas, which is most likely apocryphal, relates to this disturbance in family life and conjugal norms that Inochentie had caused.

And the Emperor asked Inochentie in front of the Synod: "Inochentie, why do you unsettle the people? The people sell their land and follow you. Women leave their husbands and children, and likewise men leave their wives, children, belongings and follow you" (*În scurt viața* 1924: 22).

And when writing from prison in the Russian Far North probably around 1916, Inochentie warns against relations between the sexes.

Brothers, love one another, and sisters do the same. Men should stay away from women, and girls from boys. Because the Devil is very cunning. Walk with pure love so that you do not give up to the Devil with your head down (*Scrisorile* 1911-1917: letter 16).[2]

[2] This corpus of letters sent by Inochentie from his various places of exile was collected, compiled and distributed by followers of Inochentie. I was presented with an electronic word document with these letters by a contemporary follower of Inochentie. The authenticity of these letters

In another letter sent from the hermitage, referred to as Golgotha in his hagiography, written to his followers at the Garden of Paradise, Inochentie urges only that those that are strong and that will thrive to follow him there (*În scurt viaţa* 1924: 47). His other followers he implores to live and pray together at the Garden of Paradise. By 1916 when this letter was probably written, the Garden of Paradise was on the way to becoming a fully-fledged community. In 1917 it is described as an estate with 45 hectares of orchards, gardens and vineyards with small houses above ground while underground the community had dug "Churches, cells and other living quarters and they were decorated beautifully and richly like the Monastery of the Caves in Kiev" (Popovschi 1926: 231-33). When Inochentie returned there in the 1917 during the revolution, the movement of people gathered pace as Inochentie called his followers to his New Jerusalem where an "unparalleled throng" was gathering of whom three quarters were said to be women (Popovschi 1926: 238). The many people that gathered there had sold their land and worldly possessions and forsaken their worldly life.

Unsurprisingly, Inochentie's critics preached against this apocalyptic message. The Orthodox theologian and 'sectologist' Botoşăneanu wrote in 1929 that Inochentism teaches that "the young should not marry for conjugal life and the birth of children is an abomination before God" (Botoşăneanu 1929: 51). The anti-Inochentist missionary manual of 1916 deals explicitly with the problem of Inochentie's teaching on marriage and virginity, and how he advises people "to turn from the bed now ready for the coming End of Days" and that Inochentie "requires virginity (remaining unmarried) from all" (Chirica 1916: 11-12). The rejection of marriage, according to the missionary manual, will "without doubt, for many bring them in turn to fornication and wickedness" (Chirica 1916: 11). Inochentists are likened in the manual to the Khlysty,[3] who broke with the marriage bed in order to engage in "spiritual love" that was judged to be, in fact, "bodily relations between a man and women but not between husband and wife" (Chirica 1916: 11). Botoşăneanu accuses Inochentists too of such sexual immorality, "Their life is therefore in commune and they called each other brothers. So it is that they are only against families with children, approving of totally free relations between men and women. Otherwise the whole structure of the sect in incomprehensible" (Botoşăneanu 1929: 51) adding that "in their underground hideouts they hold the most horrible orgies" (Botoşăneanu 1929: 51). Accusations of sexual immorality are a recurrent theme of anti-sect literature in general and

is hard to verify but in terms of style and content they are very similar to the one verifiably genuine letter that is reproduced in Inochentie's hagiography (*În scurt viaţa* 1924: 46-53).

3 The Khlysty, or followers of the "Christ Faith", were early Russian religious dissenters that renounced meat, alcohol, tobacco and sex, all things that Inochentie also preached against. They also engaged in ecstatic practices which, unlike Inochentist practice, included swirling dances (see Clay 1985; Shakhnazarov 2010; Zhuk 2004: 15).

continued throughout the Tsarist Russian and Soviet periods. As was the case with the Khlysty before them, the voice of Inochentists themselves cannot be heard in these "speculations and legends produced by hostile outsiders" (Paert 2003: 3).

Temptresses and Priestesses

The diversification of roles and the enhancement of authority of women within Inochentism was visible in various ways. The visual appearance and attire of Inochentist women was worthy of remark by contemporaries. In line with the piety and sexual abstinence required of women, their mode of dress began to diverge from ordinary village attire. Women dressed very conservatively and those that joined the community at *Grădina Raiului* are described as dressing as nuns, "They wore clothes of hemp, some of wool – all home spun, they bought nothing. The women wore black headscarves, some of the younger ones wore white ones" (Popovschi 1926: 240). Popovschi, quoting a report by missionary priests in 1912, also states that "women and girls clip their hair short" (Popovschi 1926: 121), echoing the message of Inochentie relayed by Cazacu above. The missionary manual of 1916 picks up on this point stating "Some of the craziest women followers of Inochentie clip all the hair on their head. This is not in accordance with Holy Scripture" (Chirica 1916: 19), although it may have been done in imitation of standard monastic practice for women.

Later, as the now illegal movement spread, we can find descriptions of the way Inochentist women dressed in Police and Gendarmerie reports, which were written in order help officers identify them. The Gendarme commander in Soroca County reported on the 10th October 1941 that women who are *propagandiste calificate*, "skilled propagandists", "wear black headscarves on their heads covering their foreheads and large shawls on their backs (uniformly)."[4] The official notice of wanted individuals published by the General Inspectorate of the Gendarmerie also highlights Inochentist women and girls appearance, describing them as "dressed in black clothes in the style of a nun"[5] or "completely in black with black headscarf."[6] This mode of dress amongst Inochentists women, until of course the practice was understood by the authorities, would have helped them avoid detection, passing under the radar of the authorities. The Secret Police and Military Court files from this period also offer us some visual evidence of Inochentist women's appearance. In cases that reached prosecution by the authorities, personal and community photographs were sometimes confiscated as

4 ANIC – *Archiva Nationale Istorice Centrale* fond. Inspectoratul General al Jandarmeriei dosar. 22/1941, p. 209.

5 *Buletin de Urmarire* (Wanted Notice) 1943, no. 18.

6 *Buletin de Urmarire* (Wanted Notice) 1943, no. 23.

Fig. 2: Maria Sârbu from Sireţi, county Lăpuşna, with two companions. Maria was sentenced to three months imprisonment on 22nd September 1938 for conducting Inochentist propoganda.[7]

evidence of illegal activity. The photograph printed here (fig. 2), shows three Inochentist women, one of whom is Maria Sârbu, from Sireţi, county Lăpuşna. The women are dressed conservatively and hold wooden crosses in distinctive Inochentist fashion. In the Orthodox icon tradition, the representation of individuals holding a cross in this way was restricted to martyr saints. These women, in defiance of canonical rules, portray themselves as martyrs.

In contrast with the modest and austere public image of women described above, the Romanian and Soviet press also published photographs of Inochentist women leaders that appeared to give them parity with male counterparts. 'Mothers' of God' are represented alongside Inochentie in identical 'martyr' pose (see figure 3.) and later in the movement they also appear in priestly attire (see figure 4.), breaking canonical rules and challenging patriarchal norms.

Fig. 3: Photograph published in the Romanian newspaper Romania on 25th August 1938. The caption reads "Ion Levizor (Inochentie) with one of his adepts" (Hoinaru 1938)

Fig. 4: Photograph published in the Moldavian Youth Newspaper Tinerea Moldovei 9th March 1958. The caption read "Maria Patraş (Mamunia [Mother]) and Mihail Artenii (Tatunea [Father]) in the hideout in the village of Dahnovich, Kotovsk region" (Ţopa, Chiriac 1959: 2).

Conclusion

In this chapter I have focused on the early Inochentist period up to the 1930s, however, women continue to play a significant role in contemporary Inochentist communities. The fact that women in Inochentism took on the identity of innocent victims and martyrs, and were no longer portrayed as the dangerous source of evil, represents an important transformation. De Certeau, in his classic study of possession in seventeenth century France describes a similar shift from guilty to guiltless women, from the sorcerer to the possessed (De Certeau 2000: 4).

From the various contemporary accounts and descriptions presented above, of what was a very complex picture, we can see that women's involvement was multifaceted and went beyond the usual roles that women played in Orthodox Christianity. The enhanced visibility of women and girls may have provoked some of the more extreme denunciations and scandelous accusations aimed at the movement, however, the number of reports, their diverse origin and detailed descriptions suggest that ecstatic practices and the transformation of women's sexuality were central to the movement.

It is nothing unusual in Christianity that women constitute the primary consumers of religion. The women that participated in the Inochentist communities, however, were able to take on new identities within their communities, challenging certain aspects of Orthodox Christian doctrine, peasant societal norms and the reproductive expectations of the state. The important religious innovations that took place re-shaped women's position within the movement and the communities that formed underground following Inochentie's death under the repressive policies of the Romanian and Soviet regimes.

Contemporary commentarors drew many comparisons with the practices and beliefs of earlier Orthodox splinter groups, in particular the Khlysty, the Russian mystical sect known as the Christ Faith. In his study of radical sects in Southern Russian and Ukraine, Vladimir Zhuk is able to assert that peasant dissenters, based on their new found appreciation of the biblical written text, consciously aimed at restoring "equality of status and sex in their communities, which they thought had existed amongst Christians" (Zhuk 2004: 265). Based on the evidence we have regarding Inochentism in Bessarabia, Podolia and Kherson in the early 20th century, we can make no such unequivocal claim. Inochentists read the bible much more than did their Orthodox neighbors, but their reading focused on the prophesy of the events that will unfold at the End of Days. The emergence of equality, however, seems to be a by-product of eschatological fervor and preparation for the End of Days. In contrast to Zhuk's view of Evangelical sects in post-Emancipation Russian society, who he describes as creating "their own family values and structures in order to restore morality and order in their communities" (Zhuk 2004: 266), Inochentie deconstructed the family with the aim of creating a utopian community in the shadow of the apocalypse to come. The spiritual brothers and sisters would survive the cataclysmic conditions during the reign of the Antichrist through their miraculous wells that would not run dry, their underground cells and chapels and their plentiful supply of food, the bounty of their communal labor of love at the Garden of Paradise. In this regard, there are some parallels with radical Stundists and Shalaputs, "millennial sects with communitarian principles" who were accused by the authorities of engaging in sexual experimentation (Zhuk 2004: 266). Perhaps for the same reason, because women were observed to have taken on leading roles, Inochentists, Stundists and Shalaputs were all accused of sexual immorality.

Inochentism, does not represent the first instance in the region of women being elevated to positions of leadership and exultation, amongst the Shalaputs of Nikolaev a movement arose around Marianna Stepanovna Timofeieva, the "Marianovtsy." Marianna was revered as a divine prophetess by her followers (Zhuk 2004: 115). As with Inochentism, these women figures were associated with the Mother of God, and in the case of Mirianna also with the Holy Ghost (Zhuk 2004: 116). The Shalaput "Christs" took "spiritual wives", in the same way that Inochentist male leaders were said to have done, and similarly they abstained from sexual relations with them (Zhuk 2004: 128).

Emily Baran in her study of Jehovah's Witnesses in the Soviet Union concludes that "The experience of persecution by multiple regimes solidified their rejection of secular government and that only God can provide just rule. It also strengthened their view that there was little meaningful difference between fascism and communism" (Baran 2014: 30). Inochentists in interwar and wartime fascist Romania and in Soviet Moldovia were subject to same treatment as Jehovah's witnesses. However, their response was an indigenous one that grew from a Romanian Orthodox imaginary. Divine immanence was at its heart and became expressed as embodied divinity in which both men and women could participate. In other religious communities during socialism, women took on roles that had traditionally been the preserve of men, but not to the extent that this occurred in Inochentism. The traditional means of regulating sexuality, gender roles and identities were fundamentally challenged and reordered by women who abandoned their families and domestic duties and refused to marry or reproduce. As earlier dissenting movements from Russian Orthodoxy had "constructed their religion by appropriating the available and well-known elements of Orthodoxy" (Zhuk 2004: 3), so too did Inochentists.

Contemporary sources often refer to Inochentists as originating from "the most backward part of the population" (Alexandrov 1958: 20), the rural, uneducated peasant classes. In contrast to this mainstream understanding, we can view Inochentists as innovators in a number of ways; in terms of their practices of publishing and disseminating information; their visual culture; and in terms of their structures of authority. The extent to which Inochentism ultimately proved liberational for women can be debated, however, the empowerment associated with asceticism and ecstatic practice and the possibility of a radically different life choice through which young women especially could act differently in the world represents a powerful indigenous response to women's concerns.[8]

In its beginnings, when Inochentie's revival embraced a 'peripheral possession' cult of young martyrs, in which women were seemingly in the majority, the possessed took on a privileged position within the communities. This position was also reflected in terms of the new parity that appears to have been symbolically established between 'sisters' and 'brothers' in the movement. The most striking evidence for this are the images in which men and women are shown commanding equal dignity and honor.

Part of this 'acting differently' involved the rejection of institutional patriarchal religious order – although we cannot claim that women expressed this in such terms – and in the repudiation of their civic duty to give birth, bring up, and offer to the state future citizens, soldiers and workers. The examples given above point to some alternative ways in which rural women in twentieth century Moldova performed gender, sexuality and virtue in ways that challenged the newly emerging social order and yet fulfilled their religious duty and assured their redemption at the End of Days.

Archival Sources

ANIC – *Archiva Naţionale Istorice Centrale* fond. Inspectoratul General al Jandarmeriei dosar. 22/1941, p. 209.

ANIC, *Archiva Naţionale Istorice Centrale* fond. *Direcţia Generală a Poliţiei* 206/1942 vol. 1, p. 139.

ANRM-TMC3A *Archiva Naţională a Republicii Moldova* fond. *Tribunalul militar al Corpului III armată, Chişinău* [National Archive of the Republic of Moldova – Military Tribunal of the 3rd Army Corps, Chişinău], dosar. 738-2-164 and 738-1-6846.

ASISRM-KGB – *Archiva Serviciului de Informaţii şi Securitate a Republicii Moldova, fostul KGB* [Archive of the Information and Security Service of the Republic of Moldova, the ex-KGB], personal file 020193.

CNSAS – *Consilul Naţional pentru Studierea Arhivelor Securităţii* [National Council for the Study of the Securitate Archive], dosar 15256, *Secta religioasă "Inochentişti" Anii 1928-1943*, p. 75.

---

8 There are interesting parallels with the academic debates that surround the Brahmā Kumārī movement of 1930s Pakistan. This group, which sponsored women's asceticism and had an apocalyptic vision of the End of the Days was also accused of sexual immorality. It has been suggested that the movement represents a form of "indigenous feminism" with the assertion that "the will to be free can be nourished in different ways by different cultures" (Babb 1984: 399). For debates on sexuality, asceticism and patriarchal contral amongst the Brahmā Kumārīs see Babb 1984; Chowdhry 1996; Day Howell 1998.

CNSAS – *Consilul Naţional pentru Studierea Arhivelor Securităţii* [National Council for the Study of the Securitate Archive], dosar D6880, *Secta Adventiţi de Ziua 7.a.* p. 321.

Bibliography

Alexandrov, A. (1958): *Propovăduitorii Obscurantizmului* (Preachers of Obscurantism). Chişinău: Editura de Stat a Moldovei.

Babb, Lawrence A. (1984): "Indigenous Feminism in a Modern Hindu Sect", *Signs* 9 (3), 399-416.

Baran, Emily B. (2014): *Dissent on the Margins: How Jehovah's Witnesses Defied Communism and Livid to Preach About It.* Oxford & New York: Oxford University Press.

Bâtcă, V. (1999): "Biserică Ortodoxă şi Spiritualitatea Românească în Basarabia Interbelică", *Luminătorul* 4 (43), 14-21.

Botoşăneanu, Grigorie (1929): *Confesiune şi Secte* (Bucureşti: Tipografia Cărţilor Bisericeşti).

Bucur, Maria (2007): "Fallen Women and Necessary Evils: Eugenic Representations of Prostitition in Interwar Romania" in Marius Turda, Paul J. Weindling (eds.): *Blood and Homeland: Eugenics and Racial Nationalism in Central and Southeast Europe 1900-1940.* Budapest and New York: CEU Press, 335-350.

Carpunina, I. B., A. Sibiriakov (1959): "Pocăinţa unui păcătos" (Repentance of a Sinner) in *Materiale în ajutorul lectorului ateist* (Material to Assist the Teacher of Atheism). Chişinău, 27-30.

Cazacu, Petre (2011 [1938]): *La Mănăstire, La Părinţelul* (At the Monastery, at the holy Father). Chişinău: Noua Galilee.

Chirica, Feodoie,Alecsandru Skvoznikov (1916 [1913]). *Conspecte pentru cursuri misionere norodnice de înfruntarea învăţăturii cei minciunoase a lui ieromonahul Innochentie, alcătuite de missioneri-propoveduitori a eparhiei-protoiereul Feodosie Chirica şi Alecsandru Timofevici Skvoznikov* (Syllabus for popular missionary course to counter the false teachings of hieromonk Inochentie, composed by the missioanry preachers of the diocese – archpriest Feodosie Chirica and Alecsandru Timofevici Skvoznikov). Kishinev: Eparhialnaya Tipografia.

Chowdhry, Prem (1996): "Marriage, Sexuality and the Female 'Ascetic': Understanding a Hindu Sect", *Economic and Political Weekly* 31 (34), 2307-2321.

Clark, Roland (2013): "Die Damen de Legion: Frauen in rumänischen faschistischen Gruppierungen. Trans. Andreas Rathberger"' in Armin Heinen, Oliver Jens Schmitt (eds.): *Inszenierte Gegenmacht von rechts: Die "Legion Erzengel Michael in Rumänien 1918-1938.* Munich: Oldenberg Verlag, 193-216.

Clay, J. Eugene (1985): "God's People in the Early Eighteenth Century: The Uglich Affair of 1717", *Cahiers du Monde russe et soviétique* 26 (1), 69-124.

Clay, J. Eugene (1998): "Apocalypticism in the Russian Borderlands: Inochentie Levizor and his Moldovan Followers", *Religion, State and Society* 26 (3), 251-263.

Croitaru, D. (1936): "Pericolul stilismului şi inochentismului din Basarabia" (The danger of Stilism and Inochentism in Bessarabia), *Misionarul* 8 (1-2), 120-121.

De Certeau, Michel (2000): *The Possession at Loudun.* Chicago & London: University of Chicago Press.

Dobrincu, Dorin (2007): "Religie şi Putere în România – Politica statului faţă de confesiunile (neo)protestante: 1919-1944" (Religion and Power in Romania), *Romanian Political Science Review* VII (3), 583-673.

Dragadze, T. (1993): "The Domestication of Religion under Soviet Communism" in C. N. Hann (ed.): *Socialism: Ideals, Ideologies and Local Practices.* London: Routledge, 149-56.

Engelstein, Laura (1999): *Castration and the Heavenly Kingdom: A Russian Folktale.* Ithaca & London: Cornell University Press.

Filimon, P., G. Ariton & A. Ghimp (translators) (1924): *În scurt viaţa şi faptele Părintelui Inochentie de la Balta* (The Short Life and Deeds of Father Inochentie of Balta) (Bărlad: Tip. Const. D. Lupaşcu).

Goldman, Wendy Z. (1993): *Women, the State and Revolution: Soviet Family Policy and Social Life, 1917-1936.* M Publishing, University of Michigan Library.

Hann, Chris (2010): "Introduction – Broken Chains and Moral Lazarets: The politicization, juridification and commodification of Religion after Socialism", in Chris Hann (ed.): *Religion, Identity, Postsocialism: The Halle Focus Group 2003-2010.* Max Planck Institute for Social Anthropology, 3-23.

Hoinaru, V. (1938): "Viaţa, ideile şi personalitatea călugărului Inochentie" (The life, ideas and personality of the monk Inochentie), *România* 25 August.

Howell, Julia Day (1998): "Gender Role Experimentation in New Religious Movements: Clarification of the Brahma Kumari Case", *Journal for the Scientific Study of Religion* 37 (3); 453-461.

Kapaló, James (2014): "Narratíva and kozmológia az inochentizmus ikonográfiai hagyományában", in Gábor Barna, Kinga Povedák (eds.): *Lelkiségek és Lelkiségi Mozgalmak Magyarórszáon és Kelet-Közep-Európában* (Spirituality and Spiritual Movements in Hungary and Eastern Central Europe). Szeged: SZTE BTK Néprajzi és Kulturális Antropológiai Tanszék.

Kapaló, James (2017): "'Liminal' Orthodoxies on the Margins of Empire: Twentieth-Century 'Home-grown' Religious Movements in the Republic of Moldova", *Nationalism and Ethnic Studies* 27 (1), 33-51.

Kivelson, Valerie A. (2006): "Sexuality and Gender in Early Modern Russian Orthodoxy: Sin and Virtue in Cultural Context", in John Paul Himka, Andriy Zayarnyuk (eds.): *Letters from Heaven: Popular Religion in Russia and Ukraine.* Toronto: University of Toronto Press, 100-125.

Lewis, I. M. (1989): *Ecstatic Religion: A Study of Shamanism and Spirit Possession.* London and New York: Routledge.

Kligman, Gail (1984): "The Rites of Women: Oral Poetry, Ideology, and the Socialization of Peasant Woman in Contemporary Romania", *The Journal of American Folklore* 97 (384), 167-188.

Kononenko, Natalie (2006): "Folk Orthodoxy: Popular Religion in Contemporary Ukraine", in John Paul Himka, Andriy Zayarnyuk (eds.): *Letters from Heaven: Popular Religion in Russia and Ukraine.* Toronto: University of Toronto Press, 46-75.

Korchinsky, N. A. (1934): "Selo Lipetsko i evo kultura", Krasnaya Basarabia 3, 18-20.

Nica, Antim (1943): "Viaţa Religioaşă în Transnistria", *Transnistria Creştina* 2, 9-53.

Niculescu, Andrei T. (1941): *Balta Oraşul Luminilor Transnistrene.* Bucureşti: 'Bucovina' I. E. Torduţiu.

Nistor, Ion (1991): *Istoria Basarabiei.* Bucureşti: Humanitas.
"O provocare a stiliştilor în Nordul Moldovei" (1936) *Universul* Nr. 256, 16 Sept.
O vedenie ce s'a arătat în anul 1920 (A Vision that Appeared in 1920) (1924): (Iaşi: Institutul de Arta Grafice "Versuri şi Proză").
Olson, Laura. J. & Adonyeva, Svetlana (2012): *The Worlds of Russian Village Women: Tradition, Transgression, Compromise.* Madison, Wisconsin: Wisconsin University Press.
Paert, Irina (2003): *Old Believers, Religious Dissent and Gender in Russia, 1760-1850.* Manchester & New York: Manchester University Press.
Pasat, V. (2009): Православие в молдавии: власть церковь верующие *1940-1953, 1953-60, том 1 и 2.* (*Orthodoxy in Moldavia: The Power of the Church of the Faithful 1940-1953, 1953-60, volumes I & II*) Москва: Росслен.
Popovschi, Nicolae (1926): *Mişcarea de la Balta său inochentismul în Basarabia* (The Balta Movement or Inochentism in Bessarabia). Chişinău: Tipografia Eparhială – "Cartea Românească".
Radzinsky, Edvard (2000): *The Rasputin File.* New York: Anchor Books.
Rogers, Douglas (2005): "Introduction: The Anthropology of Religion after Socialism", *Religion, State & Society* 33 (1), 6-18.
Rudiev, T. (1942): "Grădina Raiului": Impresii dintr'o călătorie misionară la Lipeţcoie, jud. Râbniţa" ("The Garden of Paradise": Impressions from a missionary journey to Lipeţcoie, Râbniţa county), *Transnistria Creştina* 1 (January-March).
Serafim [Archbishop of Chişinău and Hoţin] (1913): *Atărnarea Arhiepiscopului Serafim către Eparhie* (The Appeal of Arcbishop Serafim to the Eparchy).
Shakhnazarov, O. L. (2010): "People of the Schism, 1667-2007", in Marjorie Mandelstam Balzer (ed.): *Religion and Politics in Russia.* Armonk, NY: M. E. Sharpe, 31-53.
Shvedov, I. (1959): "Karera arhangela Mihaila", *Sovetskaya Kultura* April 4: 3.
Şincan, Anca (2012): "Silencing the Archive – A Methodological Insight into the Research for the Study 'A Day in the Life of an Inspector for Religious Denomination'", *Anuarul Institutului de Cercetări Socio Umane 'Gheorghe Şincai'* 15: 144-155.
Stahl, H. H. (1931): "Despre Inochentie şi Inochentism, fragment de convorbire cu părintele Zamă, din satul Cornova" (About Inochentie and Inochentism, a fragment of a conversation with father Zamă from the village of Cornova), *Arhiva pentru ştiinţa şi reforma sociala* 10 (1-4), 175-83.
"Tinere şi frumoase ele seduceau tineretul şi-l atrăgeau în mişcarea mitropolului Glicherie" (The young and beautiful seduce the youth and attract them to the movement of the metropolitan Glicherie) (1936): *Capitala*, September 21.
Ţopa, F., A. Chiriac (1958): "Oameni vii cu suflete", *Tinerea Moldovei*, March 2.
Trimble Alliaume, Karen (2006): "Disturbingly Catholic: Thinking the Inordinate Body", in Ellen T. Armour, Susan M. St. Ville (eds.): *Bodily Citations: Religion and Judith Butler.* New York: Columbia University Press, 93-119.
Turda, Marius (2007): "The Nation as Object: Race, Blood, and Biopolitics in Interwar Romania", *Slavic Review* 66 (3), 413-441.
Vedeniile lui Grigore Culiac şi pătimirile lui pentru mărturisirea venirii a doua a domnului Isus Hristos (The Visions and Suffering of Grigore Culeac for the Confession of the Second Coming of Jesus Christ) [undated]. Iaşi: Viaţa Românească S. C.

Worobec, Christine D. (1990): "Temptress or Virgin? The Precarious Sexual Position of Women in Postemancipation Ukrainian Peasant Society", *Slavic Review* 49 (2), 227-238.

Yakovenko, V. S. (1911a): "Psikhicheskaya epidemiya na religioznoi pochve v Anan'yevskom i Tiraspol'skom yuezdakh Khersonkoi gub", *Soveremennaya pskihiatriya* 5 (3), 191-198.

Yakovenko, V. S. (1911b): "Psikhicheskaya epidemiya na religioznoi pochve v Anan'yevskom i Tiraspol'skom yuezdakh Khersonkoi gub", *Soveremennaya pskihiatriya* 5 (4), 229-49.

Zhuk, Sergei I. (2004): *Russia's Lost Reformation: Peasants, Millenialism, and Radical Sects in Southern Russia and Ukraine, 1830-1917*. Washington DC: Woodrow Wilson Center Press.

An Indigenous Think-Tank – A Vision for Indigenous Knowledge Transmission in the 21st century

Lidia Guzy
University College Cork, Ireland

An urgent ethical question facing industrial and post-industrial societies is how to close the gap between indigenous/analogous/testimonial[1] knowledge systems and the rationalities of industrial and digital societies, governed by economic power, the exploitation of natural resources and the benefit and overall welfare of the human project. A deep dilemma undermines the possibility of a solution to this problem. On the one hand, the contemporary striving for humanity and welfare is inherently destructive to the planet and also breaches the human and environmental rights of indigenous peoples to sustainable livelihoods. On the other hand, this same hegemonic worldview is incapable of creating an imagination of interconnectedness between the indigenous, the urban, the human, the other-than-human, the earth and the cosmos, which would be necessary to achieve the *genuine* welfare of humanity in all its diversity and the earth.

Even though indigenous rights violations and indigenous cultural vulnerability are being globally addressed by NGOs such as *Survival International* since 1965 and since 1995 annually remembered at the *International Day of the World's Indigenous Peoples* as well as being documented and deplored at multiple conferences on indigenous issues,[2] the situation of indigenous peoples worldwide has not improved significantly. Attempts to include indigenous peoples' voices into mainstream policies and thinking have not engaged sufficiently with indigenous and analogous worldviews and knowledge systems. This article addresses the reasons for the lack of 'feedback' of indigenous peoples into mainstream colonial settler societies and offers possible solutions by suggesting the creation of an international indigenous think-tank. The idea for such a think-tank emerged from a research experiences in India and Brazil that encouraged a comparative and collaborative frame for indigenous research. India and Brazil were chosen as two

---

1 On definitions of indigenous, analogous, testimonial see Introduction in this volume.

2 Such as the conference entitled: *Loss of Endangered Languages, Endangered Knowledge and Endangered Environments* (1996, California, Berkley).

comparable giant nations in terms of cultural diversity, geographical scale, environmental dimension and the role of indigenous populations.

India

India is the country with the largest number of indigenous peoples in the world. The indigenous people of India are generally known as ādivāsīs, "tribals". Legal discourse in India often identifies them as members of "Scheduled Tribes" and "Particularly Vulnerable Tribal Groups" which enjoy sophisticated constitutional provisions for their protection and preservation. These groups constitute, according to the 2011 Census, 8.6% of the population: 104,545,716 out of 1,210,854,977 (1,21 billion) of the Indian population. The People of India project (1985-1995) conducted by the Anthropological Survey of India identified and located 635 distinct tribes in India, identifying among them 461 main tribes and 172 minor segments (Singh 1994) with over 700 languages belonging to language families of Austro-Asiatic, Dravidian and Tibeto-Burman (Das 2015: 16). Adivasis have their own cultural and religious traditions, observances, stories, and ideas which in recent years have gained rising academic attention (Guzy, Alles, Skoda 2015a: 12-20; Guzy, Alles, Skoda, Valk 2015b: 5-15; Carrin, Guzy (eds.) 2012; also Carrin in this volume).

The distinctive languages, cultures, worldviews, life-worlds and livelihoods of indigenous groups in India have been preserved since ancient times while coexisting with the Hindu majority society. The historical co-existence was based on the cultural institution of "jungle" kingdoms (see Schnepel 2002) which exerted a strong cultural interdependence with local tribal groups. This historical interdependency created interrelated but diversified cultural entities.

In Pre- and Post-Independence India Adivasi groups have been persistently marginalised (see Carrin, Jaffrelot 2002: 21-24). Marginalisation within the British colonial system was related to the establishment of the zamindari system (the Bengal Permanent Settlement Act) in 1793. Since then, the Adivasi territories were conferred to feudal lords for the purpose of revenue collection (Bijoi 2007: 15-27; Munda 2002). This territorial taxation incited Adivasi rebellions (see Hardiman 1987) and increased their impoverishment. Sociologically, the marginalisation of indigenous peoples can be seen in relation to the differences between Adivasi cultures, religions and kinship systems and the hegemonic Hindu caste system. Paradoxically, the post-Independence governmental purpose of positive discrimination through administratively constructed categories of "social backwardness", such as "Scheduled Tribes" or "Primitive Tribal Groups", continued to marginalise Adivasi cultures as tribal, primitive, non-sedentary and non-urban, with a pre-industrial way of life. Adivasi cultures continued to be measured by an evolutionary model of urban modernity, sedentariness and industrial development.

Indigenous movements and revolts have emerged in India since the British Rule and continue until today with recent Naxalite and Maoist insurgencies in Central and Eastern India (Shah 2006: 297–314; Misra and Das 2014). However, it is the most recent wave of globalisation of an assertive "New India" (D'Costa 2010) since the 1980's – with its subversive social exclusion or "unfavourable inclusion" of adivasi communities (see Sen 2000) and with its common breaches in indigenous and environmental rights by multinational mining corporations, which threatens the livelihoods and sustainable living of indigenous peoples in India (see Padel, Das 2010). Felix Padel's analysis (Padel 2014) and exposure of 'Development-Induced Displacement' of adivasis shows how the social structure of a tribal community is radically destroyed at every level by industrial displacement: with the change of economy from a long tradition of skilled manual techniques of cultivation and use of the forest to a new mode of life sustenance through 'unskilled labour' and 'wage labour', a dramatic degradation of life and destruction of livelihood starts. With the loss of land and control over the local environment and over water sources, adivasis are forced to migrate to urban settlements (or slums) where they are absorbed into the lowest level of social strata with exposure to the highest level of environmental pollution. While the forced re-location of communities to new habitats is traumatic and socially and culturally damaging, the re-location of sacred sites and the related intangible cultural heritage localized in them is impossible, leading to memocide[3] (Samaddar 1998) and cultural genocide[4] (Padel 2008; 2006; 2007). In the same vein, Deborah Nadal shows in her study of the forced re-settlement of the traditionally nomadic and foraging Birhor from the forests in Jharkhand and Odisha how the loss of the forest – either through progressive deforestation (ecocide[5]) or the creation of "Re-

3 According to Samaddar, the term memocide denotes the cultural dynamics of a collective and culturally destructive loss of the cultural memory of a minority society due to the influence of hegemonic value-ideas of a majority society. In the Indian context, the hegemony of Hindu values has produced a memocide in many small indigenous communities through the spread of hegemonic religious practices, ideas and hegemonic narratives.

4 Cultural genocide generally refers to a "systematic destruction of a culture or its essential indicia" (http://www.oxfordreference.com/view/10.1093/oi/authority.20110803095652845). It is synonymously used with the neologism "culturecide" and in its meaning it closely related to ethnocide as defined by UNESCO declaration of San Jose in 1981. Lawrence Davidson in his monograph on Cultural Genocide defines "When we speak of cultural genocide we are not referring to the global nature of the fast-food industry, the homogenizing of clothing styles along Western lines, or the apparent persistent desire of millions of people of non-European backgrounds to migrate to the United States or the European Union. Rather we are interested in purposeful destructive targeting of out-group cultures so as to destroy or weaken them in the process of conquest or domination" (Davidson 2012: 1); see also Elisa Novic 2016.

5 Ecocide is defined by the Earth lawyer Peggy Higgins as "the extensive damage to, destruction

served Forests" and entrance restricted "natural Parks" – (dualistic environmentalism) leads to an ethnocide[6] of a particularly vulnerable indigenous community (Nadal 2015: 39-58). Ecocide is intrinsically interrelated with the destruction of the self-esteem, value systems and the very identity of indigenous communities.

The strong contemporary social, ecological and economic marginalisation of Adivasi communities has contributed to the rise in local Adivasi resistance and political identity formation. This recent awakening of Adivasi political resistance and identity led in 2000 to a new administrative reshaping of three new Indian states (Uttaranchal, Chhattisgarh, Jharkhand). It led also to a strong internationalisation of Adivasi resistance with international agencies such as Survival and Amnesty International joining the fight against unlawful environmental destruction, exploitation and impoverishment of Adivasi communities in the course of industrialisation projects. The example of the Donghria Kondh's struggle to protect their sacred Niamgiri Hills as the geographic centre of their cosmogony (see Beggiora 2015: 51-80) against bauxite mining is a recent success story of peaceful Adivasi resistance and cultural resilience in Odisha. Due to the ongoing bad international publicity and ethical outcry, the Indian government halted Vedanta Limited Aluminium company's permits to exploit bauxite in the Khond sacred Niamgiri Hills in 2010. India's Supreme Court further ordered in 2013 that affected communities must be consulted about the project before it could go ahead. The political and judicial landmark decisions opened a new dimension in Adivasi agency, resistance, resilience and a major victory for human rights on tribal lands in India.[7]

The socio-historical context of today's situation among the Adivasi cultures shows us the complexity of the dynamics of indigeneity in India (see Devy, Davis, Chakravarty 2009), which encompasses violations of indigenous and human rights as well as the present general quest for an adequate representation of marginalised indigenous communities in India's public, political and academic discourses.

---

of or loss of ecosystem(s) of a given territory, whether by human agency or by other causes, to such extend that peaceful enjoyment by the inhabitant of that territory has been or will be severely damaged" (Higgins 2010)

6 Ethnocide means that an ethnic group is denied the right to enjoy, develop and transmit its own culture and its own language, whether collectively or individually. This involves an extreme form of massive violation of human rights and, in particular, the right of ethnic groups to respect for their cultural identity, as established by numerous declarations, covenants and agreements of the United Nations and its Specialized Agencies, as well as various regional intergovernmental bodies and numerous non- governmental organizations" (UNESCO 1981).

7 See http://www.survivalinternational.org/tribes/dongria.

Brazil

The 2010 IBGE (Instituto Brasileiro de Geografia e Estatística) Census calculates the total indigenous population in Brazil to 896.917 individuals, which corresponds to approximately 0,47% of the country's total population (200.4 million). The Brazilian Amazon is home to 280,000 to 350,000 indigenous people, of which 180,000 live traditionally, heavily dependent on the ancient forest for their sustenance, spiritual and cultural life. The 2010 IBGE Census counts 197 forest-dwelling indigenous groups, living either on reservations or in one of four national parks.[8]

Since the beginning of the European colonisation of the Americas beginning in 1492 with Columbus, Europeans collectively killed between 70 million to 100 million indigenous people (within 80 years). In the analysis of Genocide expert David Stannard this constitutes "the largest ongoing holocaust in the history of humanity" with 95% of indigenous people killed by European actions, 100% of indigenous lands stolen by Europeans, and with European-descent people becoming the most prosperous people on the planet (see Stannard 1992: X-XI). According to the anthropologist Darcy Riberio (1962: 325-346), 55 indigenous populations vanished in the first half of the 20th century alone.

In 2010, 247 peoples, speaking more than 150 different languages were documented (IBGE 2010). As a whole, the Indian population has been growing over the last 28 years, although some specific peoples have decreased in number and some others are even threatened with disappearance. Among the Indian peoples in Brazil listed by the Instituto Socioambiental (ISA), seven have populations between 5 and 40 individuals. According to Eduardo Viveiros de Castro, researcher and professor of anthropology at the Museu Nacional (UFRJ) and founding partner of Instituto Socioambiental (ISA), an Indian "is any member of an indigenous community, recognized by the latter as such. An indigenous community is any community founded on kinship or co-residence relations between its members, who maintain historical-cultural ties with pre-Colombian indigenous social organizations"[9].

According to the constitution, indigenous people in Brazil are considered "relatively capable" Brazilian citizens, having a childlike status which deserves particular protection from the state. In this sense, according to Instituto Socioambiental, the state follows a principle established by the old Brazilian civil code of 1916, based on the idea that Indians should be tutored by a state indigenous institution. From 1910 to 1967 it was the Serviço de Proteção ao Indio/SPI and

[8] Minority Rights Group International, World Directory of Minorities and Indigenous Peoples – Brazil: Overview, 2007, available at: http://www.refworld.org/docid/4954ce5a23.html (last accessed on 5 February 2015)

[9] https://pib.socioambiental.org/en/c/no-brasil-atual/quem-sao/quem-e-indio

currently it is Fundação Nacional do Indio (Funai). The aim has always been to support a full integration of indigenous communities into the national community, which means to integrate them into the majoritarian Brazilian society. The Indian Statute of the Brazilian Constitution and the rights of Brazilian Indigenous Peoples were promulgated in 1973, defining the rules on the relations of the state and Brazilian society with the indigenous communities. Even though the 1973 Statute remains in force, new approaches in the Federal Constitution of 1998, grant greater rights to indigenous peoples. The 1988 Constitution does not call for the integration of the indigenous peoples into Brazilian society anymore, ensuring them, the right to be different from the rest of the country[10].

Amnesty International, Cultural Survival and Survival International have for many years raised the problem of the lack of inclusion of indigenous peoples' voices into mainstream discourses in Brazilian educational, cultural and political life. My own experience in Brazil on an Amidila academic 2 months research trip was that indigenous issues are rarely addressed in academia, except for the Museu Paraense Emílio Goeldi in Belem or the Museu do Indio/Funai in Rio de Janeiro where there is a particular focus on exhibitions of contemporary indigenous art. A critical discourse on unsustainable progress and the impact of destructive development by Brazil's contemporary majoritarian society in relation to Brazil's indigenous people is lacking.

Indigenous Issues in an India Brazil Comparison

A collaboration between India and Brazil in relation to national indigenous issues could be ground breaking. Brazil as a country is three times bigger in territory than India, with an area of forest seven times larger than India[11], but with a much lower percentage of the indigenous people compared to India. In Brazil, these factors have resulted in the preservation and diversity of eco-cosmological knowledge systems developed throughout millennia of interaction with tropical forest environment and cultivation. In India this knowledge has been eroded by intensive incursions by non-indigenous actors. It is known that a large part of the Amazonas bio-diversity is the result of the skilful agricultural and botanical knowledge of Amerindian indigenous communities. Research by Josep A. Garí on indigenous agro-ecology for example, challenges and refutes the global perception of "wild Amazonia" and proves the sustainable indigenous impact on Amazonian ecosystems and biodiversity.

Indigenous communities conserve, use, cultivate, manage and exchange biodiversity as a fundamental component of their rural lifestyle. The indigenous agroecology comprises

10 https://pib.socioambiental.org/en/c/direitos/estatuto-do-Indio/introducao
11 http://www.nationmaster.com/country-info/compare/Brazil/India/Geography

the whole set of knowledge systems, agroecological practices and socio-cultural dynamics that shape indigenous agriculture in the context of biodiversity. The indigenous agroecology provides food security, health care, and ecosystem resilience through a local regime of biodiversity conservation and use (Garí 2001: 21).

The relative isolation of Brazilian indigenous people seems to have retained pre-Colombian eco-cosmological and agro-ecological knowledge systems over centuries which could be crucial for sustainability projects in times of ecological calamities and global climate change challenges in other parts of the world, especially India.

On the other hand, the large number of indigenous people in India can be an important indicator for the understanding of cultural resilience and resistance of indigenous people amidst threats from majoritarian cultures, societies and economies – despite similar dangers from globalisation, deforestation, legal and illegal mining and ecocide as in Brazil.

Indian civil society and the national foundational diversity discourse of Indian democracy seems to create more public awareness and understanding of issues of indigenous peoples than in Brazil. In this vein, preservation or revitalisation projects from the non-governmental as well as the governmental side have proven successful in India with a growing self-confidence amongst indigenous peoples in public space such as museums, universities and politics. The inclusion of culturally creative expressions such a ritual, performance, language and the arts in particular in the context of Indian New museology (Guzy 2009: 84-137; Chakravarty 2010: 137-150) or indigenous education (Devy 2010: 151-156) have successfully highlighted emancipatory claims of Indian marginalised indigenous communities. This emancipatory Indian indigenous expression is particularly visible in emerging indigenous animation (Douglas 2015: n.d.), indigenous art and indigenous literature (Devy, Davis, Chakravarty 2011; 2012[12]).

An in-depth comparison of India and Brazil could lead to a fuller understanding of cultural and knowledge resilience amongst indigenous/analogous/testimonial peoples. The special constitutional status of indigenous peoples in both countries provides further possibilities for a comparative legal matrix for global policy making.

International indigenous think-tank

As a vision, an international indigenous think-tank expresses and translates indigenous people's worldviews on a sustainable earth and future and offers global intellectual advice on cultural, ecological and social justice with the aim of informing global policy, higher education and legal capacities. Based on the UN

[12] http://www.adivasiacademy.org.in

Declaration on the Rights of Indigenous Peoples, adopted in 2007, an international indigenous think-tank would address the violations of indigenous peoples' rights worldwide and creatively develop answers and democratic tools to include indigenous worldviews and voices into the global mainstream imagination. Local indigenous people's worldviews on a sustainable earth and future lack a global translation into mainstream industrial and post-industrial societies and their challenges with modern insecurities and threats, such as rising socio-economic divisions, economic disparities within a growing global inequality (Pikeddy 2014) and a constant uncertainty vis-à-vis global climate change with its associated ecological calamities.

An international indigenous think-tank imagines a collaborative, interconnected world which is mutually intertwined through education and a policy based inclusion and reconciliation of different value-systems: the indigenous, the settler and the industrial. Such an international indigenous think-tank would address the challenges of respecting indigenous peoples' and human rights, respecting different worldviews and preserving a cultural, biological and ecological justice for the Earth and for the future of humanity, non-humans or other-than-human generations. The indigenous think-tank follows on from the ILO Indigenous and Tribal Populations Convention from 1957 as well as the United Nations Declaration on the Rights of Indigenous People, adopted internationally in 2007 and supported since then by the European Union. With the vision of an indigenous think-tank, MEWSC aims at enhancing the promotion of the rights of indigenous peoples as proclaimed in the UN Declaration on the Rights of Indigenous Peoples though a stronger participation of indigenous people and their worldviews in global questions of sustainability as well as the promotion of the study of indigenous resilience in order to enhance education for and about indigenous peoples and to strengthen policy making. Given the challenges posed by climate change in the Anthropocene – "a world being substantially reconfigured by human activity" (Hamilton 2014: 1) which has produced a series of unprecedented humanly-orchestrated ecological, social and cultural disasters – new skills in indigenous education and training are needed. This includes the need and wish of indigenous people to deal in a culturally and technologically innovative way with disaster management (Kalash 2017), a prerequisite for the cultural survival of ecologically and culturally endangered people.

The value of indigenous knowledge

The value of indigenous knowledge has long been recognised by anthropological research. Indigenous knowledge systems have proven to be capable of tackling national eco-politics (Conklin, Graham 1995: 695-710) and rethinking culture specific and scientific rationalities (Agrawal 1995: 413-439; Stabinsky, Brush 1996).

Indigenous knowledge is generally assumed to be the "traditional knowledge" of a group in a particular environmental and social situation, which is understood as local, orally-transmitted, practical and empirical (Ellen and Harris 2000: 2) thus context-bound and community-specific. Indigenous knowledge generally refers to the traditional ecological (Choudhury 1980; Chakraborty 1986) or medical knowledge (Shukla, Gardner 2006) of local communities.

Indigenous knowledge is harboured in language. The interrelation between knowledge and language, unique epistemological and ontological concepts and systems of communication have been acknowledged for decades by linguists, anthropologists and philosophers (De Sausurre 1919, Levi Strauss 1967-1971, Ardener 1971, Barthes 1994). The Museu Goeldi in Belem, Brazil has for example successfully used auto-documentation methods such as photography and video documentation by indigenous peoples for preservation projects of endangered Amazonian languages (Cleyton, Moore n.d.) contributing thus to the preservation of their knowledge systems, worldviews and cultures.

The vision of an indigenous think-thank focuses on this local knowledge in order to tackle global issues of a sustainable, culturally and ecologically shared human and non-human existence. It aims to close the gap between indigenous/analogous/testimonial knowledge systems and the rationalities of industrial societies, governed by discourses of power such as economic interests and national politics; agendas that lead to the exploitation of natural resources for industrial use and for the maximisation of profit and overall welfare of industrial societies. An indigenous think-tank would address the industrial worldviews' incapacity to create an imagination of an interconnectedness between the indigenous, the urban, the human, the non-human and the Earth in a sustainable process for all.

According to Albert Einstein, "the significant problems we face cannot be solved at the same level of thinking we used when we created them" (Calaprice 2000: 317). The solutions to the problems of today's world may, however, be found in indigenous critiques based on an entirely different worldview and knowledge system. By translating indigenous worldviews and their creative cultural productions and imagination, new perspectives can be found on the dilemma of an industrial welfare society, based on the cultural logic and habitus of ecocide, the history of ethnocide and continuous practice of cultural genocide.

Production of New Knowledge

Within the vision of an indigenous think-tank, new knowledge would be produced. This new knowledge combines oral forms of knowledge transmission, such as performances, rituals and oratory speech, with the use of technologically innovative methods for coping with environmental degradation. New knowledge therefore requires the adoption of programmes that combine the practical needs of ecologically endangered communities (due to deforestation, soil erosion, flood and so on) for technological knowhow with indigenous culture specific approaches to knowledge transmission and cultural resilience. The site for these programmes would be the indigenous university as exemplified by already existing indigenous university structures. An impressive example for this kind of educational experiment is the *Indira Gandhi National Tribal University*, Amarkantak, in India which was established by an Act of the Parliament of India in 2007, coming into action on July 2008. The jurisdiction of the University extends to the whole country and aims at the inclusion of the indigenous/tribal population of India into higher education. IGNTU acknowledges the need for an educational revaluation of the rich cultural heritage of tribal populations in India and it aims at the inclusion of the socially marginalised or highly disadvantaged status of these populations into higher education (http://www.igntu.nic.in/theuniversity.htm).[13]

Indigenous universities however, as Patricia Torres stated in her critique of the role and curricula of indigenous universities in Mexico (Torres 2016), are an emerging field of educational research. Settler society try to channel indigenous students into studying things only from their culture, while many of them have an interest in western science and the combination of their worldview with the available modern technologies and possibilities without losing their own cultural forms of reasoning.

The new knowledge of the proposed indigenous think tank tries to bridge the two worlds of education and knowledge: it is based on the indigenous non-

[13] With IGNTU following aims and objectives are stated:

1) to provide avenues of education, especially higher education and research facilities primarily for the tribal population of India.

2) To disseminate and advance knowledge by providing instructional and research facilities in tribal art, tradition, culture, language, medicinal systems, customs, forest based economic activities, flora, fauna and advancement in technologies relating to the natural resources of the tribal areas.

3) To collaborate with national and international universities and organizations, especially for undertaking cultural studies and research on tribal communities.

4) To formulate tribal centric development models, publish reports and monographs and to organize conferences and seminars on issues relating to tribes and to provide inputs to policy matters in different spheres.

5) To take appropriate measures for promoting the members of tribal communities capable of managing, administering and looking after their own needs by access to higher education through a university of their own.

6) To disseminate and advance knowledge by providing instructional and research facilities in such other branches of learning as it may deem fit.

7) To take appropriate measures for promoting innovations in teaching learning process in interdisciplinary studies and researches and to pay special attention to the improvement of social, educational and economic conditions and welfare of the scheduled tribes within the Union of India.

dualistic, cosmo-centric perspective expressed for example by Davi Kopenawa Yanomami's (2014) auto-ethnography *The Falling Sky*. As an indigenous apocalyptic vision, the *Falling Sky* can be read as a fundamental indigenous critique of modernity with its anthropocentric focus which has resulted in unprecedented humanly orchestrated destruction of cultures, species and eco-systems.

A new knowledge based on an indigenous critique of modernity and its apotheosis in the Anthropocene, might potentially have the power to create a new imagination of a radically interconnected human and non-human world, a worldview which, despite our incredible digital and technical capacities, has not yet been realised. The key question is "will an interconnected world-view arise fast enough and gain sufficient political, economic, and social traction soon enough to set humanity on a new course?" (Hamilton 2014: 7).

An indigenous think-tank can radically reshape solutions for an inclusive co-existence by interconnecting perspectives on the human, other-than-human, the Earth and the Cosmos with the technical worldview of modernity. By altering the relative power positions of worldviews, the indigenous think-tank could eventually set humanity on a new course of philanthropic change towards cultural, social, ecological and cosmic justice.

Indigenous think-tank as postcolonial studies

My vision of an indigenous think-tank strongly reflects the postcolonial critique of power structures (Said 1978) that mute subaltern voices (Spivak 1988) through the processes of political and intellectual colonisation (Said 1993). The anthropological discourse on literacy and orality (Goody 1968) has shown how cultural hegemonies arise out of the valuation of text as the highest technique of transmission of knowledge, eventually excluding or marginalising techniques of knowledge transmission and knowledge systems not encoded in script. The unwritten knowledge of societies without script has long been overlooked or devalued. The lack of script has become a socio-cultural pattern in the sociological and ideological marginalisation of societies dominated by orality. Indigenous/ analogous/ testimonial cultures are predominantly cultures of orality. This means that the local values and knowledge systems are enshrined in that which is oral: speech, song, the act and ritual performance. These local knowledge systems and the meanings they transmit can be understood as indigenous theories without any script. One should keep in mind that the Greek term *theoria* (deriving from Greek theorein) means contemplation or speculation expressing local systems of meaning or understanding. A system of meaning is a subjective, culturally specific, locally designed and transmitted rationality (Weber 1920). Meaning systems create sense, not in the least by means of the diverse senses: seeing, hearing, touching and the olfactory senses. Knowledge is generated and transmitted through techniques of acoustic and visual, oral or literal representation. Local or indigenous theories and knowledge systems consist of ideas and values that are sensually communicated. They use language in the form of ritual speech, the body as ritual embodiment (trance), music and dance. Mythological narratives, healing ceremonies, oracles or liturgies are clear manifestations of indigenous theories. Due to the hegemonic script-centred interest of settler societies, many of these indigenous theories of orality were ignored. Indigenous cultures worldwide, however, possess an overwhelming richness of oral and performative forms of indigenous theory. They create meaning by establishing a relation between human life and the cosmos, thus constructing particular culture specific rationalities of individual and collective action.

Indigenous/analogous/testimonial voices, their theories and their critiques of modernity have rarely been taken into serious consideration by European educational institutions or policy makers – even though the EU has fully adopted the UN Declaration of indigenous rights. The idea for an indigenous think-tank for the sake of humankind and the non-human Earth and Cosmos has not been voiced before as indigenous peoples tend to be viewed primarily as victims not as intellectual pioneers and partners, critics or ontological and philosophical thinkers. The vision of an indigenous think-tank that takes an epistemological approach evolves further the established post-colonial criticism while advancing a new interconnectedness of subaltern worldviews with the mainstream value-system and culture. Including and interconnecting with indigenous rationalities, this vision seeks to overcome the exclusion and devaluation of indigenous thinking, imagination and expression.

Conclusion – A Vision

An indigenous think-tank would tackle some of the world's most urgent problems of the Anthropocene: it would foster a change of thinking and offer a frame for the expression of an alternative imagination against the ethnocidal and ecocidal logic of a global neo-colonial industrial society. It would offer the possibility to create a truly post-colonial world and not a "neo-colonial" one where indigenous/analogous/testimonial peoples could live and where they would become equal intellectual and theoretical partners in a global eco-cosmologically sustainable world. Through the indigenous think-tank's meetings and workshops indigenous/analogous/testimonial voices and ways of thinking would be taken seriously. The experience of transcultural empathy and respect for problems and worldviews of vulnerable indigenous people has a socially and culturally empowering effect: From neo-colonial victims they would transform into a needed intellectual stimulus for a better world. An innovative engagement with indigenous knowledge, imagination and use of modern technology can lead to new models of sustainability based on the care for eco-cosmological landscapes and the moral duty to ensure a secure livelihood for indigenous/analogous/testimonial peoples.

Such an indigenous think-tank would formulate a memorandum and agenda plan for political, educational, judicial and social direct action for ecological, educational and socio-cultural justice for vulnerable indigenous/analogous/testimonial peoples and for eco-cosmological justice for the Earth and all who inhabit her.

Bibliography

Ardener, Edwin 2013 (1971): *Social Anthropology and Language*. London: Routledge.

Agrawal, Arun (1995): "Dismantling the Divide between Indigenous and Scientific Knowledge", *Development and Change* 26 (3), 413-439.

Barthes, Roland (1994*): Semiotic Challenges*. Berkley: University California Press.

Beggiora, Stefano (2015): "Indigenous Cosmogony of Kuttia Khond", *International Quaterly for Asian Studies* 46, Spring 2015, *Contemporary Indigeneity and Religion in India* (guest edited by Gregory Alles, Lidia Guzy, Uwe Skoda, Ulo Valk), 59-81.

Beth, A. Conklin and Laura R. Graham (1995): The Shifting Middle Ground: Amazonian Indians and Eco-Politics, *American Anthropologist*, New Series, Vol. 97 (4), 695-710.

Bijoi, C. R. (2007): "Adivasis of India. A history of discrimination, conflict and resistance", in: Aditi Chanchani, Mamata Dash, Rosemary Viswanath et al. (eds.): *This is our homeland. A collection of essays on the betrayal of Adivasi rights in India*. Bangalore, 15-27.

Calaprice, 2000. *The Expanded Quotable Einstein.* Princeton: Princeton University. http://press.princeton.edu/chapters/s6908.pdf (last accessed in May 2015). Press.

Carrin, Marine, Christophe Jaffrelot (eds.) (2002): *Tribus et Basses Castes. Résistance et Autonomie dans la société Indienne, Collection Purusartha*. Paris, 21-24.

Carrin, Marine, Lidia Guzy (eds.) (2012): *Voices from the Periphery. Subalternity and Empowerment in India*. New Delhi: Routledge India.

Chakravarty, Kalyan Kumar (2010): "The Living Museum Movement in India. From Heritage Interpretation to Heritage Action?" in: Guzy, Hatoum, Kamel (eds.): *From Imperial Museum to Communication Centre? On the New role of Museums as Mediators between Science and Non-Western Societies*. Würzburg: Königshausen & Neumann, 137-150.

Cleyton, Ellison, and Denny Moore (n.d.): *Samples of documentation work done by the linguistics Division of the Museu Goeldi*, Belém (www.museu-goeldi.br/linguistica).

D'Costa, Anthony (2010): *A 'New India'? Critical reflections in the long twentieth century*, London: Anthem Press.

Das, N. K. (2015): "Indigeneity, Anthropology and the Indian Tribes: A Critique", *Journal of Adivasi and Indigenous Studies* (JAIS) II (1), February 2015, 11-34.

Davidson, Lawrence (2012): *Cultural Genocide*. Rutgers University Press.

Devy, Ganesh N., Geoffrey V. Davis, Kalyan K. Chakravarty (eds.) (2009): *Indigeneity, Culture and Representation*. New Delhi: Orient Black Swan.

Devy, Ganesh (2010): "The Song of Orpheus. Reflection on the Museum of Voice", in: Guzy, Hatoum, Kamel (eds.): *From Imperial Museum to Communication Centre?*

On the New role of Museums as Mediators between Science and Non-Western Societies. Würzburg: Königshausen & Neumann, 151-156.

Devy, Ganesh N., Geoffrey V. Davis, Kalyan K. Chakravarty (eds.) (2011): *Voice and Memory. Indigenous Imagination and Expression*. New Delhi: Orient Black Swan.

Devy, Ganesh N., Geoffrey V. Davis, Kalyan K. Chakravarty (eds.) (2012): *Narrating Nomadism. Tales of Recovery and Resistance*. New Delhi: Routledge.

Douglas, Tara (no date): *Pardhan Gond adoption of new media* 3 (1), 18-27 www.southasianist.ed.ac.uk.

Douglas, Tara (2015): *Tales of the Tribes: Animation as a Tool for Indigenous Representation*. A thesis submitted in partial fulfilment of the requirements of Bournemouth University for the degree of Professional Doctorate.

Garí, Josep (2001): *Biodiversity and indigenous agroecology in Amazonia: The indigenous peoples of Pataza. Etnoecológica* 5 (7), 21-37.

Goody, Jack (ed.)(1968): *Literacy in Traditional Societies*, Cambridge.

Guzy, Lidia (2008): *Par e Sur – Sounds of the Goddess from the Boro Sombar region of Eastern India*. Berlin Museum Collection, Lars-Christian Koch (ed. of the CD-series), Mainz: Wergo Schott Verlag.

Guzy, Lidia (2009): "India", in: Guzy, Hatoum, Kamel: *Museum Islands. On the New Role of Museums*. Berlin: Panama Verlag, 83-137.

Guzy, Lidia, Rainer Hatoum, Susan Kamel (2010): *From Imperial Museum to Communication Centre? On the New role of Museums as Mediators between Science and Non-Western Societies*. Würzburg: Königshausen & Neumann.

Guzy, Lidia (2013): *Marginalised Music. Music, Religion and Politics from the Bora Sambar Region of Western Odisha*. Basel/Berlin: Lit.

Guzy, Lidia, James Cuffe (2015a): *Special Issue Emerging Adivasi and Indigenous Studies Irish Journal of Anthropology*, Guest editor Lidia Guzy, General Editor: J.B. Cuffe, Irish Journal of Anthropology 18 (2) 2015 ISSN: 1393-8592 http://anthropologyireland.org/index.php/ija-journal/journal-archives/81-2015/106-2015-2.

Guzy, Alles, Skoda, Valk (2015b): Special Issue Contemporary Indigeneity and Religion in India, *International Quarterly for Asian Studies December Issue* (together with Greg Alles, Uwe Skoda, Uelo Valk) http://asianstudies.arnold-bergstraesser.de/en/node/127819.

Hamilton, Patrick (2014): "Welcome to the Anthropocene", in: Diana Dalbotten, Gillian Roehrig, Patrick Hamilton (eds.): *Future Earth—Advancing Civic Understanding of the Anthropocene, Geophysical Monograph 203*, 1-8. American Geophysical Union: John Wiley & Sons, Inc.

Hardiman, David (1987): *The coming of the Devi: Adivasi assertion in Western India*. Delhi: Routledge.

Higgins, Polly (2010): *Eradicating Ecocide: Exposing the Corporate and Political Practices*. London: Shepheard-Walwyn.

Levi-Strauss, Claude (1967): *Mythologiques 1, Le Cru et le Cuit*. Paris: Plon.

Levi-Strauss, Claude (1967): *Mythologiques 2, Du miel aux cendre*. Paris: Plon.

Levi-Strauss, Claude (1968): *Mythologiques 3, L'Origine des manières de table*. Paris: Plon.

Levi-Strauss, Claude (1971): *Mythologiques 4, L'Homme nu*. Paris: Plon.

Kalash, Taj Khan (2017): "Ecological Living in Peril: The Case of Kalasha Society in Hindu Kush", at conference *Shamanism and Eco-cosmology. A cross-cultural perspective*

(27 &28th April 2017) at Panteion University of Social and Political Sciences, Athens. (oral presentation, unpublished paper).

Kulirani, B. Francis, Kamal K. Misra, Kishor K. Basa (2015): *Tribes and Analogous People In India: Contemporary Issues*. Delhi: Gyan Publishing House.

Mann, Charles C. (2005): *1491: New Revelations of the Americas before Columbus*. New York: Knopf.

Minority Rights Group International, World Directory of Minorities and Indigenous Peoples – Brazil: Overview, 2007, available at: http://www.refworld.org/docid/4954ce5a23.html (last accessed on 5 February 2015).

Munda, Ram Dayal (2002): *India's Protection and Promotion of Tribal Rights: Obligations under ILO Convention on Indigenous and Tribal Peoples, 1957 (No. 107)*, paper submitted at Indigenous Rights in the Commonwealth Project South and South Asia Regional Expert Meeting, 11th–13th March 2002.

Nadal, Deborah (2015): "Housing Ancestors. The Reorganization of Living Spaces among the Birhor of Jharkhand and Odisha" in Guzy, Alles, Skoda, Valk (eds.) (2015): Special Issue Contemporary Indigeneity and Religion in India, *International Quarterly for Asian Studies* December Issue, 39-58.

Novic, Elisa (2016): *The Concept of Cultural Genocide. An International Law Perspective*. Oxford University Press.

Padel, Felix, Samarendra Das (2010): *Out of this earth: East India Adivasis and the Aluminum Cartel*. New Delhi: Orient Blackswan.

Padel, Felix (2014): "Resisting Cultural Genocide in an Age of Investment-Induced Displacement. In Dissent" in: Kamal K. Misra, N. K. Das (Eds.): *Discrimination and Dispossession: Tribal Movements in Contemporary India*. New Delhi: Manohar.

Pikeddy, Thomas (2014): *Capital in the Twenty-First Century*. Harvard: The President and Fellowships of Harvard College.

Ribeiro, Darcy (1962): "Social Integration of Indigenous Populations in Brazil" in: *International Labour Review*, 325-346.

Saussurre, Ferdinand (1916): *Cours de linguistique générale. Édition critique*. Paris: Payot.

Said, Eduard (1993): *Culture and Imperialism*. London: Chatto & Windus.

Said, Edward (1978). *Orientalism*. New York: Vintage.

Schnepel, Burkhard (2002): *The Jungle Kings*. New Delhi: Manohar.

Shah, Alpa (2006): "Markets of Protection. The 'Terrorist' Maoist Movement and the State in Jharkhand, India", *Critique of Anthropology* 26, 297-314.

Sen, Amartya (2000): "Social Exclusion: Concept, Application, and Scrutiny" *Social Development Papers No. 1*, Office of Environment and Social Development Asian Development Bank. Manila: Asian Development Bank.

Singh, K.S. (1994): *People of India -The Scheduled Tribe. National Vol. III*. Delhi: ASI and Oxford University Press.

Spivak, Gayatri Chakravorty (1988): *In other words. Essays in cultural Politics*. New York, London: Routledge.

Stabinsky, Doreen, Stephen B. Brush (eds.) (1996): *Valuing Local Knowledge: Indigenous People and Intellectual Property Part*. Washington: Island Press.

Stannard, David (1992): *American Holocaust: The Conquest of the New World*. Oxford University Press.

Torres, Patricia (2016): "Indigenous Knowledge and Higher Education in Mexico", keynote at *Latin American Indigeneities* Workshop at University College Cork, The Marginalised and Endangered Worldviews Study Centre (MEWSC), Study of Religions Department & The Centre for Mexican Studies of Spanish, Portuguese and Latin American Studies, 6 Oct 2016, (unpublished paper, oral communication).
UNESCO (1981): *Unesco and the struggle against ethnocide.* Declaration of San Jose. Paris UNESCO.
Weber, Max (1920): *Wirtschaft und Gesellschaft*. 5th rev. (ed. by Johannes Winckelmann). Tübingen.

The 'Father', the Intellectual, and the Artist: The Lives of Three Indigenous Adi Activists of the Donyipolo Movement, Northeast India

Claire S. Scheid

Abstract

This article examines the restructuring of the indigenous Donyipolo faith among the Adi by offering a tripartite biographical human perspective that briefly chronicles the lives and contributions of three of the movement's central figures: Talom Rukbo (the 'Father'); Oshong Ering (the Intellectual); and Komeng Dai (the Artist). By doing so, this piece intends to add a personal element to the history of the new Adi religious system, which has been 'formalised' as the indigenous faith of Donyipolo (Sun-moon). Based on local publications, individual interviews, and conversations with the families of these men, Donyipolo has been examined 'behind the scenes', revealing the manner in which the reformation's direction was impacted by personal lives in the community – and, in turn, influenced the personal lives of these community members. These three men were instrumental in the revolution and the restructuring of Donyipolo, in large part, is a direct result of their experiences and contributions. Their narratives are further utilised to determine how the Adi shape indigenous hagiography and forge their own links between the movement's contributors and 'sacredness' in Donyipolo.

Introduction

The Adi are indigenous to the Northeast Indian state of Arunachal Pradesh and follow a religion called Donyipolo. With a rich metaphysical ontology and a vast breadth of variation within praxis, Donyipolo is centered on the Sun (*Donyi*,[1] female energy) and the Moon (*Polo*, male energy). Non-human powers, *uyu*, contribute to Adi navigation of daily life and are intertwined with the natural habi-

[1] There is not yet one codified system to represent the Tibeto-Burman Adi language. In this paper, I employ a simplified transliteration system. When quoting from other authors who have used different systems, their transliterations have been retained.

tat – the mountainous jungles of the Eastern Himalayan foothills. Over the past decades, the Adi have 'institutionalised' Donyipolo in an attempt to preserve it, introducing the creation and distribution of prayer books and instructional texts; the construction of places of worship; the design and distribution of iconography; and the determination of new roles for ritual specialists, responsible for changes in the methods of prayer, ritual, and 'healing'. These new structures of worship, occurring as the boundaries of the formerly isolated Adi heartland became increasingly porous, were enacted by a group of Adi community leaders with the foresight and practicality to reform the faith.[2] The lives of these revolutionaries additionally chronicle great changes in the northeastern state of Arunachal Pradesh. Their stories can thus be viewed as maps that allow us to navigate the Donyipolo revival from the perspective of individual lives.

Dunaway states that folklorists have long seen the value in *memorats* (personal narratives) (1992: 40). Such a method, one that relies on oral interviews and individual histories, is in keeping with the principles of the interactive ethnographic process espoused by Briggs, attempting to understand larger cultural beliefs by speaking particularly with members of the culture about these beliefs (*e.g.*, Briggs 2008). Herzfeld's work (*e.g.*, 1997) is often discussed as a classic example proving the relevance of 'ethnographic biography' (see Herzfeld 1997), the premise of which is built on by Jackson (2008), who equates this approach with Sartre's 'singular universal'[3] and argues for the necessity of individualised studies of people rather than an overarching focus on one culture that relies purely on larger brushstrokes. Jackson contradicts White's controversial commentary on the similarity of biographies of Pueblo Indians – that they are 'about as personal as the life history of an automobile tire' (as quoted in Jackson 2008: 377-397) – by stressing that even 'tire marks' may appear similar but 'each has an idiosyncratic tread and unique pattern … identifiable as belonging … *to a particular vehicle, to a particular person*' (Jackson 2008: 397) – an observation that should be apparent to ethnographers working closely with informants in the field and one that is certainly the case among the Adi. Somers further argues for the merits of what she calls 'narrative identity', calling for a re-evaluation of the construction of identity formation by connecting 'identity politics' and the 'social construction of identity'

---

2 The founder of the Donyipolo Yelam Kebang (Faith Council), Talom Rukbo, deliberately set out to reformat the Adi belief system from a 'faith' to a 'religion'; he viewed 'religion' as being more structured than 'faith', particularly through its use of religious texts (Borang 2002: 3).

3 Sartre's 'singular universal' argues that a human is not an 'individual' but rather a 'singular universal' – 'totalized and thereby universalized by his period, he retotalizes it by reproducing himself in it as a singularity. Universal by the singular universality of human history, singular by the universalizing singularity of his projects, he demands to be studied from both sides.' Jean-Paul Sartre, *The Family Idiot: Gustave Flaubert 1821-1857* (trans. Carol Cosman; 5 vols.; Chicago: University of Chicago Press, 1981-1993) 1: 7-8. As quoted in Jackson 2008: 380 (footnote 9).

(Somers 1994: 23). An individual indigenous life is a valid and unique narrative, and the state of being indigenous should not be seen as producing homogeneity in identity. There is great value to be found in the biography of a given indigenous person, perhaps even more so than in studies focused instead on the groups as a whole.

Moving in this vein, this piece begins with a summary of the experiences and works of Talom Rukbo, the founder of the movement; follows with a biographical sketch of Oshong Ering, Adi intellectual and contributor to the movement; and concludes with a discussion of the life and art of Komeng Dai, the creative force behind the images that have become the 'public face' of Donyipolo. Particular challenges occur in attempting biographies in the Adi setting: contradictory dates are provided; different perspectives offered by various subjects make locating consistent narratives difficult; and – as this piece relies both on local publications and extensive interviews[4] – the written word, as it has sprung within this first literate generation, is sometimes different from oral tellings of the same material. Yet by presenting brief biographies of these three men, different snapshots of the role of the Donyipolo reformation through these human lives emerge, supporting Mintz' assertion – championed by Dunaway – that 'the anthropological *life history* situated an individual life within a concept "of how people are at once products and makers of social and cultural systems within which they lodged"'[5] (Mintz 1984: 306, as cited in Dunaway 2002: 40). Contemporary Donyipolo simultaneously shaped, and was shaped by, the community members who practice the faith.

This article concludes with an exploration of the manner by which these life narratives have been shaped into Adi hagiography – particularly posthumously – corresponding organically to the idea of Campbell's 'monomyth', that which makes a hero's journey. The depictions that emerge of these mens' biographies inform us about the Adi construction of 'the special life' and highlight the interwoven nature of the revival and the individual Adi within this context.

---

4 Interviews with Oshong Ering, the families of Komeng Dai and Talom Rukbo, and others who knew these men were conducted in 2013, 2014, and 2015 in East and West Siang districts, Arunachal Pradesh, as part of a larger project investigating the Donyipolo Yelam Kebang (Faith Council) (see Scheid 2015). Interviews were conducted in the English and Adi languages; the text that appears as quotes in this article was given in English with the exception of the interviews with the family of Komeng Dai, which were translated with the assistance of Dugge Gammeng. Local publications about these men (*e.g.*, Borang 2013, 2002; Ering 2005) further assisted in the compilation of their life narratives.

5 Sidney Mintz (1984): 'The Anthropological Interview and the Life History,' in Dunaway and Baum, (eds.) *Oral History: An Interdisciplinary Anthology*. Nashville, Tennessee, USA: American Association for State & Local History, 306.

Fig. 1: Altar image of Talom Rukbo in Lamrung Gangging, Solung Ground. © *Scheid 2014*

Fig. 2: A modern gangging near Jine, the historical site of Rukbo's birth. © *Scheid 2014*

Talom Rukbo – The 'Father'

The most venerated figure within the Donyipolo revival – considered to be its 'Father' and its founder – is Golgibote Talom Rukbo (1937/1938-2001). 'We gave him the title Golgibote [describing] a[n] herb called Golgi Roksok which cannot go extinct; even fire cannot destroy it' (Taluk Tamuk, first president of the Donyipolo Faith Organization; as interviewed in Koyu *n.d.*, *The Life and Times of Golgi Bote*). The closest English translations for 'Golgi Roksok' would perhaps be 'Perpetual Bloom' or 'Everblossom', making Rukbo the 'Everblossoming Leader'. Rukbo's contributions were so significant that he himself has become an icon of the religion: his pictures are placed on altars, and his life celebrated annually and always remembered.

Rukbo was born to Rukpaying (father) and Odam (mother) on 30 October 1937 (1938) in Jine, where today the Kelek Government School stands in Balek Village, five kilometres from Pasighat, the largest Adi town (Borang 2013: 8).

Omak Rukbo, nephew of Talom, recalls that Odam 'hurried back from the field to give birth [at] 3.30 or 4.' (O. Rukbo 2015: 13). The birth was assisted by a man named Papang Yomso (known also as Nonong Papang) who looked after young children and thus was considered qualified to help with the delivery. When he was born, Talom was crying very loudly, and Papang told Odam 'it was the first child (baby) out of a hundred ever I attended who made me shocked and fearful by its loud frightening cry. It has a uniqueness. I therefore, keep its name as Olom (later on Talom) – meaning to make frightening shock' (O. Rukbo 2015: 13). This was the first of a number of events viewed as culturally unusual that surrounded Rukbo and which have today been woven into hagiographic folklore about him.

Oson Rukbo, son of Talom, recalls that his 'grandmother lived to more than 100 years' (Interview Pasighat 2014). Talom's elder brother Tagen Rukbo states: 'We were a big family of many brothers and sisters – but among the siblings two of us were the only surviving brothers' (Koyu *n.d.*, *The Life and Times of Golgi Bote*). As a youth, Rukbo was very involved in cultural activities, sports, and song and dance – a 'born leader' (Interview Pasighat 2014). He would ask travelers from neighboring tribes to perform and tell stories, harboring always an interest in heritage and tradition (O. Rukbo 2013: 14). Further, he organised sporting events intended to bring the community together (O. Rukbo 2013: 14). He attended Sadiya school in Assam (Interview Pasighat 2014), Government High School Pasighat (Koyu *n.d.*, *The Life and Times of Golgi Bote*), and St. Edmund's College in Shillong,[6] Meghalaya, matriculating 1 March 1957 and graduating 19 September 1961 (dates in Borang 2013: 8[7]). In Shillong, he participated in a North-East Frontier Agency[8] initiative to translate textbooks into Adi; though this initiative was later abandoned due to its use of Devanagari script (Adi today is written in Latin script), it reflects his early commitment to literacy for his people.

Rukbo had married Ongat, daughter of Jipit (mother) and Kobang (father) in 'class 8 or 9', around the year 1950, and she conceived during his final year in Shillong.[9] She had been named Ongat as she was the last of twelve children, Ongat meaning 'done, last, finished' in this context. She recalls, 'I was in my tender age [when we married], at the time of the great earthquake of 1950. We had an arranged marriage. I ... gave birth to our first child when he came back as Language Officer. I did not go with him to his posting place, and [stayed] behind to look after my in-laws' (Koyu *n.d.*, *The Life and Times of Golgi Bote*). Oson Rukbo, their son, recalls in an interview that Jipit – mother of Ongat –

6 Koyu n.d., *The Life and Times of Golgi Bote*, states that he attended St. Anthony's College, Shillong, but other sources (Borang 2002, Borang 2013) record St. Edmund's College.

7 Throughout this paper, I specify the origin of dates as sometimes they conflict between source materials.

8 The North-East Frontier Agency (NEFA) was administered by Great Britain and later India, before becoming the (Indian) Union Territory of Arunachal Pradesh in 1972.

9 It is not clear which of Rukbo's time in Shillong she is referring to here.

was a powerful ritual specialist (*uyu miri*), and that all but Ongat and one brother died. These deaths were attributed to the *uyu* – 'spirits' – belonging to Jiping, who would 'take' these children, 'eating' them. According to Oson, 'When her [Jiping's] spirit would eat people, she used to vomit out, fingers would vomit out and also the hair' (Interview Pasighat 2014). It was believed that she 'ate' most of her children and other community members as well.

After working briefly as a teacher at Pasighat High School, Talom Rukbo began a long series of government positions, both in Shillong, then the headquarters of the North-East Frontier Agency, as well as in various posts across the state of Arunachal. He served in Shillong as an Assistant Political Officer (beginning 2 January 1962; Borang 2013: 8) then worked as the Language Officer at Pasighat from 1963-1969 (Borang 2013: 8)[10] He was posted in Pangin, Arunachal, in 1965 as Sub-Area Organizer Home Guard (Sashastra Seema Bal, the Armed Border Force). On 2 January 1971, Rukbo became the Deputy Director of Information and Public Relations for the North-East Frontier Agency, assuming the post in the Shillong headquarters before becoming Special Officer Cultural Affairs Pasighat on 2 March 1971, continuing in this role until 1977. During his tenure in this position, in 1973, he revitalised the *Bogum Bokang* – the highest level of indigenous self-governance – in Aalo, West Siang.[11]

During his post in Pangin, he began travelling to remote villages, gathering stories, *Abangs*,[12] and other traditional expressions of Adi identity and belief. Omak Rukbo recalls another memorable event that has helped cast Talom in a supernatural light within the community.

> Holding the responsibility on his shoulder to awaken the people sleeping in the dark, [he] set out from Boleng to Li:sing-Mé:sing village with his companions. An hour before dusk, when he took a short while [*sic*] rest, suddenly a fierce, violent and thundering sound came from the top of the mountain and echoed down towards [the] plain. Everyone stood standstill with fear. If visible, it was like a meteor having a long tail and made a very peculiar sound like … UM UM UM. That very sound frequently echoed in his ears and showered a tremendous inspiration to feel himself that he might have a spiritual potentiality to make his dream into [reality]. Truly, from thence, whatever he wrote commented and displayed had been warmly welcomed and supported by the people wholeheartedly. This paved him a way towards success. (O. Rukbo 2015: 16)

In 1980, Rukbo ran for an MLA (Member of Legislative Assembly) position. Although he was unsuccessful, he was still revered in the community, and the people took to heart his ideas and teachings. 'Many people used to tell in funny

---

[10] Koyu n.d., *The Life and Times of Golgi Bote*, states that the position of Language Officer was between 1960-1961.

[11] See also Scheid 2015 for a biographical sketch of Talom Rukbo's work history, 131-132.

[12] *Abangs* are metaphysical oracle narratives that chronicle the history and mythology of Adi ontology; they are performed in long recitation, usually by ritual specialists.

way that "if anyone wants to fill up one's empty belly with words, then better go to Talom Rukbo, he will serve the best,"' recalls his nephew (O. Rukbo 2013: 17). Harboring the attitude that 'service for society is nobler than government service' (O. Rukbo 2013: 15) Rukbo became secretary of the Adi Cultural and Literary Society, (Pasighat) in 1980, where the Donyipolo reformation was born. It was also the location of his workshop, where he did much of his writing (Koyu *n.d.*, *The Life and Times of Golgi Bote*).

While Ongat, his wife, was illiterate, Rukbo, was a prolific writer, penning poems, stories, plays, and texts about the Adi and Donyipolo. His concentration was legendary:

> His wife [Ongat] told me that one day, before sunrise, he entered his personal room and did not come out even for breakfast in spite of repeated calls. His wife prepared to go to the field. When time arrived, she asked him to take care of the tins (containers) filled with rice which were kept in his room. He didn't say anything, but simply nodded as if he had heard her. In fact, it was a coincident nodding that he had an expression in his own writing satisfactory. ... In the evening, when his wife came from the field, she found the rice scattered all over the floor of the room messily. This had been done by goats. On the other hand, surprisingly, Golgibote was found to be fixed in usual concentration. More surprisingly, the mother goat fell dead just behind him caused by over-eating, but he didn't even notice it. Rest of the goats were lying restfully on the verandah after spreading all around. This dirty scene irritated her to whip him, but no word; no response could be heard from the writer. After sometime when she shook him, he just commented 'Donyipoloism is our religion and world must know it. I knew nothing about the happening just I know about my presentation in the writing. So don't blame me please.' His wife could make no more argument and retired to her room, but he continued to work. (O. Rukbo 2015: 15-16)

Poems such as 'The Adi are about to go [to] waste' and 'Beware' (see Borang 2002: 4) paint a very clear picture of a man who feels that his culture is threatened both from external forces and the inability of internal forces to fight against them. Rukbo's poems also reflect his affection for his own community, his interest in furthering women's rights, and his sorrow at humanity's damage to the earth and the environment (see Borang 2002: 4). Obang Tayeng divides Rukbo's personal writings into five types: 'epitaphs, nature poems, patriotic, satires, and spirituals' (O. Tayeng 2013: 58). He also used in his works many words from the *Abangs*, incorporating 'priestly' Adi, terms that the layman would not be familiar with – both as a means of preserving this privileged tongue and of propagating it. Once formalisation initiatives started among the Adi, Rukbo, of course, contributed significantly to the text of the prayer book, the *Angun Bedang* ('Way of Light', 'Enlightenment', 'Illumination') and wrote instructional guides for the new religion of Donyipolo.

Rukbo had been the first to realize that the Adi needed religious texts if their culture was to survive, a conclusion he came to as part of his participation in the International Association for Religious Freedom (IARF) conferences which he attended in various cites across India (and, later, in 1990, in Hamburg, Germany). This awareness led to much discussion about terminology, steered in part by Oshong Ering, profiled later in this paper, and paved the way for other changes such as the construction of *ganggings* (prayer halls); the codification of ritual and holidays; and the creation of images of deities by local artist Komeng Dai, also profiled later in this paper.[13] In the promotion of this new religion, Rukbo and his protégé Kaling Borang traveled widely and actively reached out to neighboring groups, laying the foundation for a full-scale religious restructuring across the state. He was extremely busy during these years, his son Oson recalls, and did not have much time to spend with his family. But Oson is not resentful of this – 'what my father has done is a very good thing for Adi people' (Interview Pasighat 2014).

In 1999, Rukbo became very ill. He had for some time before been hard of hearing, but this new illness debilitated him, making it difficult for him to continue his work (Interview Pasighat 2014). His wife, Ongat, said that he told her that if he ultimately died on 30th or 31st December – traditionally Donyipolo Day, the first of which had been held in 1986 – 'then I am a true son of God; if not, I am a mere mortal' (Koyu *n.d.*, *The Life and Times of Golgi Bote*).

Rukbo died on 30 December, 2001, at 1:15 pm –

> after receiving some pieces of *eso* (*mithun*)[14] meat tied to a rope with intestines handed over by a group of ladies who were the true followers of his teaching and principle. As soon as the meat was handed over to his hands, telling, that it was of their own self expense, not by contribution from any generous person, he just nodded his head without any utterance and tried to express a peace and contentment on his face, then and there, pallor on face overtook and took away his life. Through this, it is inferred that his heart and mind firmly held up his breathing to keep commitment true that he made 15 years ago [with the founding of the Donyipolo Yelam Kebang (the Donyipolo Faith Council)]. (O. Rukbo 2015: 17)

As in Rukbo's life, small 'miracles' surrounding his death contributed to community lore about him. His hands were perceived by Omak Rukbo (his nephew) and Tajom Tasung (current Donyipolo Yelam Kebang Head Secretary) as being unusually flexible after death, able to grasp the money that mourners were placing in them. Omak writes that his whole body seemed uncannily movable even three nights after he passed away (O. Rukbo 2013: 17-19). A halo also appeared on the last photograph taken of Rukbo's coffin. At first, his wife believed it to be a water drop on the film, but it was sent to technical experts for analysis and 'no defect

---

13 For a full overview of the Donyipolo reformation, see Scheid 2015 and Chaudhuri 2013.

14 *Mithun* is a type of gaur cattle central to Adi trade and identity.

[was] found in it. It means a halo above the head.' (O. Rukbo 2013: 19). This photograph is now enshrined in Boying *Gangging* Pasighat.

Fig. 3: Picture of the 'halo coffin' in Boying Gangging; the small 'halo' is at the center top. © *Scheid 2014*

Fig. 4: Son Oson Rukbo stands next to of his father's stone grave marker. © *Scheid 2014*

Rukbo is buried on his home estate, and today his wife's burial hut stands next to his.

Fig. 5: Nearby is Ongat Rukbo's straw grave hut. The building behind hold's Rukbo's tomb. © Scheid 2014

Golgibote Talom Rukbo's contributions to the movement must not be underestimated and are, indeed, perpetually in bloom. The cause engulfed his private life, and yet the reformation would not have been furthered without this sacrifice. Nephew Omak speaks of Rukbo's double family legacy: 'If his pen was his wife, then papers were his children and relatives. If his mind was source of earning, then society was the wealth' (O. Rukbo 2013: 18).

Oshong Ering: the Intellectual

Fig. 6: Oshong Ering in his home in 2014. © Scheid 2014

Oshong Ering, the only living man profiled in this piece, is the intellectual of Pasighat. Revered, experienced, and remarkably articulate, he speaks Adi, English, and Assamese fluently along with holding a basic knowledge of Sanskrit and a number of other Indian languages due to his administrative trainings in Ranchi, Bihar, Orissa, Kolkata, and other subcontinent stations (Ering 2005: 33-35). He was the first to complete a full course from Pasighat High School and among the first to attend college in Shillong. He is also among the first few in Arunachal Pradesh to become literate. He was for many years a respected member of the Indian Administrative Service, the premier administrative civil service in India. Unlike Rukbo, Ering does not describe himself as a particularly religious man, although he was central to the Donyipolo reformation. Ering persuaded Rukbo to focus on social causes – 'I advised him to engage in social works ... we decided to [begin publishing in the 1970s] ... on Donyipolo' (Interview Pasighat 2014).

Born in the village of Roing near Pasighat between 1932 and 1937,[15] Ering was the third son of Adul (father) and Gomyi (mother). Ering spent his childhood exploring the jungle, participating in community hunting, acrobatics, song and dance, maturing within the normal *dere* (dormitory) system.[16] He recalls in his autobiography, *The Lingering Memories*, the terror of the Great Earthquake of 1950 (Ering 2005: 10-13) and three occasions on which he nearly drowned (Ering 2005: 21-24). He traveled to Pasighat with his father in 1940 (or 1942[17]) for early schooling, then studied in Sadiya before returning to the newly established Pasighat High. Ering had an arranged marriage planned – he was to marry his sister-in-law in a system typical among the Adi (*birme apeng*) – but he told her of his reservations and his future plans to travel to Shillong, thus avoiding this union. He matriculated at St. Edmund's in Shillong with only 200 rupees, unaware of the challenges to be faced in a large city with Irish, Italian, and German instructors teaching in English (Ering 2005: 8-9). Like Rukbo, he participated in the NEFA textbook translation project, but later proposed his own transliteration system over Devanagari (Ering archives). While in Shillong, he also developed a friendship with eminent anthropologist Verrier Elwin,[18] which he recalls often in interviews (Interviews Pasighat 2014, 2015).

---

15 He writes that his 'illiterate parents accounted with difficulties that I was born sometime in the year 1932-33. But my teacher might have recorded my date of birth as on 1st day of February 1937' (Ering 2005: 1).

16 As summarised from his autobiography Ering 2005: 1-2.

17 Ering gave the date as 1940 in a 2015 interview (Pasighat) and as 1942 in his autobiography (Ering 2005: 7).

18 Verrier Elwin (1902-1964), English anthropologist, is widely considered to be the 'founder' of indigenous studies in India. A charismatic researcher, he began his time in India as a priest but soon became an advocate for indigenous peoples, including in the Arunachali context: through his friendship with Nehru, he helped form governmental policies that took into account tribal needs and societies. He continues to be revered in Arunachal Pradesh and across India.

> [I met Elwin in] 1955. A small letter came saying to come and meet him. [I arrived at his home] in Mawlai [the Khasi area of Shillong]. I did not know whether he was Elwin, and he said, yes, yes, come. ... He was typing [when I arrived] – two typewriters, one in this corner here, one there. He was typing, and when he became tired of typing, he came. ... He asked me about stories; he collected from us so many stories. (Interview, Pasighat, 2015)

As he remembers in his autobiography, Elwin asked him many questions about the challenges facing NEFA tribes.

> Do you like to die early peacefully? Do you like to die hard by struggling? How do you see the changing society of the tribes? Do you feel suffocated of various modern developmental programmes of the administration? Do you feel that these developmental schemes are imposed on you? Would you feel comfortable if your tradition and faith are side-tracked or ignored? Have you been converted to any religious-ism? (Ering 2005: 17)

Ering reminisces that when Elwin asked him whether he wanted to 'die early peacefully' or 'die hard by struggling' he thought he was speaking of physical life and replied that he would rather not die at all – or, if necessary, would prefer a long life (Interviews Pasighat 2014, 2015). But Elwin was speaking metaphorically, engaging Ering on the challenges facing the Adi and their neighbors. They spoke of the Adi system of self-governance, *kebang*, among other things. The two remained in touch during Ering's time in Shillong and his conversations with Elwin shaped his own approach to his administrative and intellectual initiatives among the Adi.

Having avoided early marriage, after his return from Shillong in 1959, he wed a woman of his choosing. Her later illness, coming on suddenly when she was in her thirties, would go on to greatly influence his life.

> Thus, my whole life is dedicated to her cause. Her life-long sickness and my struggle have taught me to face the challenge of life fearlessly. I have gathered courage through experiences. Failure and success is to be judged by others, I go on fighting. Intensity of suffering and humiliation emanating from her agony will purify me and my soul. Compassion and tolerance, God embolden me. When the struggle will end, God knows. Til then, I go on struggling. (Ering 2005: 44-45)

One of his wife's pregnancies corresponded with the 1962 Chinese aggression against Arunachal Pradesh. Ering was instructed to stealthily gather information, and he was forced to leave for this journey. Ultimately, he assessed that the Chinese were primarily interested in the Tibetan areas rather than Adi settlements.

> After three and a half months, I returned to Pasighat. This period was spent sometime in the forests, villages and administrative centres. ... My wife teased me for not informing her of my whereabouts ad I had to make lame excuses to her. ... I learnt coding and decoding of cipher messages and map reading of the area, but my personal security was

left in the dark. I might have come within the ken of Chinese binoculars at Tuting and if they came to know that I was in the possessions of government classified documents; they could have trapped me endangering the national security. Since I was young and innocent of such a possibility, I did not think of anything then. I marched from place to place covering 40 to 50 kms per night. (Ering 2005: 28)

In 1974, he underwent judicial training (Ering 2005: 36) and in 1982 he was given a post at Mohanbari Supply Depot of Arunachal Pradesh as Assistant Director of Supply. He additionally assisted in the eradication of poppy farming, which was responsible for opium addiction among many Adi. In interviews, he recalls overseeing a judicial trial in Pasighat in which the invocation of Donyipolo was utilised: in certain dispute settlements, Donyipolo is invoked to define the innocent party. The results for the guilty are often violent pain or death, occurring naturally through Donyipolo's wrath. In this instance, boiling water was used to determine truth: the two men placed their hands in the water and whoever was left unburnt was to be considered in the right. In this case, both men had to be taken to hospital for their burns. Ering stopped this formal practice in his division following this event (Interview Pasighat 2014).

Ering, like Rukbo, wrote prolifically. In his archives, housed in the home of his younger daughter, his works include 'The Adis in Search of Donyi-Polo', 'The Religion of the Tanis', 'Adoption of Roman/English script for Tanii [*sic*]/Adi language', 'Marriage and Divorce', 'Donyi-Polo: The Enlightened Deity', 'Adi Belief and Faith', 'The Traditional Institution of Tribal Self Administration of the Adis', 'Solung Festival with Modern Perspective', 'Myths and Stories of the Adis', as well as writings on Matmur Jamoh, a freedom fighter of the Adi. He additionally composed an English-language musical production entitled 'the Eternal Voyage' (Ering archives).

In the 1980s, Ering participated in the selection committee for the Donyipolo Yelam Kebang and was involved in advising the Adi Cultural and Literary Society in the early days of the religious formalisation. However, he has remained wary of Hindu influence in the organisation, and his focus seems to be more on preserving the culture and tradition of the Adi than on restructuring its form. In 1990, he attended the International Association for Religious Freedom conference in Hamburg, Germany, alongside Talom Rukbo and Galo leader Thumpak Tee. Ering recalls vividly his time there – the many questions from foreigners, the talk he gave (he was asked to speak more loudly and slowly), the point he made that women had rights in the Adi community (Interviews Pasighat 2014, 2015).

Now about eighty years of age, he is a frequent interviewee for researchers and consistently shares his knowledge by speaking with visitors. He serves as chairman of the Dying Ering foundation, 'a society for human development towards a better living and livelihood' (Ering 2005: back cover). Through his assistance, many of the Adi historical traditions have been preserved and passed on not only to the

Fig. 7: Oshong Ering in his home. © Scheid 2015

community but also to foreign visitors. One is reminded of his response to Elwin's question – would he rather die quickly and painlessly or slowly – and his response that he would rather his culture not die at all. His answer has been evidenced in his life, one which has contributed immeasurably to the preservation of the Adi faith while also helping guide the Adi forward into a new and globalised age.

Komeng Dai: the Artist

Fig. 8: Courtesy of Dai and Tasung families.

Osam Dai Tasung, younger sister[19] to Komeng Dai, describes how he received his name:

[19] There were three additional siblings between Osam and Komeng, but they died. Additionally,

I will tell you why Komeng Dai goes by Komeng Dai. ... There is one *arik* (field) named Langkom. When [the workers were] at the field, Komeng Dai's mother gave birth to Komeng Dai, while working. After birth, she put Komeng Dai in a *botok* (local umbrella). And she cut the umbilical cord by herself. And put some cloth. And said *I will put Komeng Dai here and I will go to the field because I have not completed my work. If I return to [the] village, there will be taboo* [here, consisting of 2-3 days without work]. *So I will finish whatever [work] I am doing.* After [giving birth to him] she directly started her work again. The field's name is Langkom and he was birthed there. So his name was Komeng. (Interview Pasighat 2015)

Dai was born in the village of Adi-Pasi in 1948.[20] From his birth Komeng was partially deaf. Both his sister Osam and brother Tagom remember that he would blame the circumstances of his birth for this handicap. Tagom recalls that he would often try to convince Komeng that 'there are so many deaf people in the world', hoping that Komeng would not view the condition as a handicap, but, nonetheless, Komeng could be difficult. Komeng let the condition interfere with his advancement, often responding '*ngo nurung kamang*' ('I can't hear'; lit. 'I don't have ears').

In 1951, several members from Dai's family, including Komeng (but not elder brother Tagom) moved into Pasighat from the village. Komeng later began his schooling in nearby Balek. He was admitted into the boys' hostel in class six. He was so interested by art that he neglected his studies. At the time, Tagom was the only sibling bringing in an income: 'I told him, "concentrate on your studies, you must pass class ten or twelve for your future," but he didn't listen to me. ... I tried to convince [him] many times to study first then do what you want' (Interview Pasighat 2015).

'Since [I first knew] Komeng Dai, from that time, he would draw,' recalls his sister. He had an artistic nature; all who speak of him stress that he never studied art but possessed an inborn talent. Eventually this passion led to a prestigious scholarship offer for Komeng to pursue art education in Kolkata. However, fears about his lack of hearing ultimately prevented this. His mother was concerned in part that the 'people in the plains may kill him' (Interview Pasighat 2015) and he himself harbored a self-consciousness about his deafness that hampered such a commitment away from his home.

Komeng's artwork covered an array of subjects pertaining primarily to hunting, fishing, and jungle traveling. He also painted portraits of his family as well

there were three siblings elder to Tagom Dai – himself four years older than Komeng – but they also died. There was one sibling between Tagom and Komeng; it is unclear whether he or she is still alive.

20 Osam estimates 1948; Dai's elder brother Tagom says it might have been in the month of August.

as portraits of community members.[21] He additionally illustrated some graphic novels, in which he incorporated storylines into series of images with texts.

Fig. 9: Courtesy of Dai and Tasung families.

Fig. 10: Courtesy of Dai and Tasung families.

Talom Rukbo was aware that Komeng was a talented artist so he invited him to an *Abang* recitation organised by Rukbo and Subuk Tasung, then the Special Cultural Officer. The *Abangs* are spoken in a 'priestly' Adi dialect that is sometimes difficult or impossible for younger generations – or non-specialists – to understand. But Rukbo told Komeng: 'you hear the *Aabangs* and you try to paint' (Interview T. Tasung Pasighat 2015). Komeng then designed and created a number of *Abang* illustrations, many of which are today housed in Lamrung *Gangging*, Pasighat. Komeng worked increasingly with the Donyipolo Yelam Kebang, providing visual depictions of Adi characters and narratives. In 1984, he became a core member of the Adi Cultural and Literary Society, forming part of a group that Kaling Borang refers to as 'Staff Artists'. The 'Staff Artists' also included mu-

[21] Some of these are preserved in Pasighat market (*e.g.*, in the fabric store).

Fig. 11: Courtesy of Dai and Tasung families.

Fig. 12: A painting by Dai in Lamrung Gangging. © *Scheid 2014*

sicians such as Tain Tamuk and Manik Pao, all based out of Lamrung *Gangging*, which housed the Society – and, as mentioned above, Rukbo's office.

Tagom, however, remained concerned about Komeng's participation.

[When Talom Rukbo] and Komeng Dai became friends and they started this art, drawing, painting, and I also said to TR that 'first he should study'. At that time, I was posted far from Pasighat and I took some leave. . . . I [s]aid to Talom Rukbo, 'you are destroying his future. I thought that if he was working with you, he should need some qualification for that also, then also his life will have some improvement, what will he do now [after all the Donyipolo painting was done]?' But they didn't listen. Donyipolo party were requesting me to let him keep painting for them. I said 'don't say like this to me. I know that [Komeng] will never understand what I need but at least he should pass class 10.' And Komeng Dai said, 'I don't want to study. I will work with them.'

Doing this art thing and Donyipolo culture never left him. He may be not 'mentally fit' but his imagination is so good. And he worked with Talom Rukbo. He didn't need too

Fig. 13: Depiction of traditional emo (poison) collection from the high peaks by Dai. In Lamrung Gangging, Pasighat. © *Scheid 2014*

much advice from Talom Rukbo because his imagination is also good. That's why the Donyipolo party didn't want to leave him. I said to them, 'you Donyipolo people don't listen to me. What have you done for him? He also doesn't have any passbook.'[22]

And I said 'Ok, you are working with them so you should do good work. Whatever you want to fulfill [later], you can't do that because you have no education. [Whatever you want to do] but stay well'

Although considered handsome, Dai never married and was subject to mood disturbances and long silences. He drew a self-portrait in which he called himself *turna uyu* – 'living ghost'[23] – 'by looking in the mirror he has drawn it' (Interview T. Tasung Pasighat 2015).

In the late 1980s, Komeng's elder brother Tagom was transferred to Pasighat and took leadership of his household, living next with Komeng and another younger brother at Jawaharlal Nehru College Campus in Pasighat where the family had a small field.

Komeng's images of *Kine Nane*, *Doying Bote*, and *Dadi Bote*[24] – like many of his other illustrations – are today widespread across Arunachal, reproduced in each *gangging* (prayer hall). Once Komeng had created each image, a photograph of it was taken and then printed for distribution. These three deities are only several of a vast pantheon of deities to be found in Donyipolo, but it is they who have since come to epitomize the movement and exist in widespread repro-

22 'Passbook' refers to banking ability.

23 *Uyu* is a term that generally refers to the non-human. In this case, Osam Dai Tasung translated '*turna uyu*' as 'living ghost' so that is the translation employed.

24 These three deities are prominent in the 'formalised' Donyipolo. Kine Nane is the deity of agriculture; Doying Bote is the deity of humans and wisdom; Dadi Bote is the deity of animals.

Fig. 14: Courtesy of Dai and Tasung families.

duction. Most *ganggings* use Komeng's iconography of these gods on their altars, sometimes with other deities as well; in other cases, local artists have repainted Komeng's design themselves for altar display or, in rare cases, designed a new interpretation. In general, however, Komeng's pieces dominate the illustrations in contemporary Donyipolo. 'What the deities look like are imaginary – in the same way all illustrations of deities are imaginary,' says Oson Rukbo (Interview Pasighat 2014). However, as his father Talom had argued, it aids in worship to have an anthropomorphic figure through which people can connect with the divine (Rukbo *n.d.*: 12).

Another output of Komeng's collaboration with the Donyipolo administrators is the Donyipolo concentric circle design. According to Tajom Tasung, the results came as direct collaborations between Komeng, Rukbo, and Subuk Tasung.

> They all sat together and they decided. Donyipolo is not seen. [We] don't know [what] he looks like. But He[25] must be bright, something like bright – and out of that ray comes … light of Kiine Nane, Doying Bote, Dadi Bote. Out of the [Donyipolo group's] imagination, they came up with this round [design].

25 Sometimes, Donyipolo is referred to as 'He', even though it represents the synthesis of male and female. In early prayers, such as those preserved in the archives of the International Association for Religious Freedom, this is also the case.

Fig. 15: Dai's design in Golgibote Gangging, Itanagar. © Scheid 2013

As explained by Takong Miki, *tabe*[26] of Yingkiong *Gangging*, the white in the center of the circle represents *Donyi Among* (the Sun place; the Sky place) – a positive place where one will go after death if one does good work; the yellow circle represents forgiveness, a value that should be cultivated; the green circle represents *Tani Among* (a land of idealised humans; a world with greenery); and the black represents the human Tani[27] who live a dark world of ignorance.[28] The circles are surrounded by rays coming out that superficially represent the sun; yet it is also representative of *Donyi miki seri ne; Polo migoe sero ne* (the sun is all-seeing; the moon is all-seeing) (Interview Komkar 2015).

[26] In this context, *tabe* refers to the ritual specialist who oversees *gangging* (prayer hall) services.

[27] The Adi are one of the Tani group who trace their shared heritage to Abo-Tani (lit. Father-Man).

[28] In some of the concentric circle designs to be found across Arunachal, there are additional circles of varying colors and orders; this particular *tabe* was explaining the version that he considered to be 'official'.

Fig. 16: Donyipolo circle design, Pangken Gangging. © *Scheid 2015*

Fig. 17: Courtesy of Dai and Tasung families.

In 1993 or 1994,[29] six months after the death of his mother – an event from which his brother reports Komeng did not emotionally recover – Komeng began to travel between villages to feed, by bottle, a calf whose mother had also died.

[29] An official certificate from the Adi Cultural & Literary Society says Dai died in 1993; some family members report 1994.

On August 5,[30] he drew a picture of himself with this calf. He had gone to Char Ali, as always, to collect the milk to give the calf. He died later this same day.

> When [his body was discovered] warm, I said to [my brother-in-law] that we must take him in car to hospital. … We carried him on my back, and put him in the car, and we came back. … I instructed people to keep his [belongings] in one room because people will now come and collect his belongings [as per Adi tradition] … but I [myself] was distracted with his dead body and our father was too old and our mother had died. [Thus is was hard to manage which of his art was kept or taken.] … When he died, all the village people took all his paintings. (Interview Tasung family Pasighat 2015)

On the anniversary of his death, as per Adi tradition, the calf – now a cow – was sacrificed to travel to *Uyu Among* and be united with Komeng.[31]

Komeng Dai's art is now integral to the Donyipolo reformation, found in Adi villages throughout the state. The Adi Cultural and Literary Society issued him a posthumous citation 'in recognition of his remarkable contribution towards the preservation and reformation of Adi culture, literature, and faith'.[32] His mission to work with the Donyipolo reformers impacted his own life greatly and created a legacy of unique portrayals of Adi life and religion.

Fig. 18: Tagom Dai and his wife with their portraits drawn by Dai. © Scheid 2015

[30] Adi Cultural and Literary Society Pasighat, Citation of Dai's death, dated 1 September 1993.

[31] In Adi thought, if an animal is sacrificed, it will join the herd of whom for which it was sacrificed. However, if it dies in the jungle, it will live its afterlife in the herd of the *uyu* (non-human entity) by whom it was claimed.

[32] Adi Cultural and Literary Society Pasighat, Citation of Dai's death, dated 1 September 1993.

Narrative Analysis

In many ways, this paper is the beginning of a larger attempt to 'systematize' via historical records the 'formalisation' of Donyipolo. It does not explore the lives of the many others who contributed to the Donyipolo reformation: Kaling Borang, community and Donyipolo Yelam Kebang (Faith Council) leader; Mameng Dai, revolutionary poet and participant in the International Association for Religious Freedom (IARF) conferences; musicians Tain Tamuk and Manik Pao, who wrote the melodies for the prayer songs; Thumpak Tee, Galo intellectual and IARF-Hamburg participant; Ogom Dai, the first *taabe*, ritual specialist in the formalised religion; Subuk Tasung, early cultural officer; Taluk Tamuk, first DPYK president; B. Pertin, IARF participant; Tajom Tasung and Oyin Moyang, influential administrators of the current DPYK regime ... the list of important contributors is long. But these three – Rukbo, Ering, and Dai – can be seen as archetypes through which the revolution occurred: the unique synergy between Rukbo's vision, Ering's intellect, and Dai's artistry gave birth to the movement.

The necessity of inclusion of personal biography in this case is three-fold: 1) it adds human perspectives to the study of a community movement, as has been seen above; 2) it begins to inform us about how Adi lives are recorded during a time of transition; and 3) it allows us to draw distinctions between the portrayal of the living and the already deceased, thus highlighting the construction of Adi hagiography. Therefore, it is worth paying further attention to the means by which revolutionaries' histories are presented – and the difference in the 'mythical' representation of the dead versus the more secular depiction of the living. Both Rukbo and Dai are now described as having almost supernatural events occurring in their lives: Rukbo is portrayed as a unique child; his actions are reported to have been supported by strange thundering sounds; he predicted his death date as mandated by Donyipolo; his body showed remarkable flexibility after his passing; and a halo appeared on the final picture of his coffin. Dai fits the prototype of the tormented artist, deaf and moody, unfocused on practicalities, yet so adept at pen and paint that he transcended cultural requirements and was chosen by Rukbo to create the faces for the divine. In the case of Dai's close relationship with his calf, the calf can be viewed as an avatar; the two both lost their mothers early and later died on the same date (separated by a year). One is reminded of Frazer's commentary in his seminal *The Golden Bough* – 'when a person's life is conceived as embodied in a particular object, with the existence of which his own existence is inseparably bound up, and the destruction of which involves his own, the object in question may be regarded and spoken of indifferently as his life or his death, as happens in the fairy tales' (Frazer 1890: 812). Rukbo, similarly, was so intertwined with the Donyipolo reformation that exhaustion from it brought him illness and a premature death, yet the movement would decidedly not have occurred but for his devotion to it.

It is possible, therefore, to begin to deconstruct Adi narrative and to identify the particular markers that indicate 'importance' in life. To progress further in an archetypal analysis, these markers seem to align with Campbell's 'monomyth', with each man enacting a personal 'hero's journey' – beginning in ordinary worlds, undergoing trials to achieve gifts, and ultimately deciding whether to bring this gift back to his original home (Campbell 1949). Of course, Campbell's work describes the process by which a person becomes a founding mythic figure for a culture, once his career is viewed, usually retrospectively, as fundamentally transformative.

The 'ordinary world' into which these men were born was the indigenous Adi world, and, for all three, the 'unusual world of strange powers' by which they were challenged was the 'Westernised' world of contemporary Indian civilisation: Rukbo was faced with a mainstream religious framework into which his indigenous faith did not fit; Ering was transformed by his higher education and the articulate questions of Elwin; Dai was unable to complete normal standard education or pursue art training in Kolkata, in part because of his own demons, including his perception of his deafness. Yet each 'subdued' the new world in his own way: Rukbo, the 'Father', realised that he must restructure his religion into the forms understood by the new world; Ering, the intellectual, realised that a formal 'Western' foundation must underlie Rukbo's visions, should the new world be able to understand them; and Dai was able to express hitherto abstract and non-representational aspects of the faith in ways that were concretely apprehendable by local Adi worshippers and which yet brought Donyipolo into a 'representational tradition' in line with several of the world's more populous religions. All three suffered through 'trials' as they struggled to assimilate the new cultures, and all, in the end, as this paper has demonstrated, have returned a 'boon' – the salvation of the Donyipolo religion, in a new form – to the Adi people.

The chart below represents the 'mythic' similarities found in the stories of these men, which begin to reveal the constitution of Adi hagiography.

	Rukbo	Ering	Dai
Unusual birth	√ Loud crying	<Unknown>	√ In the field
Early precocity	√ Many interests	√ Academic	√ Art talent
Traditional training	√ School, college in Shillong	√ School, college in Shillong	<School refused, art training refused>
Transformative, Spiritual experience	√ Many examples (e.g., thundering sounds)	√ Assumed: transcendent experience through schooling	√ Assumed: highly spiritual content in artwork

Extraordinary physical stamina/focus	√ Legendary concentration	√ Prolific and varied scholarly output	√ Artistic skill
Predicts own death	√ 30 or 31 December	<Unknown>	<Via calf drawing?>
'Miracles'	√ Multiple	<Unknown>	√ Calf avatar
Eternal life	√ 'Sainthood' in Donyipolo	Assumed (upon death): return to *Donyi Among*	√ Sacrifice of calf to eternal Komeng

Thus, in the telling of their lives – particularly for Rukbo and Dai – the hero's profile emerges, lending itself to deification as Donyipolo has transitioned into a new form. Oshong Ering, though self-described as not particularly 'religious', has lived a secular yet parallel journey – and no doubt accounts of his intelligence, foresight, and contributions to the Adi community will yield a comparable posthumous narrative.

Through examining the biographies of these three men, we are offered a new lens for the comprehension of the reformation, confirming that the contributor's individual lives' have been unique and varied. From a literary and hagiographic perspective, it manifests that they have each, in a way, lived a 'hero's journey' – one whose results are inseparable from their own lives. They each wielded individual tools: the vision (Rukbo), the groundwork (Ering), and the artistic talent (Dai). The intersection of the trajectories of these three men formed the core for the founding of the Donyipolo Yelam Kebang and the preservation of Adi culture and faith in its new form; their contributions to the movement, similarly, were core aspects of their individual lives.

Acknowledgements

I very much thank the families of Talom Rukbo, Oshong Ering, and Komeng Dai, particularly Oson Rukbo, Tagen Rukbo, Osam Dai Tasung, Tagom Dai, Tajom Tasung, and Ponung Ering Angu; also Oshong Ering himself, Thumpak Tee, Kaling Borang, and Oyin Moyang. I am grateful for the translation assistance of Dugge Gammeng and Kalen Pertin. I also thank Kaling and Rebecca Tamut and the Donyipolo Yelam Kebang for their hospitality and assistance throughout this project. This research was funded by the Graduate College of Arts, Celtic Studies, and Social Sciences, National University of Ireland – University College Cork and by the Government of Ireland Irish Research Council Postgraduate Scholarship.

Bibliography

Borang, Kaling (ed.) (2002): *Golgi Bote Talom Rukbo: His Thoughts and Deeds*. Pasighat, Arunachal Pradesh: Central Donyi-Polo Yelam Kebang.

Borang, Kaling (ed.)(2013): *Én-Géna Pu:né (The Leading Star): A Commemorative Volume on Golgíboté Talom Rukbo.* Guwahati, Assam, India: Heritage Foundation.

Briggs, Charles (2008): "Disciplining Folkloristics", *Journal of Folklore Research* 45 (1), 91-105.

Campbell, Joseph (1949 [1968]): *The Hero with the Thousand Faces*. Princeton: Princeton University Press.

Chaudhuri, Sarit K. (2013): "The Institutionalization of Tribal Religion: Recasting the Donyipolo Movement in Arunachal Pradesh", *Asian Ethnology* 72(2), 259-277.

Dunaway, David K. (2007): "Method and Theory in the Oral Biography", *Oral History* 20 (2), 40-44.

Ering, Oshong (2005): *The Lingering Memories*. Pasighat: Siang Literary Forum.

Ering, Oshong (n.d.): Ering archives [personal manuscripts]. Pasighat, India.

Frazer, Sir James George (1922 [1969]): *The Golden Bough: A Study in Magic and Religion*. London: The Macmillan Company.

Herzfeld, Michael (1997): *Portrait of a Greek Imagination: An Ethnographic Biography of Andreas Nenedakis*. Chicago: The University of Chicago Press.

Jackson, Michael D. (2008): "Between Biography and Ethnography", *The Harvard Theological Review* 101 (3/4), 377-397.

Koyu, Tape (n.d.): *The Life and Times of Golgi Bote*, Tani Darang (director). Documentary film. Pasighat: Donyipolo Yelam Kebang.

Rukbo, Talom (n.d.): *Donyipoloism through Questions and Answers.* Pasighat, India: Adi Cultural and Literary Society.

Scheid, Claire S. (2015): "Talom Rukbo and the Donyipolo Yelam Kebang: Restructuring Adi Religious Practices in Arunachal Pradesh", *Internationales Asienforum* 46 (1-2), 127-148.

Somers, Margaret R. (1994): "The Narrative Construction of Identity: A Relational and Network Approach", *Theory and Society* 23, 605-649.

Indigeneity and Religious Conversion in Siberia: Nenets 'Eluding' Culture and Indigenous Revitalisation

Tatiana Vagramenko

Numd'Siarvy Ne, the Bride of God

It was the cold and blizzardy spring of 2011 when I stayed in Marina's house in a snowbound village of Beloyarsk, across the Polar Urals. Marina was a short, thin and sickly looking Nenets woman in her early fifties. Several years ago she abandoned her forty-some years of nomadic tundra life and moved to the village. A wise woman, known as a bearer of indigenous knowledge and a gifted storyteller, she was, as a child, sick with cirrhosis of the lungs, which sometimes was interpreted by her relatives as a shamanic illness. Besides, her father always prevented her from getting married, insisting that Marina should stay spouseless. And for Marina's family this was a sign that she might be a *Numd' siarvy ne* – the bride of God, a woman promised and devoted to the main Nenets deity called Num. "They think I am a shaman, always ask me to tell them something," Marina once said to me, "But I don't know who I am. I don't beat the drum, what can I tell 'em?" She also inherited the clan's sacred sledge (*khe' khan*), where Nenets people traditionally keep their sacred objects. This supposedly made her responsible for keeping the clan gods and correspondingly for safeguarding the clan's wealth and luck.

However, Marina changed the course of her life and soon after she settled in a village she was converted to Protestant Christianity becoming one of the most active members of a local Baptist community. "You will be happy", many years ago these were the last words of Marina's father to her, before he died. "I don't know why he said that, 'you will be happy'. Maybe, he might have had a revelation, because I am with God now, and *Num'd' siarvy* means a bride of God. Truly, a believer is a bride of Christ. Maybe that was the prophecy, that I will be chosen by God and become a believer."

In 2006, when I first arrived in Yamal-Nenets Autonomous Area (North-Western Siberia), I was surprised by the level of agitation – in public discourse and everyday life – concerning the issue of Evangelical conversion in the tundra.

Everyone discussed the appearance of "sects". From everywhere I could hear stories about wandering missionaries who burned Nenets "idols" (traditional ritual objects and sacred sites) and destroyed Nenets culture, about Nenets converts who had given up their ancestors' gods, who sacrilegiously violated tundra traditions and hence would soon die in poverty being punished by gods and people. There was gossip about weird sectarian meetings in homes; about tundra Nenets children in residential schools who gathered in bathrooms to pray and to read the Bible; about "sectarian chums" in the tundra which were better to avoid when migrating with the reindeer stock. Local authorities were alerted to visiting missionaries and the police carefully watched the activities of Protestant communities mushrooming throughout the vast tundra of Yamal peninsula and the Polar Ural Mountains.[1]

The Nenets people turned out to be open to religious change, and during the 1990s and 2000s many Nenets, both nomadic and settled, were converted to various types of Protestant Christianity. This appeared unexpectedly, given that Siberian Nenets are popularly viewed as strongholds of "indigenous traditional culture", successfully resisting outside influences. For instance, against the background of a general post-Soviet decrease in indigenous traditional economy, the Nenets provide the most striking example of flourishing nomadism (what is popularly called "the Nenets phenomenon"). They reveal one of the highest levels of engagement in nomadic lifestyle and subsistence economy (reindeer herding, fishing, and hunting), of native language competence, and finally, of preserving traditional religious practices and sacred sites (see Mukhac̦v et al. 2010: 10;Stammler 2005: 66ff.; Liarskaya 2003; Vakhtin, Liarskaya 2004).

"When *Lutsa* [Nenets term for Russians] in 1917 were destroying and burning their towers or cupolas, their churches, we used to hide our deities", Irina told me, a Nenets woman, referring to a period of the battle against religiosity in Soviet times. The struggle against shamanism and other indigenous religious traditions also became one of the priorities of Soviet modernity and "socialist construction" in Siberia and the Russian North (Forsyth 1992: 287ff.; Suslov 1931; Skachkov 1934). "The Nenets people have small religion, closer to nature, so we could preserve everything", Irina continued, "During the 1970s, as soon as *Lutsa* drove up to a *chum*, as soon as one could hear bells of a Red sledge [representatives of the Soviet authorities], we hid everything... We took away sacred sledges and kept them in the forest so that no one could see... "

1 The Nenets people belong to the group of the so called "indigenous less-numerous peoples of the North of the Russian Federation" (one of 44 listed in this group). Historically they inhabit the tundra of the European North, North-Western-Siberia, and the Taimyr Peninsula, with smaller groups living in the taiga of the Polar Urals and the territory between the Ob' and Taz rivers.

However, since the post-Soviet period, the territories of the Polar Ural and Yamal tundra have become a zone of intensive Evangelical missionary activities with frequent cases of conversion to Protestant Christianity among native people. And while "traditional" Nenets customs and beliefs, sacred sites and ritual practices were being promoted on a public level as a foundation of Nenets survival, the rural Nenets often eagerly embraced the Christian Evangelical message, challenging commonsense perspectives on the resilience of Nenets traditional culture.

Protestant conversion often met with violent anti-conversion attitudes from native society and local authorities. Non-converted Nenets often took a relentless stance against their converted fellows. Protestant Nenets were now believed to be betraying their "people", their ancestors' legacy, and hence, they were considered to be not Nenets enough. The loss of their authenticity was at issue.

The generally hostile anti-conversion attitudes in native society evoked by religious rearrangements corresponded with ambiguity in the missionary milieu. Nenets religious conversion raised the issue of native culture and its place in Christian life. As religious conversion was understood to be a radical change in Nenets' personal life, it provoked the question of what to do with the native culture, whether to reject it as heathendom or at some point to contextualise the Christian message within it. Is native tradition actually a barrier on the path to salvation or, on the contrary, should it supplement and enrich Christian culture? Missionaries and converted Nenets developed various, sometimes conflicting, responses to these questions, which in turn caused tensions within the missionary movement, as well as determining social relations in the tundra.

The issue of the compatibility of Christianity with Nenets life and culture in many respects defined the development of missionary strategies, as well as native responses. This is the question that triggered social conflicts and inspired new modes of collaboration, that sometimes made Nenets families fall apart and created new life strategies, that influenced local public discourse as well as regional policy toward missionary activities, and eventually, as I show below, that mobilised a language of indigeneity and stimulated ethno-consciousness.

In this paper I analyse the process of the Nenets construction and reconstruction of their authenticity, and their strategies of "reasoning-out" (Gable, Handler 1996; Bruner 1994). I explore Nenets engagement with Christian logic and Christian ideology and the most wrenching challenge that it carries – the experience of a Damascus Road conversion.

Post-Soviet Indigenous Activism

Post-Soviet social, political, and religious changes, the growth of nationalism and regionalism based on ethnic distinctions in Russia extended to the indigenous peoples of Siberia and stimulated the emergence of *indigeneity* as a political and cultural trend in Siberia (Gray 2005). The new wave of neo-traditionalism and more politicised indigenous activism re-emerged in the public arena and turned into the revitalisation of ethnic-based autonomous districts and republics in Siberia, with their own legislative bodies and the foundation of indigenous organisations addressing indigenous issues and defending indigenous rights (Schindler 1997; Pika 1999). Various local indigenous societies, associations, museums and folk ensembles flourished in Siberia and the Far North. They promoted the idea of revival of indigenous cultures and languages, and the protection of native lands and environment.

The construction of indigeneity is interwoven with the construction or revitalisation of indigenous religiosity. Religion has become a tool for the mobilisation of cultural and ethnic identities, and plays a crucial component part in Siberian indigenous activism (Balzer 2002, 2008; Humphrey 1999). As Andrei Znamenski argues, spiritual revival becomes "a planned ethnocultural enterprise" (2007: 346). Thus, during the 1990s, in the context of such ethnocultural revival of indigenous Siberia, shamanism and the multiplicity of local religious beliefs and practices began to come out into the public sphere, resonating with the wider political-economic context of post-Soviet Siberia, as one of the ways to "re-indigenize" people and place (Znamenski 2007: 345; see also Balzer 2005, 2008). According to Eva Fridman (2004), shamanism became "sacred geography" – it territorialised ethnicity, produced, legalised and sanctified locality and its borders, and rooted people within it, thus making them "indigenous".

The Nenets people produced their own images of "Nenets religion" and "Nenets shamanism", which were constructed as ethnic symbols (see Lar 1998). A galaxy of Nenets writers and poets, folklore groups, local festivals and exhibitions, celebrations of indigenous holidays – all these created a foundation for the promotion of pristine Nenets traditional culture, and hence, for the development of a more politicised revitalisation movement.

The image of 'Nenets religion' became a trend driven mainly by politically and socially active indigenous intellectuals, who attempted to reify Nenets traditional culture and religion as the foundation of Nenets indigeneity, as the essential condition for Nenets survival. It became one of the parts in the polyphony of indigenous land- and rights-claims.

Numerous sacred sites have become visible tokens of Nenets indigenous religiosity, as well as special targets for regional policy. An internationally supported project on mapping and protection of sacred sites and sanctuaries in the tundra of the Yamal area was intended "to promote the preservation of indigenous cultures" (Znachenie 2004), particularly in the context of the rapidly growing industrial development of the Yamal tundra (see also Yefimenko 2004). In some respects this practice sought to mark the borders of indigenous lands, thereby not merely to promote Nenets indigenous culture, but to re-root it within particular territorial boundaries. Whatever violated the symbolic and physical borders of indigenism was jealously accused of being an invasion of indigenous privacy.

However, the violation of the indigenous sacredness came not only from external influences (such as the expansion of the extractive industries in the North), but from *inside* of the native society. On the map of indigenous sacred sites, the borders were challenged not only by global developments, but by internal variability of the culture and its potential for radical and enduring change.

Burning the Sacred: Evangelical "Crusades" to Siberia

The Post-Soviet process of "unmaking and making of relations" (Humphrey 2002) implied multidimensional trajectories. With the opened frontiers, new opportunities have been created for cross-cultural interaction revealing a global religious marketplace. Siberia became one of the most striking spots of recent changes on the Russian religious map, and was associated with an increasing presence of various Protestant denominations and churches in its vast territories (Krindatch 2004: 131; Dudarenok 2005; Brumbelow 1995). Since the mid-1990s, scholars have begun to register the growing influence of evangelical movements among the indigenous population of Siberia and the Far North (Wiget, Balalaeva 2007; Rybakova 2009; Pelkmans 2009). Here, "at the end of the earth", there exist people whose "paganism" still lives on in the form of numerous sacred places as well as in everyday life. A great number of missionaries from within the post-Soviet space as well as from different foreign countries (from Western and Northern Europe, United States, Canada and even from Cameroon, Australia and Korea) began their activities in the Polar Urals and Yamal, making it a "battlefield" of different missionary principles and strategies, thus transforming and rearranging the Siberian religious landscapes. As a result of current missionary activities, a highly competitive multi-religious landscape has developed in the Russian Arctic, with diverse religious domains.[2]

[2] Missionary initiatives during the 1990s and 2000s were not the first cases of evangelisation among the Nenets. As far back as the 17th and 19th centuries the Nenets had already experienced encounters with Russian Orthodox missionaries. During the 19th and early 20th centuries special Orthodox missions were established targeted at evangelizing among the Nenets people. However, the Nenets see no links between Russian Orthodoxy and Protestant Christianity, regarding them as completely different and unrelated religions. The long and complicated Soviet history of struggle against any religious beliefs and practices, including Orthodox Christianity, created a gap between 'before' and 'after'. And those traces of Orthodox tradition (like Orthodox icons or the image of St. Nicholas as one of the gods in the Nenets pantheon) are now regarded by many Nenets as part of their 'traditional beliefs'. Nowadays, the Russian Orthodox Church is publicly represented as traditional against the background of non-traditional, hence foreign and alien, evangelical missionary movements. However, the Orthodox Church does not have intensive missionary work among the natives in the tundra, and Orthodox adherents in

The growing Protestant movement came in contradiction to the politics of indigenism and indigenous movement, which was based on the promotion of native traditional religion(s) and shamanism. At the beginning of the conversion era in the Polar Urals, the anxiety over missionary activity was particularly enhanced by a number of cases when the Christian rupture and born-again impulse led to a rigorous denial of "traditional Nenets culture" – whatever it might be that converted natives understood by these words: from burning Nenets sacred sites and ritual artefacts from the home to the point of giving up an entire nomadic way of life and settling down in villages and towns.

The anti-native-culture position occasioned a series of complex confrontations and negotiations between different religious communities, evoked tensions within the native society in general, as well as raised heated debates in regional public discourse.

Nadia, a Nenets woman living in the tundra, a mother of nine children, told me her conversion story:

> And when we were baptised, we returned to our *chum*, took all our idols and went out with all my children in the night to the forest – we were afraid that people would see us – then threw petrol on the idols and burned them. We were so afraid that people would find out about that. But rumours spread quickly that we had burned our idols. People swore at us that we were out of our minds, that our children would all die soon.

The practice of burning sacred articles (Nenets: *khekhe*) was believed to be a significant part of the religious experience, an expressed sign of full conversion (cf. Vallikivi 2011). Similar to the case of Alaskan Natives observed by Kirk Dombrowski in his ethnography "*Against Culture*" (2001), the practice of burning "idols" was, for the Nenets people, an expressed ritualisation of discontinuity, or as Joel Robbins (2003: 224) calls it, "rituals of rupture". The Nenets converts rigorously followed the Christian rupture impulse of being "born again", emphatically denying those symbols and practices of their "traditional culture", now regarded as "heathen". They burned traditional sacred articles and sacred sites and ceased observing tundra rituals.

Conversely, from the perspective of native society, Nenets converts were accused of not being *Nenets* enough, of being morally corrupt and socially dangerous. Ultimately, some native converts were forced to give up the nomadic life in the tundra and to move to sedentary space. "If you are Baptists you are no longer Nenets". This dichotomy became a foundation for most discussions and tensions aroused around religious conversion. A person who is "no longer Nenets" is thereby under threat of losing social continuity, losing ties with the indigenous community and, consequently, the stability of his/her livelihood.

---

the North are mainly Russian incomers.

It was a much publicised massive burning of "idols" by one Khanty[3] family in the Baidarata tundra (Southern Yamal) that triggered the most acute tensions within the nomadic society. This Khanty clan was considered one of the most powerful shamanic families in the region. Their clan "idols" were considered to be the "strongest" and many Khanty and Nenets people venerated the "gods" of this particular family. However, when the majority of the family members were converted to Charismatic Christianity, they started burning their ancestral sacred sites. Below is the story of a participant in those events, Valia, a Khanty woman who was the first in her extended family to be converted to Charismatic Christianity:

> When people repent, they stop worshipping idols. You can't imagine how many idols we destroyed! We destroyed all our clan's [sacred] sledges [...] Eventually we did that, we burned this big sledge, we all were praying so much, because we were so terrified! The sledge was so huge, unusually huge! Sacred! But we destroyed it, even though we all were so afraid of these idols. [...] Sveta, my sister, and her daughters took their [sacred] sledge and towed it into the forest. In the forest they poured petrol over it and destroyed it. Sveta said that she had mortal fear... So I said to her, "Don't play with it! Come on! Give it to me! I destroyed all my idols, all my icons; I destroyed even that 'grandfather' [a ritual image of her deceased relative]. And look, nothing happened to me. Look, God protects me!"
>
> You know, miraculously, it is those families who have come to God, who had the biggest idols and the strongest shamans. And all of them have now burned their idols and God has protected them. Igor too belongs to a famous shamanic clan. [...] We have been worshiping them [idols] all our lives. We were afraid that something terrible could happen to our families, but moreover, we were afraid of the people around us, that they would do something bad with us.

Later on, when the practice of burning "idols" became widely known, native society was agitated by stories about the punishment of the sacrilegious. In Se-Yakha tundra (Northern Yamal) rumours circulated that soon after a young woman had burned her family "idols" her mother disappeared. Her frozen dead body was found several months later, half eaten by dogs. This lamentable death was interpreted as the spirits' punishment for burning "idols". In another part of the tundra there was an accident when a converted man fell victim to a bear, which attacked and crippled him. "A bear was a sign for him, surely it was a sign for him to stop attending the sect", people said.

But of course, converts were much more afraid of the people around them than spirits and animals. Born-again natives whose parents disinherited them and took back all the reindeer; converted families left alone by their kin, without

[3] The Khanty are an indigenous people of western Siberia. The Siberian Polar Ural tundra historically has been the territory of strong Khanty-Nenets communication, resulting in a general historical and cultural Khanty-Nenets community.

crucial support; husbands punishing their wives for ritual disobedience – they surely knew about all these stories when they were burning "idols". A tragic story was narrated to me by an old missionary who has been working among indigenous people in Yamal for many years. He told the story of a young woman, converted to the light of Christianity. She was originally from a shamanic family and her close relative was a shaman. Her dead body was found in a cemetery, tied to one of the graves. "She was ritually killed – little by little, by seven knots, strangled by that shaman, because she gave up her ancestral faith and accepted Christ in her heart", whispered the missionary to me.

Christianity and Nenets Re-Indigenisation

"Who will we eventually become – Russians, Nenets, Baptists?" a Nenets believer mused to himself one day as we were conversing, adding then, "We are lost among cultures".

At times, finding themselves on the frontier of worlds, having been accused of losing their "*Nenetsness*", their indigeneity, under the threat of being excluded from the native society, converted Nenets began to reconsider their previously intolerant stances towards native culture.

Religious conflicts and cultural tensions eventually stimulated converted Nenets towards revising their indigenous legacy and articulation of cultural and ethnic boundaries, which led to the reshaping of Nenets indigeneity. The dynamic of religious conversion brings what Marshall Sahlins (2005[1992]; 1999) refers to as "a self-consciousness of indigenous culture" or self-conscious movements of cultural differentiation and essentialisation, when new believers themselves become aware and defensive of what they call their "indigenous culture".

A Nenets woman from the Polar Ural tundra, who was a member of the Baptist community, justified her doubted authenticity and demonstrated that she had a distinct culture: "Somebody accused us that we have forgotten our gods and don't worship them anymore. But in general, we preserve our culture all the same, we never forget our culture. Although I don't follow [Nenets ritual tradition], I follow my culture". "Culture" becomes a reified entity, a property that is in need of defending (thus appropriating the western meaning of "culture", cf. Jackson 2007: 232). They articulate, revise, and re-assemble the notion of "Nenets traditional culture", while trying to suit it to their Christian life. Hence, new cultural constructions are put into play, such that the taken-for-granted pattern turns into ethno-consciousness. "The objectification of identity, in short, appears here to have produced a new sensibility, an explicit new awareness of its essence, its affective, material, and expressive potential", as Jean and John Comaroff point out (2009: 2).

While legitimising the idea that converted natives are, nevertheless, entitled to have Nenets identity and Nenets culture, they have begun to mobilise and concretise their indigeneity, both as ethno-consciousness and as political agency. When converted Nenets find themselves in danger of losing their Nenets authenticity and experience the threat of exclusion from the native society, when they are accused of not being Nenets or "traditional" enough, they develop a strategy of *re-indigenisation,* i.e., they seek to recover their indigenous culture and identity (Jackson 2009). Converts' claims to having rights to Nenets native culture and Nenets identity have become a strategy to ensure their threatened ethnicity and to return their lost authenticity, which they need for the legitimisation of their power (Gable, Handler 1996: 568). Conversely, by re-articulating and re-defining the notion of "Nenets traditional culture", Nenets converts have developed new schemes that allow them to make sense of their chosen religious path in their Nenets life.

They bring Christian ontology and Nenets ideas into dialogue as part of a strategic manoeuvre for empowerment and claims to authenticity.

Re-Indigenisation as Ethno-Consciousness: Nenets Ethno-Theology

Communication between the two systems of meanings (native culture and Christianity) is transferred into a deeper symbolic and categorical level. Missionaries and converted natives undertake serious conceptual work on translating, interpreting and reevaluating both traditional categories and Christian ideas. The ultimate goal of such negotiation is to build a bridge and reconcile Christianity and Nenets culture.

Converted Nenets develop what Michael Scott (2005) terms "*ethno-theology*". By this term he defines the process of indigenous theological speculations and constructions where Christian converts "evaluate indigenous ideas and practices in relation to those of Christianity and situate ancestral identities and histories within Biblical history" (2005: 102). Similar to Scott's observation, Nenets Christians select and reinterpret the content of Christianity in a way that allows them to reconcile their pre-converted past with their born-again present.

This is how the project of *Nenets Christianity* was developed – the idea of a specially developed ethnic version of Christianity. It carried a message of the salvational role of Christianity in Nenets history, where Christian faith was believed to transform and to restore the Nenets as the god-blessed people. In his study of the Swedish Faith Movement, Simon Coleman argues that such a contextualisation approach that celebrates "the virtues of locality and patriotic attachment" nevertheless contributes to a globalizing orientation: "Faith rhetoric appropriates symbols of nationhood in a way that is entirely appropriate to an imaginative construction of the possibility of trans local influence and empowerment" (Coleman

2000: 209). The localizing approach has become a way of translocal empowerment for the Nenets too, whereby they envision the specific place of the Nenets people in the history of Christianity and in world history in general.

The main advocate and promoter of this adapted Christianity, translated and contextualised within Nenets culture, was the Evangelical church "*Blagaia Vest*", based in Salekhard city, the capital of Yamal-Nenets Autonomous Area. The initial aim of the project was to reconsider the previous rigorous conversion strategies and missionary principles that frequently brought social conflicts and tensions to the Polar Urals and Yamal, and to make those strategies more compatible with local cultures in order to make it easier for the native people to accept Christianity without rejecting the key patterns of their culture.

A Russian Evangelical missionary, one of the advocates of Nenets Christianity, in 2006 generalised his understanding of the project in the following way:

> They [nomadic natives] are not ready to accept [Christianity] with our context, they are not ready to accept our culture. We need somehow to get the message across, but substitute the packaging [*podmenit' upakovochku*]. Let them keep their own culture. If I respect their culture and pray to God in their language, it will be the same anyway. We'll just correct things a little [. . .] In other words, I am totally convinced that Nenets culture should be fully preserved, fully. Their language, their prayers, and even their rituals, you know. We need to bring the Gospel while not disturbing their culture.

He continues with the story of a missionary who witnessed a Nenets traditional reindeer sacrifice and instead of refuting the ritual, he used the tactic of negotiating between the "heathen" ritual and Christian ideas: he tried to convince them that the ritual just performed was actually good and right – as good and right as the Old Testament is – but now he had brought the New Testament; and then he continued with his usual preaching.

Appropriating missionaries' ideas on the compatibility of Protestantism and Nenets traditional culture, some converted Nenets have gone further and argued that the new ethnically framed Christianity is not merely possible but will be the foundation for native survival and will prevent the destruction of native traditional culture. When I first met Mikhail in 2006, a Nenets who became an Evangelical missionary in Yamal, he said:

> Today there is a new page of history in our [Nenets] life – everything has changed and Christianity has arrived. I am telling you, here and now, history is happening, something entirely new that has never happened before in the world. It is the history of the awakening of the people, of the entire people!

Several years later, in 2011, he confided to me that he had seen God's foresight: Christ does not want Nenets to believe like Russians, he wants to see the creation of Nenets churches, "within their own culture"; God wants the glorification in

Nenets language and culture. Hence, Mikhail saw the preservation of nomadic culture and the creation of Nenets churches as the fulfillment of God's will.

Disenchanting Traditional Culture

But what to do with all those native symbols and practices that at the beginning of the conversion era were regarded by the majority of converts and missionaries as heathen?

At times, one of the discursive methods that enabled "traditional culture" in Christian life to be kept became the *disenchanting* of traditional culture. In the discursive negotiation between Christianity and native culture, the "dangerous" symbols and practices become de-sacralised, and "culturalised", i.e., they are taken out of the sphere of the "religious" and brought into a sphere of "culture", translated now as secular or "rational" patterns (cf. Broz 2009; Vaté 2009). Here, again, the culture and religion discourse is a key concern. As Virginie Vaté notes, "[D]issociation of 'culture' and 'religion' appears to be a way for converts to reconcile their indigenous identity with Christianity" (2009: 49). Examining the contextualisation of Protestant Christianity among the Chukchi, Vaté argues that missionaries replicate the typical Soviet rhetoric, "national in form, Socialist in content", developing their missionary strategies as "national in form, Christian in content" (2009: 48).

In order to prevent social tensions evoked by conversions in the tundra, some missionaries and converts have developed the technique of interpreting "pagan" practices and notions rather as etiquette or ethnic features, rationally or even scientifically grounded. The religious meanings are denied or believed to be completely lost. The "Nenets religion" is eventually turning into "Nenets philosophy". "All these are not heathen but ethnic – all these rituals, customs, prohibitions", was the most common justification tool I heard in native Christian communities.

A Korean translator of the Bible into the Nenets language, who has been living in Sale hard for many years and is now one of the most sincere advocates of Nenets culture, argued:

> When you ask them [why a woman is not allowed to cross the space behind a fire place in a *chum*] – nobody will answer you. It is simply a custom now, simply a custom. Even if it used to have a previous religious meaning, nowadays they [Nenets] separate it, hence, it is simply their custom [. . .].
>
> It is philosophy, Nenets philosophy. They purify with smoke [meaning ritual purification *kŷv- kŷv*] – it is a science, but not religion. We should respect this. There always is a reason we just don't know it yet [. . .] It kills bacteria, it is necessary, and if you destroy it people in the tundra will get sick [. . .].

The multiplicity of native ritual practices and traditions that previously were regarded as "heathen", were rationalised and essentialised – "the culture" now is not a "heathen" construct, but something that runs in people's blood and is inherent in their genes.

At times, Nadia, the born-again Christian who was the first who burned her ancestral "idols" and began to follow the most rigorous attitudes toward "Nenets heathendom", returned to her "Nenets culture" and tried to justify it, following the same logic of *disenchanting*. When I stayed the third time at Nadia's *chum* in autumn 2011, she recalled her conversion story again. This time, the framework and intonation of the story differed from that one narrated to me five years earlier. When I heard it for the first time in 2006, she told me mostly about burning her ancestral "idols" and her liberation from society's traditional prohibitions and restrictions on behaviour. The message of rupture dominated throughout her narrative. Something significantly changed in her story as re-narrated a few years later. Nadia told me that she had returned to following some traditional customs, making excuses for her previously rigorous attitude toward "the culture". The story she told was about the prohibition against crossing the space behind the fire place, near the *symsy* pole that traditionally marks the sacred space in a Nenets *chum*. Nadia told me that some converts were sure that their conversion allowed them to stop following this prohibition and so she also stopped. "But this place [in a *chum*, behind a fireplace] is like a kitchen for us, we keep groceries and kitchen utensils there", she argued. And then she asked me: "You don't step over dishes and groceries in your kitchen? So we don't either. We used to call it a sin, in Nenets *hyvy*. But now I don't call it a sin – it is just something inappropriate [*neudobno*]". Then she told me about the Nenets prohibition against stepping over clothes and men's tools. In the same way, she removed a veil of "sinfulness" while interpreting these practices:

> To step over [clothes and tools] is uncomfortable too. How can I step over my child's pants or shirts?! I won't call it a sin, but at the same time I won't feel comfortable to put these clothes on my child afterwards [. . .] *Hyvy*, I used to call it a sin, but now I am in God, so I won't cross over men's lassos [*arkan*], not because it is a sin, but because it is unpleasant [*nepriiatno*] and inappropriate.

The woman who five years ago courageously said, "Now we can do everything [. . .] We have gotten rid of fear", has now restored all these customs back. She argued that she needed them because she believed that all these regulations keep order in tundra life. She criticised her daughters-in-law, saying that they are "too modern" and do not follow the tundra code of conduct, violating the regulations surrounding male and female social spaces; she now taught them to live as of old. At the same time, she remained a sincere believer, one who read the Bible, who prayed, who attended community gatherings, and who taught me how to live a truly Christian life.

Nadia disenchanted her culture, thus legalising it in her life in Christ. She functionally revaluated the system of knowledge and meanings underlying those traditional practices, now basing them on new concepts such as "ethnic", "rational", "genes". She stretched traditional categories, impregnating them with new values. She needed that to maintain continuity-in-change.

Conversion of History: The "Old Testament" Nenets

"A group's vision of its future... arises out of its embedded understanding of its past", argues Jean Jackson (2009). Likewise, Marshal Sahlins points out that when people undergo culture change, encompassing "the existentially unique in the conceptually familiar", they embed their present in the past (1985: 146).

This is what converted Nenets are doing when bridging Christianity and their traditional system of knowledge. Some of them do not see in Christianity and Nenets culture merely compatibility or complementarity, but essential unity and continuity. They have come to embed Christian logic and the Christian message in their social and personal histories, thereby not only defending their "culture", but sacralising it in Christian terms. In this framework, Christianity is represented as reflecting the most profound aspects of genuine Nenets culture, and the conversion experience brings the reformation or purification of authentic "Nenetsness" and *Neneiil'* – true Nenets life. This approach allows Nenets to embrace Christianity by focusing on the essential community of their native tradition and Christian patterns rather than on the conflicting "heathen" discourse.

One of the most common techniques of symbolic bridge building between Christianity and the Nenets world is the representation of traditional Nenets culture as the *Old Testament* and non-converted Nenets as Old Testament or Biblical Nenets. In such a framework, converted Nenets represent themselves as having been custodians of God's law all along, those who primordially belonged to God's plan for humanity and whose "traditional culture" and ancestors' religion are "expressions of imperfect but innate inclinations towards Christian truth" (Scott 2005: 109).

Hence, Nenets culture is not regarded as simply heathen anymore nor Nenets people as backward, but rather as prophetical, who have always lived according to the old Jewish laws. This approach is not unique to Nenets conversion; it can also be traced in some other cases of missionary-indigenous encounters where indigenous culture is represented in Biblical terms and is compared with Old-Testament Hebrew culture, thus ensuring the continuity between pre- and post-converted lives (Badmaev et al. 2006: 97-99; Broz 2009: 23; Vaté 2009: 51-53; Wiget, Balalaeva 2007; see also Scott 2005).

It is noteworthy that it is the image of reindeer and Nenets nomadic life that has become a crucial means for translating "Nenets culture" as Old-Testament. The reindeer, around which Nenets nomadism and their general world-view is concentrated, has become an important symbol in Nenets Christian life as well. In Nenets tundra life, the reindeer is a source of food, transport, clothes, housing, and economic exchanges. It is, in general, a dominant category of Nenets culture, and the majority of Nenets tundra regulations and rites seek to guarantee the safety of the reindeer. As a Nenets woman from Yar-Sale village expressed it, "Reindeer are life, reindeer are everywhere, they are all around in [Nenets] life. Reindeer, reindeer, reindeer".

In Nenets Christian life the reindeer have become a token and a measure of God's blessings (a true believing Nenets is blessed with a wealthy herd), and a form of church tithe. The reindeer is a Biblically pure animal and reindeer herding is reminiscent of the ancient Jewish pastoral society; thus through the reindeer and nomadism Nenets have gained legalised status within Christianity.

Nenets rituals and sacrifices, for example, are considered analogous to ancient Hebrew rituals. Nenets love to read the Old Testament and interpret Hebrew nomadic pastoral society as a prophetic description of traditional Nenets society, comparing Hebrew shepherds with Nenets reindeer herders.

Mikhail, a Nenets missionary, used this technique as the main strategy in his justification of Nenets culture:

> The Old Testament is still alive among us, because we, the Nenets, live according to the Old Testament [...] Take the Nenets people – they are nomadic people. They have cattle – reindeer. And take Israeli people – they used to be nomads too. Then, in the Old Testament there are such notions as clean and unclean animals. And Nenets people too have the same notions! Birds, fish. Scavengers are unclean animals, as well as all those who eat someone else's flesh. Whitefish [*muksun*] have proper scales – everybody understands that it is a clean animal. But pike is unclean. We also have peaceful sacrifices: when we wish to thank God we can bring, for example, berries, cloudberries [...] That is, we have the same system in our culture.

When I stayed in Beloyarsk village, in a community of converted Nenets, we often read the Bible and this reading was the best way to call up old memories of Nenets tundra life. Beginning with "we also used to live according to the Old Testament", Marina, my hostess, then described various Nenets traditional rituals, customs and myths. Nenets prohibitions of the use of some species of animals and birds for food were reminiscent for readers of the ancient Jewish distinction between pure and impure animals. All Nenets rituals and behavioural regulations surrounding women during their periods and childbirth could now be justified by the Old Testament notion of ritual impurity and defilement of a woman and the Jewish idea that her impurity "infects" others (contamination by menstrual blood). Reading the Flood story, Marina told about *sikhirtia,* the Nenets mythical small underground people with conical heads that are believed to be the Nenets' predecessors. She explains the legend of *sikhirtia* through the Biblical image of the Flood:

Sikhirtia is closely connected with the Biblical story about the Flood. All the earth was flooded – everything, and the land where the Nenets lived, was also flooded. And when the water had gone all the people had died. But *sikhirtia* must have survived, hidden under the ground. But the water stayed for a long time, therefore they stayed under the ground for a long time and did not see the sun. It might be because of this that they are now afraid of sun light. So everybody died, but these conical ones survived.

Alternative Soteriology

In this way, traditional Nenets culture is not simply legalised within a Christian system, but is *sacralised* – the Nenets are *God's chosen people* whose duty is to fulfill God's will in the modern world, who prophetically are meant to find salvation.

Nenets "born-agains" see the Christian idea of God as referring to the main spiritual being in their indigenous cosmology,[4] and draw freely on such ideas in elaborating their justification of "traditional culture". A Nenets believer argued:

The Nenets are very spiritual people. They believe in gods, they believe that there are good and bad gods. And they understand that there is a Supreme God, the Creator. And when they hear the Gospel, they already understand that the Bible's God and their own God are one and the same.

Eventually, their "ethnicity" was replaced by "spirituality", as some Protestant missionaries argued that the Nenets "are not Nenets, but spiritual people". An Evangelical minister from Salekhard expressed it:

It turned out that these people [the Nenets] have the greatest, the richest culture, which is close to Biblical visions. These people don't need to discover that God does exist, unlike the Russians who used to live in an atheistic society and believed that they came from monkeys. The Nenets and all their culture are soaked with spirituality [. . .] They have a clear understanding of God the Creator – it is Num. They have their understanding of evil and sin. They have a Biblical conception of sacrifice for the sake of God's forgiveness and propitiation [*umilostivlenie*] [. . .] They are highly spiritual people.

4 This approach goes as far back as the nineteenth century Russian Orthodox mission among the Nenets, when one of the local spiritual beings of the Nenets cosmology – *Num* (Nenets: *num'* – sky) – was constructed according to the concept of the supreme deity, as the major God of heaven, responsible for human life and the guardian of moral order (Khomich 1979; Kostikov 1930; Veniamin 1855: 56-57). And *Nga* – the spirit related to the underground world – was conceptualised as the Devil or moralised evil.

Tundra life and non-converted nomadic Nenets are regarded as closer to Christianity than everybody else in the modern world, because they essentially have been living in the Old Testament. Even though some of the natives continue to live according to the Old Testament, believing in "idols" and resorting to the help of shamans, their lives were regarded by their convert fellows as prophetical.

Native born-agains re-narrated their personal stories and local histories, while internalising Christian values and key concepts such as *prophecy*, *salvation*, *predestination* and *damnation*. They revised their histories, situating them within Christian *soteriology*. Hence they did not merely embed their present in the past, but plunged it into their future – foreseeing their own, specifically Nenets, role in carrying the Christian message out into the world.

Religious conversion entails the creation of new oral histories, the invention of new family stories and hence a new history of salvation. When Nenets people told their Christian testimonies and personal conversion narratives, they usually started by telling stories not about themselves, but about their grandparents and great grandparents, reconsidering their ancestors' lives as God's prophecy and Providence.

In winter 2011 I arrived in Aksarka village, where Liudmila lives – an indigenous Charismatic leader and an internal missionary of her extended family. I intended to visit her and to listen to her conversion narrative. It was a six-hour story – the story of the conversion of her entire clan. Noteworthy that she began her story by telling about her grandfather who lived at the beginning of the twentieth century – a reindeer herder, a famous shaman who had never heard such words as Charismatic, or even Christianity, and knew only a little about the Russian god. It was the story of the miraculous salvation of her grandfather, who had been lost in the sea, drifting on an ice floe for three days. For Liudmila, it was a prophetical sign of the future conversion of the entire clan:

> He never knew God as we know Him now. But he began to pray to God the Father, because he realised that there was no sense anymore to ask "idols" for help – none of them could help him now. So he began to pray, "God! Save us! Help us!" [...] And then God made a path for him – a path made of ice that led him to the coast [...] Imagine, we are all destined to be saved, Satan knew that from the clan of this man a big branch [of Christians] would come out. Because there are many believers in our clan nowadays. And Satan wanted to cut this branch down, to uproot it. Our grandfather prayed not even knowing God, and God replied to him. It was a miracle.

Then Liudmila continued with her father's story, who was also a reindeer herder and who inherited the ancestral shamanic gift. He participated in World War II, where he saw for the first time Russians praying to their God, to "some Jesus". At the moment of crossfire between the Germans and Russians, he followed some

Russian soldiers and knelt down invoking God's name. Liudmila narrated it as follows:

> There was heavy fire from the German side. And my father often told us, "People around cried, 'God, save us!' And I knew too that God the Father helps, since he saved my dad out of the sea. And I also kneeled and prayed. And I heard God's voice, 'Don't be afraid, you will return home alive'".
>
> You see, he did not know God, but God talked to him anyway. Afterwards, he had so many revelations in his life, he did not know the Bible but he had such big revelations about the spiritual world [...] There was a miraculous salvation – God saved my father and therefore all his offspring, because He knew that through him his offspring will be reckoned and will be saved as Christians.

While re-narrating the oral history, native Christians constructed an *alternative soteriology*, in which God prevented the Devil's intent and saved those whose offspring would be future religious leaders. It is significant that such key concepts as prophet, priest, shaman, God's chosen leader have been developed into a common semantic field. "Simply because now we do not have a worthy priest... But we had one, and we called him a shaman", said Liudmila.

To sum up, along with *disenchanting* "native culture" as the means to justify it in Christian life, it is also the sacralisation of "the culture" and immersing Christian logic and Christian concepts into the native history that worked as the strategy for reconciling Christianity and indigenous identity. Moreover, this strategy was developed by native converts and missionaries in a way that it became a means for empowerment, replacing the conventional "second-classness" of the Nenets (and Khanty) by the notion of their chosenness and exceptional/ prophetical status within the Christian paradigm.

Politicising Conversion: Re-Indigenisation as Political Agency

As an outcome, the attempts to contextualize the Christian message within Nenets culture have led to a "recovery" of ethnic identity in a way that mobilised indigeneity as a political tool, where indigeneity reveals political agency, its social and political usage.

New indigenous churches in the Polar Ural region and Yamal peninsula registered NGOs and conducted various projects in support of nomadic indigenous people. They also supported native cooperation in *obshchiny* (indigenous clan-based fishing or herding communes) and inspired indigenous political claims.

In the widely known land conflict between the cooperative "Krasnyi Oktiabr" (based in the city of Vorkuta, Komi Republic) and private reindeer herders of the Polar Ural tundra, the Baptist missionaries were often mentioned as one of the stimuli for the conflict. The tension revolved around the land issue: the cooperative management complained that numerous Nenets private reindeer herders pastured their herds on the lands that belonged to the cooperative. They demanded the private herders either leave the pastures (due to the harsh polar mountain environment they in fact had no other place to go) or join the cooperative (in which case their herds would not belong to them anymore and would be a property of the cooperative). The head of the cooperative publicly accused the Baptist missionaries in propagandizing among the nomads that the latter should refuse to comply with the law, also instigating the herders to claim that these lands actually belong to them, and the tundra as a whole belongs to indigenous peoples. He argued that, following the missionaries' instructions, private herders claimed their land back and made complaints about the violation of their rights as *indigenous people*.

Indeed, this new political indigenous mobilisation was often viewed as an expression of opposition sentiments, running counter to the paternalistic approach of the local authorities towards the indigenous population. A Charismatic minister from Salekhard generalised it as follows: "Here [in the Yamal area] Protestants are treated badly by local administrations, because we teach indigenous people to speak proudly, they get more confident. But nobody needs that here". Conversely, using almost the same terminology, one of the leading politicians in Salekhard blamed Protestant missionaries for teaching nomadic Nenets the basics in law (*pravovoi likbez*), hence making "sectarian" Nenets hard to communicate with:

> They [converted Nenets] become so competent [*gramotnye*] [...] An absolutely uneducated reindeer herder or fisherman tells you, "Why do you force me to believe in other religions? According to the Constitution I have rights to choose for myself!" And our *FS-Beshniki* [Federal Security Service workers] were thereby put into a corner. They cannot do anything.

Anatolii, an Evangelical missionary in Salekhard, told me a story about how he and his mission-church helped converted Khanty fishermen unite into a fishing *obshchina* and their subsequent struggle with local authorities:

> [We] helped them organize a fishing community; we registered it and took care of all juridical things for them. They say, "They will kill us!" But I said to them, "Nobody will kill you". And when they'd already started fishing themselves, their previous boss [*khoziain*] saw them fishing on the same part of the river [*peski*], and he shouted at them, "What are you doing here?!" But I said to them, "Don't be afraid and answer him that this land is yours and you are its rightful masters". And since that time they have become rightful masters of their river.

Another Evangelical community in Salekhard has registered an NGO with a typical name – Association of Indigenous Peoples of the North "*Nasha Zemlia*" (Our Land). In cooperation with some charity organisations, the church conducted different social and humanitarian aid projects in support of nomadic indigenous people.

As an outcome, some converted natives are now engaged in social and political initiatives and play an appreciable role in the region's social life. Peter, a missionary who is Nenets by origin, at the same time is the organiser and the head of two native communities in the Yamal-Nenets Area – the reindeer herding cooperative "*Yasavei*" and the indigenous *obshchina* "*Obnovlnnaia Zhizn*" (Renewed Life). And he is also engaged in the activities of the indigenous association of the Nenets people "*Yamal – Potomkam*" (Yamal to Its Descendants) as the head of one of its departments. One of the Khanty's leading Charismatics is the people's deputy in the local municipality. Both consider their social and political activity as part of their Christian mission.

Although the majority of native born-agains are not so active in the social and political life of their region, their new religious experiences and their practice of justifying and defending 'indigenous culture' influence the increasing indigenous awareness.

In general, the situation is not unique for the Polar Urals and reflects many other cases of Protestant conversion in the context of colonial and post-colonial encounters. As observed by a range of scholars, the interrelation of neo-Protestant missionaries and native cultures in Latin America and Africa have frequently resulted into the so-called "indigenous awakening" and politicizing indigeneity (Gallaher 2007; Parker Gumucio 2002). In Latin America of the late twentieth/early twenty-first century, new-wave Protestant missions have been particularly successful in regions with a high population of indigenous peoples (Dow 2005). And as scholars argue, the "emergence of indigenous" here, the constitution of indigenous ethnic identities, ethnic claims and in general the eruption of an indigenous movement onto the political scene have been profoundly influenced by the great expansion of indigenous neo-Protestantism, as well as Catholicism revitalised by liberation theology (Trejo 2009).

In post-Soviet Siberia too, scholarship reports that oftentimes Protestant leaders are at the vanguard of the local indigenous revival (Broz 2009: 23-24; Vaté 2009: 41). However, it would be an exaggeration to look at Nenets conversion as a developed political opposition or indigenous movement, but rather what Jean Comaroff (1985: 194-196) calls a mode of "ritualised resistance" – rarely explicitly expressed – resistance not as established political action, but resistance as consciousness. Here, in the tundra of the Polar Urals, following the logic and approaches of post-Soviet indigenous movements, the Protestant conversion experience has become a new channel through which to integrate the transnational indigenous culture discourse.

Conclusion

The religious conversion experience stimulated the Nenets people to begin the self-conscious construction and articulation of cultural and ethnic boundaries and the reshaping of Nenets indigeneity. Nenets have been selective in what they have accepted and what they have rejected in international Evangelicalism, indigenising, appropriating and recycling heterogeneous values, concepts, and practices in the construction of alternative versions of the past and the future. They sought to indigenise new meanings and practices in ways that allowed them to enforce their own cultural order in a drastically changing world (cf. Sahlins 1999). Thus, the immersion of Christian logic and Christian concepts into Nenets indigenous culture eventually worked as a means for indigenous empowerment. It became an alternative strategy for grassroots revitalisation movement, on par with more politicised indigenous activism based on the revival of the old traditional practices, shamanism or the promotion of Orthodox Christianity (which was often regarded by the Nenets as part of their historical tradition).

Nenets converts have become involved in the process of re-assemblance of the notion of "native culture". To borrow from Humphrey J. Fisher (1973: 28; 1985: 156), drifting between the "Phoenix Knight" of their native system of meanings and the "Juggernaut" of the Christian message, Nenets born-agains have adapted and developed traditional cosmology, modifying and developing their own categories, symbols and practices to the extent that it has acquired a legitimised status and a meaningful, livable function again.

They have developed a strategy of re-indigenisation, and have legitimised their rights to have Nenets identity and Nenets culture, thereby mobilising their indigeneity as ethno-consciousness and political agency. While developing an alternative way of world-building, the Nenets ensure their own survival, they embed the present in their past and construct a new project of the world future and salvation in which they play a crucial role.

References

Badmaev, A. A., Ch. O. Adygbai, V. A. Burnakov, D. M. Mansheev (2006): *Protestantizm i narody Yuzhnoi Sibiri: istoriia i sovremennost'* (Protestantism and the Peoples of Southern Siberia: History and Present). Novosibirsk: Institut arkheologii i etnografii SO RAN.

Balzer, Marjorie Mandelstam (2002): "Healing Failed Faith? Contemporary Siberian Shamanism", *Anthropology and Humanism* 26 (2), 134-149.

Balzer, Marjorie Mandelstam (2005): "Whose Steeple is Higher? Religious Competition in Siberia", *Religion, State & Society* 33(1), 57-69.

Balzer, Marjorie Mandelstam (2008): "Beyond Belief? Social, Political, and Shamanic Power in Siberia", *Social Analysis* 52(1), 95-110.

Broz, Ludek (2009): "Conversion to Religion? Negotiating Continuity and Discontinuity in Contemporary Altai" in Mathijs Pelkmans (ed.): *Conversion after Socialism. Disruptions, Modernisms and Technologies of Faith in the Former Soviet Union.* NY, Oxford: Berghahn Books, 17-37.

Brumbelow, Gary (1995): "The Other Side of Russia: Evangelical Ministries in Siberia", *East-West Church & Ministry Report* 3 (Spring), 1-3.

Bruner, Edward (1994): "Abraham Lincoln as Authentic Reproduction: A Critique of Postmodernism", *American Anthropologist* 96(2), 397-415.

Coleman, Simon (2000): *The Globalisation of Charismatic Christianity. Spreading the Gospel of Prosperity.* Cambridge University Press.

Comaroff, Jean (1985): *Body of Power, Spirit of Resistance. The Culture and History of a South African People.* The University of Chicago Press.

Comaroff, Jean, John L. Comaroff (2009): *Ethnicity Inc.* The University of Chicago Press.

Dombrowski, Kirk (2001): *Against Culture. Development, Politics, and Religion in Indian Alaska.* University of Nebraska Press.

Dow, W. James (2005): "The Expansion of Protestantism in Mexico: An Anthropological View", *Anthropological Quarterly* 78(4), 827-850.

Dudarenok, Svetlana M. (2005): "K voprosu formirovaniia 'novogo' konfessional'nogo prostranstva na rossiiskom Dal'nem Vostoke" (On the Formation of "New" Confessional Space in the Russian Far East) in: *Svoboda sovesti v Rossii: isotricheskii i sovremennyi aspekty*, Vol. 2 (Moskva) http://www.rusoir.ru/03print/04/14/index.html (last accessed on 3 October 2008).

Fisher, Humphrey J. (1973): "Conversion Reconsidered: Some Historical Aspects of Religious Conversion in Black Africa", *Africa: Journal of the International African Institute* 43(1), 27-40.

Fisher, Humphrey J. (1985): "The Juggernaut's Apologia: Conversion to Islam in Black Africa", *Africa: Journal of the International African Institute* 55(2), 153-173.

Forsyth, James (1992): *A History of the Peoples of Siberia. Russia's North Asian Colony. 1581-1990.* Cambridge University Press.

Gable, Eric, Richard Handler (1996): "After Authenticity at an American Heritage Site", *American Anthropologist* 98(3), 568-578.

Gallaher, Carolyn (2007): "The Role of Protestant Missionaries in Mexico's Indigenous Awakening", *Bulletin of Latin American Research* 26(1), 88-111.

Gray, Patty A. (2005): *The Predicament of Chukotka's Indigenous Movement. Post-Soviet Activism in the Russian Far-North.* Cambridge University Press.

Humphrey, Caroline (1999): "Shamans in the City", *Anthropology Today* 15(3), 3-10.

Humphrey, Caroline (2002): *The Unmaking of Soviet Life: Everyday Economies after Socialism.* Cornell University Press.

Jackson, Jean E. (2007): "Rights to Indigenous Culture in Colombia" in: Mark Goodale, Sally Angle Merry (ed.): *The Practice of Human Rights. Tracking Law Between the Global and the Local.* Cambridge University Press, 204-241.

Jackson, Jean E. (2009): "Traditional, Transnational, and Cosmopolitan: The Colombian Yanacona look to the past and to the future", *American Ethnologist* 36(3), 521-544.

Khomich, Liudmila V. (1979): "Vliianie khristianizatsii na religioznye predstavleniia i kul'ty nentsev" (The Influence of Christianisation on Religious Ideas and Culture of the Nenets) in: *Khristianstvo i lamaizm u korennogo naseleniia Sibiri (vtor. pol. XIX – nachalo XX veka).* Leningrad: Nauka, 12-28.

Kostikov, L. V. (1930): "Bogovy oleni v religioznykh verovaniiakh khasovo" (God's Reindeer in Religious Beliefs of the Khasovo) in: V.G. Bogoraz-Tan, D.A. Zolotar¸v, Ya. P. Koshkin et al. (eds.): *Etnografiia,* Vol. 1-2. Moskva-Leningrad, 115-132.

Krindatch, Alexey D. (2004): "Patterns of Religious Change in Postsoviet Russia: Major Trends from 1998 to 2003", *Religion, State & Society* 32(2), 115-136.

Lar, Leonid (1998): *Shamany i bogi* (Shamans and Gods). Tiumen'.

Liarskaya, Ye.V. (2003): "Severnye internaty i transformatsiia traditsionnoi kul'tury (na primere nenstev Yamala)" (Contemporary Boarding Schools and the Transformation of Traditional Culture (the Nenets of Yamal)), Dissertation, European University at St. Petersburg.

Mukhach¸v, A. D., G. P. Khariuchi, A. A. Yuzhakov (2010): *Kochuiushchie cherez veka: olenevodcheskaia kul'tura i etnoekologiia tundrovykh nentsev* (Migrating through Centuries: Reindeer Culture and Ethnoecology of the Tundra Nenets). Salekhard-Yekaterinburg.

Neumann Fridman, Eva Jane (2004): *Sacred Geography: Shamanism among the Buddhist Peoples of Russia,* Bibliotheca Shamanistica, Vol. 12. Budapest: Akadémiai Kiadó.

Parker Gumucio, Cristian (2002): "Religion and the Awakening of Indigenous People in Latin America", *Social Compass* 49(1), 67-81.

Pelkmans, Mathijs (ed.)(2009): *Conversion after Socialism. Disruptions, Modernisms and Technologies of Faith in the Former Soviet Union.* NY, Oxford: Berghahn Books.

Perevalova, Ye.V. (2004): *Severnye khanty: etnicheskaia istoriia* (Contemporary Khanty: Ethnic History).Yekaterinburg: UrO RAN.

Pika, Alexandr (ed.) (1999): *Neotraditionalism in the Russian North: Indigenous Peoples and the Legacy of Perestroika.* Ed. in English by Bruce Grant. Canadian Circumpolar Institute (CCI) Press.

Robbins, Joel (2003): "On the Paradoxes of Global Pentecostalism and the perils of continuity thinking", *Religion* 33, 221-231.

Rybakova, Olga (2009): "The Evangelist Communities of Magadan Oblast", *Sibirica* 8(3), 1-21.

Sahlins, Marshall (1985): *Islands of History.* Chicago: University of Chicago Press.

Sahlins, Marshall (1999): "What Is Anthropological Enlightenment? Some Lessons of the Twentieth Century", *Annual Review of Anthropology* 28, i-xxiii.

Sahlins, Marshall (2005): "The Economics of Develop-man in the Pacific" in: Joel Robbins, Holly Wardlow (eds.): *The Making of Global and Local Modernities in Melanesia. Humiliation and the Transformation and the Nature of Cultural Change.* Aldershot: Ashgate Publishing, 23-41. (Originally published in the journal *Res* (1992) 21, 13-25.

Schindler, Debra L. (1997): "Redefining Tradition and Renegotiating Ethnicity in Native Russia", *Arctic Anthropology* 34(1), 194-211.

Scott, Michael W. (2005): "'I Was Like Abraham': Notes on the Anthropology of Christianity from the Solomon Islands", *Ethnos* 70(1), 101–125.

Skachkov, I. F. (1934): *Antireligioznaia rabota na Krainem Severe* (Antireligious Work in the Far North). Moskva: "GAIZ".

Stammler, Florian (2005): *Reindeer Nomads Meet the Market. Culture, Property and Globalization at the "End of the Land".* Lit Verlag Berlin.

Suslov, I.M. (1931): "Shamanstvo i bor'ba s nim" (Shamanism and the Struggle against It), *Sovetskii Sever* 3-4, 89-152.

Trejo, Guillermo (2009): "Religious Competition and Ethnic Mobilization in Latin America: Why the Catholic Church Promotes Indigenous Movements in Mexico", *The American Political Science Review* 103(3), 323-342.

Vakhtin, N.B., Ye.V. Liarskaya (2004): "Yazykovaia situatsiia i problemy obrazovaniia" (Language Situation and the Problems of Education) in: V.A. Tishkov (ed.): *Sovremennoe polozhenie i perspektivy razvitiia korennykh malochislennykh narodov Severa, Sibiri i Dal'nego Vostoka: Nezavisimyi ekspertnyi doklad.* Novosibirsk: Izdatel'stvo Instituta Arkheologii i Etnografii SO RAN, 133-148.

Vallikivi, Laur (2011): "What *Does* Matter? Idols and Icons in the Nenets Tundra", *Journal of Ethnology and Folkloristics* 5(1), 75-95.

Vaté, Virginie (2009): "Redefining Chukchi Practices in Contexts of Conversion to Pentecostalism" in *Mathijs* Pelkmans (ed.): *Conversion after Socialism. Disruptions, Modernisms and Technologies of Faith in the Former Soviet Union.* NY, Oxford: Berghahn Books, 39-57.

Veniamin (Smirnov), Archimandrite (1855): "Samoedy mezenskie" (Mezen Samoyeds) *Vestnik Russkogo Geograficheskogo Obshchestva* 3, 77-140.

Wiget, Andrew, Olga Balalaeva (2007): "Crisis, Conversion, and Conflict: Evangelical Christianity, Rapid Change, and the Eastern Khanty", *Sibirica* 6(1), 1–29.

Yefimenko, Alona (2004): "Sacred Sites and Sanctuaries in Russia" in Erich Karsten (ed.): *Properties of Culture – Culture as Property. Pathways to Reform in Post-Soviet Siberia.* Berlin: Dietrich Reimer, 159-168.

Znachenie okhrany sviashchennykh mest Arktiki: Issledovanie korennykh narodov Severa Rossii. Moskva: AKMNSS i DV RF(2004) (English version: The Project report in English: The Conservation Value of Sacred Sites of Indigenous Peoples of the Arctic: A Case Study in Northern Russia. Report on the state of sacred sites and sanctuaries. CAFF Technical Report. No. 11. 2004. http://library.arcticportal.org/1302/1/Technical-Rep-no.-11.pdf (last accessed on 15 July 2013)).

Znamenski, Andrei A. (2007): *The Beauty of the Primitive. Shamanism and the Western Imagination.* Oxford University Press.

Zuev, V.F. (1947): "Opisanie zhivushchikh v Sibirskoi gubernii v Ber¸zovskom uezde inovercheskikh narodov ostiakov i samoedov" (The Description of the Heterodox Ostyak and Samoyed People Living in Beriozov District of Siberian Province) In: *Materialy po etnografii Sibiri XVIII veka*, Vol. 5. Trudy Institua etnografii AN SSSR.

---

[4] All mistakes or inaccuracies responsibility of Gillian Watt.

The Globalisation of World Views: Indigenous communities and Alternative Tourism collaboration?

Gillian Watt

(with collaboration from Roberto Moreira, and others from Misiones province Argentina)[1]

Introduction

This article is based on ethnographic fieldwork in the Misiones province of Northeast Argentina, the focus of which is the potential for dialogue and possible collaboration between alternative tourism initiatives and Mbyá Guaraní communities in Misiones. This fieldwork report presents some findings from a six month project funded by Erasmus Mundus, Academic Mobility for Inclusive Development in Latin America (AMIDILA) entitled '(Neo) Shamanic Dialogue in Misiones Argentina: Indigenous Mbyá Guaraní agency and globalisation'. The project aimed to document and analyse encounters between indigenous Mbyá Guaraní groups in Misiones, Argentina, and non-indigenous tourists and visitors to the region. Through short ethnographic fieldwork visits to the Mbyá Guaraní communities, tourism businesses, and individuals, the project aimed to map and investigate transcultural exchange of world views within tourism. Because of the limited time frame, the project was restricted to a general overview with a focus on 'alternative' forms of tourism of the kind that 'travellers' (*viajeros, pasajeros*) might experience. This kind of tourism might involve visits to indigenous communities by travellers and tourists interested in indigenous knowledge systems, rituals, and the use of ritual plant medicines such as ayahuasca and others. My research interests were inspired by research in South East Brazil where a representative from an international 'New Age' contemporary or Neo-shamanic group (*Camino Rojo* – Red Road) contacted Guaraní villages to exchange shamanistic ritual practices (Langdon, De Rose 2012). A 'Medicine Alliance Network' was formed as a result of three groups: Red Road, the Brazilian ayahuasca religion Santo Daime, and a Guaraní group from Clearwaters Village. The three groups not only influenced each other's rituals but also inspired other players to subsequently become involved, such as lowland Quichua and Shuar from Ecuador and members of *sangoma*, a South African shamanic tradition. The development of this Medicine Alliance resulted in a revitalisation of Guaraní ritual and cultural life, a positive affirmation of Guaraní identity, and an improvement in social and economic conditions (Langdon, De Rose 2012). My research aimed to investigate whether there have been (or whether there is potential for) similar alliances amongst the Mbyá Guaraní in Misiones province, Argentina, that might bring similar beneficial outcomes for this group.

My central research questions focused on how the globalised spread of neo-shamanism as a dialogical category has affected the Misiones Mbyá Guaraní, if at all, and whether there are potential benefits for this extremely marginalised and disenfranchised group through encounters and exchanges with non-indigenous people who are involved in Neo-Shamanism or wish to explore indigenous ritual practice.

The research project aimed, through an exploration of the interchange between indigenous voices and knowledge systems and tourist/visitors (who, in many ways, are representatives of hegemonial forces), to investigate the potential for new solutions to local problems with the explicit idea that this re-examination of globalising influences might lead to indigenous empowerment rather than further oppression. This article reports on some aspects of this fieldwork. I will describe how the research focus developed and changed with the challenges of being in the field; and then how ongoing research and facilitation aims to develop some practical measures for the improvement of social conditions for an Mbyá Guaraní (henceforth referred to as Mbyá) community in Misiones province, Argentina through a collaboration with a 'new age' non-indigenous 'ecovillage' also based in Misiones. In a more general sense, I suggest that in some cases the globalisation of worldviews has the potential to result in benefits to indigenous people and also benefits to marginalised non-mainstream communities of non-indigenous in a process of collaborative exchange.

Context

Argentina, which is the second largest nation in Latin America (after Brazil), has a relatively low indigenous population at 3% (Seymoure 2012) compared to countries such as Bolivia or Peru which have 62% and 46% respectively.[2] Argentina has been subject to deep European influences and has a strong middle class. The history of indigenous genocide in the formation of the Argentine nation state makes

2 For Bolivia see UNDP2006 at http://www.ilo.org/indigenous/Activitiesbyregion/LatinAmerica/Bolivia/lang--en/index.html International Labour organisation web page Bolivia (last accessed on 20th Aug 2015) and Peru see http://lt.umn.edu/earthducation/expedition4/indigenous-cultures/Earth Education Expedition 4 2012, Indigenous Cultures web page (last accessed on 20th Aug 2015).

grim reading (see Trinchero 2006) and as Trinchero (following Foucault 1976) indicates (2006: 121) it has left "'stigmas remaining in its body'". Although Argentina voted in favour of the UN declaration of the Rights of Indigenous Peoples 2007, the situation remains desperate for many — especially those in Misiones province. The Mbyá originally lived in forest that is now demarcated as being within Misiones province and the neighbouring Corrientes province as well as beyond Argentina's borders in Brazil and Paraguay.

This project focused on the province of Misiones alone. Misiones comprises only 1.1% of land within the national boundaries of Argentina (Seymoure 2012: 15). It contains a portion (11,300 squared km) of what remains of the Interior Atlantic Forest which once covered one million square kilometres of Brazil, Paraguay, and Argentina (Seymoure 2012). This forest is under threat from logging and agribusiness as well as, in places, an increase in tourism (*e.g.* upmarket hotels, especially in the Iguazu Falls region, which is a UNESCO World Heritage Site). Misiones is a province that is bordered on three sides by Brazil, Paraguay, and the Argentine province of Corrientes. It is a marginal province by virtue of its geopolitical boundaries which create a finger shaped projection in the North-east of Argentina. The history of the Latin American Jesuit Missionary project from 1608 to 1767 (Rolin 2004) is evident in Misiones, as the several ruins of the Jesuit 'Reductions' are UNESCO World Heritage Sites and valuable tourism interests. There was also a substantial wave of European immigration to Misiones from the late nineteenth century to the middle of the twentieth century leading to a population consisting of a wide range of immigrant nationalities and allegiances.[3] Also, since the Second World War, there are immigrant populations from Japan, Laos, South Korea, and Taiwan (Rolin 2004). Therefore, Misiones is a province of frontiers and borders where "debates over identity form part of everyday life" (Enriz 2010: 1). It has a population of 1,111,443 (in 2010, World Data Atlas 2015). In the midst of this tension of the assertion of immigrant, ethnic, national, and provincial identities, the Mbyá live in mostly rural marginal communities. This is a group that for many years moved through the Paranense or Atlantic semi-deciduous forest region (which was originally a part of the Amazon forest complex) but are, for the most part, presently unable to continue a nomadic lifestyle due to forest removal, fragmentation and degradation.

Misiones has a sub-tropical climate and has an average year round temperature of 20°C/68°F. Summer temps can be as high as 40+ degrees centigrade; however, winter temps (June, July, August) can drop low enough to warrant the need for external heating and covers for the body especially at night time. There is no distinct dry season, and humidity is mostly high.

---

3 There are immigrant groups from Austria, Brazil, Denmark, England, Finland, France, Germany, Italy, Lebanon, Norway, Paraguay, Poland, Russia, Spain, Sweden, Switzerland, Syria, and Ukraine (Rolin 2006).

The Mbyá may be defined in the first instance by their membership of the Tupi-Guarani linguistic family[4] (a linguistic family common in the rainforest of central South America). There could have been as many as 1.5 to 2 million Guaraní people in the southern cone before European conquest and subsequent colonisation (Seymoure 2012). Like many indigenous, there is a long history of persecution starting from the first colonisers of the sixteenth century who controlled them by interference, forced relocation, and slavery. However, the Mbyá group were not assimilated into the Jesuit mission project in Misiones with other Guarani groups (Seymoure 2009, Cebolla Bad 2012). The substantial and generally inaccessible forest at that time provided refuge for the Mbyá until the mid-nineteenth century when the newly formed South American nations of the area started the exploitation of the forest habitat. Although, even at this early stage, some Mbyá were involved in seasonal employment, they remained relatively autonomous, especially as regards political control, religious leadership, and world view and lifestyle, with large areas of forest still remaining available (Gorosito Kramer n.d.). Settlements were changed every five or six years for various reasons, including depletion of resources in the area (Cebolla Badie 2012). However, the more recent and aggressive exploitation of habitat through forest clearing, tobacco production and introduction of exotics (the latter two also bringing intense use of pesticides) with accompanying expulsion of Mbyá communities has led to the forced adoption of more permanent settlements (Gorosito Kramer n.d.). At present, there are estimated to be 6,500 Mbyá in Misiones (Enriz 2010). The Mbyá live in family-based communities, surviving through subsistence farming, government assistance, some salaried work, and a small income from tourism, mainly the sale of artisan crafts — wooden animals and basketry — and ornamental plants (orchids) that they gather from the remaining forest (Von Hau, Wilde 2009; Roburg, Seymoure 2012). As mentioned before, the Mbyá group were not part of the Guarani group that were assimilated by the Jesuit project in Misiones (Seymoure 2009; Cebolla Badie 2012,) although tourism marketing does not make this very clear. The Mbyá now live mostly in areas demarcated for them by the government or on land owned by private non-indigenous. Many live in roadside communities on the main roads (*Rutas)* that traverse the province.

The World Bank reported, according to Roburg and Seymoure 2012 (p. 16), "[...] that Mbya Guarani communities suffered from worse living conditions than indigenous communities in other provinces". Few Mbyá communities hold title to their land, a situation that is further compounded by wider issues of what comprises 'territory'.[5] National and Provincial legal frameworks in Argentina tend

[4] The Tupi-Guarani linguistic family consists of 51 different language types (www.ethnologue.com/subgroups/tup%C3%AD-guarani%C3AD-0 Ethnologue-Languages of the World. Last accessed on 18th August 2015).

[5] Indigenous notions of 'territory' can be and often are different from non-indigenous: "We

not to include concepts of territory and indigenous governance that encompass preservation of the forest, nor fundamentals such as environmental resources of, for example, water, the subsoil, etc. (Von Hau, Wilde 2009).

Many Mbyá live with persistent material destitution and high poverty indices (Sy 2013),[6] as well as food insecurity, lack of self and cultural esteem, and alcoholism. Land loss as a result of logging, expansion of monoculture forest for the paper industry, and agribusiness, contribute to their disenfranchisement, and also to a diminishment in health. Many traditional medicines are lost with deforestation and lack of access (Sy 2013), as well as significant loss of livelihood (food animals and plants). The average life expectancy is 40 years and the greatest number of deaths occur among children (Valente 2006; Seymoure 2012).

Government welfare programs and NGO assistance, although vital, especially in situations of food insecurity, are also problematic because such programmes foster binding reliance on a dominant culture and ideology which simultaneously continues to damage indigenous lives and cultures and have introduced divisions that have weakened Mbyá representation as indigenous (Gorosito Kramer n.d.). Moreover, Mbyá continue to suffer serious health and social problems despite a 'boom' in interest from Europe for academic research and NGO 'projects' concerning the Mbyá (Cebolla Badie n.d.). Sometimes 'aid' may also be inappropriate; for example, government donated wooden houses are very cold in the winter (pers. comm., community member near Santa Ana, Misiones, August 2015); and the charitable giving of unwanted mass produced branded clothing only encourages a rejection of Mbyá culture, especially amongst the young. Lack of running water and sanitation can also be problematic. Despite all of this, in the International Work Group for Indigenous Affairs Annual Yearbook on Argentina, the Mbyá are mentioned only briefly in 2011 and 2012 (www.iwgia.org).

Methodology

This research employs classic ethnographical approaches. In other words, it takes a "holistic approach to the study of cultural systems" (Whitehead 2005: 4). I explored processes and meanings within localised and globalised/globalising cul-

occupy a cultural space with various ceremonial grounds and cemeteries... and there is respect towards nature... but we as indigenous peoples are not owners of these lands, we are part of a natural system and it is us who belong here" (Quote from Mbyá person from Von Hau, Wilde 2009: 18).

6 Mbyá leaders question narrow definitions of poverty "We value our culture – this is our wealth" (Mbyá bsence of material status symbols... in the words of a cazique (leader) 'one is poor because of not having [access to] the forest anymore'" *Von Hau, Wilde 2009: 18), leader Puerto Iguazu 11th July 2015) and "frequently emphasise that being poor is not confined to the a

tural systems and aspired to an interpretive and reflexive research process. I took detailed field notes with 'thick' description in fieldwork journals. I also documented interviews through audio recordings, obtaining written consent from my participants.

I positioned myself in the tourism sector within the 'backpacker' and 'hostel' demographic (ages commonly early twenties to late thirties, Euro-American and Argentinian predominantly). I presumed this would be the tourism demographic most likely to be seeking alternative or spiritual tourism. I use the term 'alternative' tourism to mean that which "emphasises avoidance of environmental damage, scaling down, the issue of who benefits, and cultural sensitivity" (De Kadt 1990: 1) and spiritual tourism broadly to mean a "tourism characterised by a self-conscious project of spiritual betterment" (Norman 2012: 20). The aim of my study was to obtain a general overview of tourism that involved the Mbyá in the Misiones region, exploring the possibilities that might be opened up by tourism encounters between 'Neo-Shamanism' (by groups or individuals) and Mbyá ritual practice, and focusing where possible on 'alternative' tourism initiatives.

The time limits of the project (six months April to September 2015), combined with various challenges in the field, meant that the research remained at an exploratory level. All interviews were unstructured but I had various themes that I introduced into each interview. These were: involvement in tourism that includes or facilitates contact with the Mbyá; whether tourism benefits the Mbyá; and the kinds of tourism thought to be best suited/beneficial to the Mbyá. Also in some interviews, and where appropriate, I sought opinions on Mbyá involvement in alternative tourism projects initiated by non-indigenous.

I conducted nine in-depth interviews which altogether included four women and six men. The age range was 23 years to 58 years. Some interviews took place in 'ecovillages' – a term I am using to describe rural based intentional communities[7] owned or run by non-indigenous people. These (usually rural) communities aspire to lifestyles that might include, self-sufficiency, spiritual development, organic gardening, Neo-shamanic rituals, communal living, self-built dwellings, and often a desire for (or an idealisation of) world views involving relationality with

[7] "An 'intentional community' is a group of people who have chosen to live together with a common purpose, working cooperatively to create a lifestyle that reflects their shared core values. The people may live together on a piece of rural land, in a suburban home, or in an urban neighborhood, and they may share a single residence or live in a cluster of dwellings. This definition spans a wide variety of groups, including (but not limited to) communes, student cooperatives, land co-ops, cohousing group, monasteries and ashrams, and of farming collectives. Although quite diverse in philosophy and lifestyle, each of these groups places a high priority on fostering a sense of community – a feeling of belonging and mutual support that is increasingly hard to find in mainstream Western society". From F.I.C. Fellowship for Intentional Community http://www.ic.org/wiki/intentional-communities-lifestyles-based-ideals/ (last accessed on 20th September 2015).

the natural world (plants, animals, stones, etc.). These ecovillages accepted tourists and *viajeros* ('travellers') as volunteers, interns, or paying guests. I interviewed five people involved in ecovillages in Misiones, three of whom were the owners of the land (two Argentinian and one North American) and two of whom were visitors/tourists/*viajeros* (English and Colombian). I also interviewed a medical doctor who has worked for several years with Mbyá and who offers opportunities for internships and visits from *viajeros* and 'alternative' tourists. I interviewed one person who was a '*viajero*/tourist' (from Uruguay), especially interested in indigenous ritual and worldview. I interviewed one Argentine tourism provider in the town of Puerto Iguazu (an intensely touristic location due to the UNESCO heritage site of Iguazu Falls) who worked with a Mbyá community and individuals. I interviewed two Mbyá persons, one a schoolteacher and community representative, another a leader (*cacique*) of a community significantly impacted by encroaching tourism businesses.

In addition I documented many conversations with tourists and people involved in the field of 'alternative tourism'. As an 'outsider' it was possible to take a somewhat detached and observational role, particularly regarding attitudes towards indigenous people, and related observations regarding colonial histories and expressions of Argentinian national identity. These observations were documented in detail in fieldwork journals. I had aimed to conduct several more interviews with Mbyá; however the process and experiences of fieldwork revealed that this would not be straightforward or as easy as I had hoped.

Fieldwork experiences

Various research challenges emerged early in the fieldwork. The southern hemisphere autumn in mid-April 2015 when I arrived in Misiones, is the beginning of the 'low' season for tourism. Posadas, Misiones' capital city, is not typically on the tourism circuit but it is the biggest starting point in the area for the exploration of the extensive ruins of the Jesuit reductions in the area, and is also a transport hub for buses and planes to Iguazu Falls as well as providing several connections to other areas of Misiones and the rest of Argentina (*e.g.* Buenos Aires, Cordoba etc.). However, during this low season there were few tourists. The weather was cool, and, though I had been advised on the presence of many Mbyá selling artisan products to tourists in the Plaza de San Martin and other touristic sites in the centre of the city of Posadas, there were not any Mbyá there at this time and artisan markets were closed.

Posadas is a frontier city, separated from Paraguay by the River Parana and has a population of approximately 300,000. It is clear on arrival that there is a strong European descendent population with many people who are naturally 'blonde' and who have pale skin. It retains much of its colonial past with many old buildings remaining. One of its more recent developments is the construction of La Costanera, an esplanade that runs along the edge of the Parana River opposite Encarnación. Here on sunny evenings it is possible to see large numbers of people walking, taking exercise (many with I-pods, or portable music systems), sitting in groups drinking the national drink *Mate* or walking with small dogs. There are two main Plazas, Plaza 9 de Julio[8] and Plaza San Martin,[9] which have both been upgraded in recent years to provide leafy and pleasant areas in the city centre. In May 2015, I saw a small group of Mbyá Guarani selling baskets on La Costanera and another in Plaza San Martin selling baskets and wooden handcrafted animals. In both instances barefoot Mbyá children looking for small change (*monedita*) and/or cookies (*galletita*) in shabby and sometimes torn clothes ran amongst the well and casually dressed non-indigenous Argentinians of Posadas. There was a striking contrast between the indigenous and non-indigenous. In San Ignacio, an hour by bus outside the city and one of the main sites of the ruins of the Jesuit reductions, there were small groups of Mbyá women and children sat on the ground near the heritage site, selling hand-carved wooden animals and ornamental plants. Next to them was a line of neat wooden kiosk-like stalls managed by non-indigenous also selling handicrafts. Words such as 'browbeaten' and 'downtrodden' sprung to my mind when I saw the groups of Mbyá women and children sitting on the ground nearby. I tried to engage the women in conversation but was met with mostly silence and the occasional shy smile. At the main entrance to the ruins, which have had a dramatic upgrade in recent years and are on the international tourist circuit, huddled a little group of five young barefoot children in torn, dirty, and shabby clothes trying to sell small natural crystals from the forest and tiny orchid plants. Again they were asking for food and money and again well-dressed Argentinian and international tourists walked past them to pay the (substantial, in the case of internationals) entrance fee to the interpretive centre where 'Guaraní' artifacts and recorded singing could be enjoyed and beyond which the ruins themselves can be viewed.

I decided to go to the Office of Guaraní affairs (*Dirreción Provincial de Asuntos Guaranies*) in Posadas[10] to introduce myself and seek advice on making contact with communities and inform them of the research project. I was told by a representative there that there was no cultural tourism of the kind that I was interested in (that is, sharing of rituals with tourists); there was no use of ayahuasca in the communities here; and there were not the structures in place that would allow for the development of a 'cultural tourism' of this kind apart from a small scale

8 The date that commemorates Argentina's Independence Day.

9 Commemorating Jose San Martin an Argentine leader in the fight for Independence from Spain.

10 I was later to find out that this organisation may not be representative of Mbya in the region (see Roburg, Seymoure 2012).

operation in a community in Puerto Iguazu.[11] There was, however, I was told, touristic development involving Mbyá songs and music and musical instruments. At this time, the significant limits of short term research projects were revealed to me through a newspaper article written by Cebolla Badie (n.d.) who pointed out that in recent years many people from Europe have come to develop projects with the Mbyá but that these were mostly short term and superficial (although helpful in drawing attention to the Mbyá who for many years remained 'invisible').[12] Also many projects are not that helpful or informed (Cebolla Badie, pers. comm. June 2015) and possibly set up dependencies that add to problems of social disenfranchisement and self-esteem.[13]

At this point, plagued with many dead ends and obstacles, it seemed that mine was just another short-term project that would do and contribute very little to the lives of the Mbyá people and that, despite my aspirations to 'help' and promote inclusive development, perhaps I was no help at all — just another well-meaning European who did not speak the Mbyá language nor fully understand the situation, with an agenda that did not relate to the needs of the people concerned.

It was at this time that I fortuitously came across an article in a provincial newspaper which revealed the apparent presence of five ecovillages (*ecoaldeas)* in

---

11 In a community called Fontin Mborere.

12 *"En los últimos años hubo un boom de investigaciones sobre los mbya, ahora es como que hay muchos "expertos" hablando de la comunidad mbya y en realidad la mayoría de estas investigaciones son muy lights. Es decir, nadie se ha dedicado durante lapsos determinados de tiempos a estar el lugar. Estar en el campo es la marca de la antropología, de la investigación etnográfica. En general toda esta gran cantidad de tesis y de investigaciones que salieron ahora son con estadías cortas de tiempo donde nadie conoce el idioma.Otra cuestión es que son repeticiones del trabajo de otros autores, trabajan eso y lo repiten sin a veces constatar o verificar esa información"*. Cebolla Badie, M., Misiones Para Todos. misionesparatodos.com/cebolla-badie-hace-20-anos-los-mbyas-eran-casi-invisibles(last accessed 25th September 2015) no date given.

13 For example even in the 1970s such problems were emerging with 'help' from outside: as this extract from an Mbyá poet shows:

"...And the forests, the forests are not beautiful anymore.
Now the forests are ugly
We do not have our forests anymore
The animals we used to know are gone now
The deer, the wild pigs, all the rest
Even if they are still there we do not kill them
I cannot find myself anymore
I cannot find myself here anymore
If the governor can do it,
if this is something he can do,
let him give me some place with many animals
Even if they are not forests
I do not want them to lend me anything else
I do not need any more tools..." 'Pai Antonio' Antonio Martinez 1979

Misiones (*Primera Edición* 2015), several of which offered ayahuasca and other ritual ceremonies originating in indigenous communities. From this point, I decided to enhance the scope of my research to include the presence of alternative non-mainstream forms of colonisation. I directed my investigation towards exploring the potential of such communities to benefit, or at least be less damaging to, indigenous world views and lifestyles. I wondered whether these ecovillages might aspire to similar lifestyles and worldviews that (broadly speaking) indigenous people do. Did these groups communicate with the Mbyá? Was there any kind of exchange or collaboration here? How did these groups align interests in indigenous worldviews (via ayahuasca and other ceremonies) to their manner of 'colonising' (albeit possibly in an alternative and less exploitative way)?

Mamaroja (Red Mama) was the first ecovillage I stayed in. Mamaroja is an experiment in self-reliant homesteading and simple living. This project "was born of our desire to live in a happy and harmonious way, free to explore our full potential as creative and intelligent beings. We want to live true to our ideals and honest with ourselves. For us, this means living close to nature, making choices with ecological consciousness, and building a comfortable, peaceful place conducive to growth and sharing" (www.mamaroja.org).

Mamoroja is in an isolated position outside a small town in the centre of Misiones province, embedded in a humid forested valley and bordered by two small rivers. It is an educational project offering internships and courses in sustainable living, adobe house building (*bio-construcción*) made from the abundant red clay soil of the region, yoga retreats and "sacred medicine cleansing and ceremonies" (www.mamaroja.org). Many international and national visitors, and tourists, will pass through Mamaroja, on courses, or as volunteers.

> Mamaroja is down a red earth track. ... Through a gate with the Mamaroja sign you walk past a small vegetable patch that looks a bit overgrown, then through trees to a large open plan corrugated roof over a cob structure. Sturdy large wooden tables, wooden branches hold up the roof crossways, larger ones at the corners. A concrete floor. Hammocks strung between posts. Shelf units, books, jars, a 'pantry', bottles, plastic tubs under tables marked with labels for different kinds of compost ('rabbits', 'chickens', 'compost'). A parrot, dark green and non-talking flies across the kitchen/living space which is open-sided with single back wall constructed of cob. Two sinks set into wood, wooden cupboards, etc. No windows as such, as all open to the elements. A large round fireplace with logs and benches made with pieces of wood immediately in front of the construction. A single solar panel facing north to pick up the rays. A hill in front with many tall trees rising up the ridge. Three cats live in the far corner in front of the pantry. Two dogs. A lemon tree next to the fire pit. Bunting, dreamcatchers, wind chimes; books on plant consciousness and shamanism; the weathered skull of a cow attached to a piece of wood by the fire. At the back of the 'room' a large wooden carving of a Native American head in full ceremonial headgear. The background sound of rushing water from the nearby river. (Author's Fieldwork Journal I, June 12th 2015)

Mamaroja is owned and managed by a woman from the US and a man from Argentina. Both have a deep interest in indigenous shamanic ceremony with the use of plants and other natural substances as well as a commitment to sustainable and community living. One of my first questions to them was whether, when they set up their project, they consulted with the local indigenous.

An important part of us doing the work here is doing community service out of Mama Roja. And we thought being here, working with the most marginalised people, who are the Guarani, would be something that would benefit Misiones and they might be the people most open to these ideas which mainstream think are crazy but you know... earthen building, mud houses, mud huts, people living in the jungle in mud huts but you know the Guarani have been building out of mud for thousands of years and they were semi-nomadic people. And so, we thought we would do an exchange of some sort with like getting ideas from them, like what materials they use at the very beginning when we were just experimenting with earthen building as it is used here in Misiones. We had a base of earthen building skills from other places, but it's really location based, like how you use the earth and the materials. So we thought we would get involved with the Guarani communities and do work with them to find out what techniques they used, and how they built and where they look for materials and all of these things. It wasn't easy to make contact with the communities and then we sort of got sidetracked with experimenting, trial and error, on our own land and talking to our neighbours and talking to the people in this particular valley which are not Guarani people, they're colonists like us, but from a long time ago. (Kimberley, Mamaroja, 30th July 2015)

That there are difficulties in making relationships in a short time with the Mbyá was becoming very clear to me. The Mbyá are an essentially 'private' group when it comes to contact with 'white' people (generally referred to as '*los blancos*'). The history of mobility to further reaches of forest as a result of contact and habitat destruction, plus a history of persecution and prejudice from non-indigenous, combines with a cultural identity that is "intrinsically embedded within the natural world they live in and cannot be separated from the *monte* or *kaagui*[14] because the forest is a sacred place that represents a place of God's creation and presence. Consistent with this belief, the *monte* has always been a place without whites and not for whites" (Seymoure 2012: 33).

There is also in Misiones a persistent prejudicial and uncomprehending attitude to the Mbyá worldview and lifestyle which is likely to discourage positive views of contact. In conversation with a taxi driver in a tourist town, I came across what may be widespread misunderstandings of Mbyá indigenous world views generally: "They don't want to work, they are lazy, they steal, they only want to beg and get benefits from the government, they only pretend to be poor, they just want to drink alcohol, they don't make the handicrafts they sell — they buy them in cheaply from Peru, they get up at 10 in the morning", etc. (summarised from

[14] Forest (*monte* = spanish; *kaagui* = Mbyá).

author's field notes). In conversation with a community leader from this same area an often repeated phrase from him was that "it's complicated" ("*es muy complicado*") (Interview 11 July 2015). The multi-layered problems facing the Mbyá in Argentina are certainly complicated. However, it has to be assumed that the world of '*los blancos*' will not easily stop its encroachment upon indigenous lives and therefore, the creation of new ways of empowerment and agency need to be explored. This thought guided my conversation with the owners of Mamaroja:

Q. Do you think there's any potential in the idea that should indigenous groups and an eco-village... [collaborate] — do you think there's any potential in empowering both groups? What do you feel about that? In that this is kind of a marginalised lifestyle and maybe a lot of the mainstream doesn't really understand what you might be doing?

A. Yes, but in the eco-village we choose to be marginalised. And the difference is they are marginalised by the system and by history. It's a very different situation. We choose this, they don't choose that. They never had the option to choose, they were pushed to that. And I don't know how to integrate that you know to integrate, like to be more... (Marcelo, Mamaroja 30th July 2015)

A. But the people that come into our little marginalised community, that 'come', who are not pushed, are people who are looking to... they're reaching out from the centre of the culture, you know, reaching out to look for a reconnection because something inside the mainstream culture is not satisfying them. So they're looking for something else and they're looking to get back to these earth-based ways of living. You know, you're still an intelligent being, you're still pulling the building blocks that you've been given from inside of a culture, but you're taking them and looking for something bigger than that, something beyond the tools that you were given in university or society or through your job or whatever it is and looking for something else that reconnects you and so we reach into these pushed-away, marginalised societies to find, to seek what wisdom they might still have because the indigenous groups have and have had a connection to and a way of listening and being with this planet that we're at desperate need to understand how they do that. We pushed them down and suffocated them and covered their ears and covered their eyes for so many years, that hopefully there's still some wisdom there that we have to turn back to now. All indigenous communities that carried their stories along, carried their ways along and that I think is what's going to help, that wisdom, along with this other wisdom that we've gained as humanity... something has to come together to do this, what Joanna Macy calls 'The Great Turning' you know the revolution of moving, like reaching over this hump of ignorance that we're just digging ourselves into. (Kimberley, Mamaroja 30th July 2015).

The lifestyles pursued in ecovillages, such as can be found in Mamaroja, and indigenous lifestyles may have much in common, despite fundamental differences in knowledge systems and world views.

Another ecovillage I visited, which I will call 'Nature Haven' (not its actual name), was offering a more tourist-orientated service in terms of a rural hostel situation deep in a forested natural environment. This was owned and run by an

Argentinian non-indigenous woman who wanted to create an alternative life style. As in Mamaroja, at the ecovillage Nature Haven there was an 'Eastern' influence with yoga playing an important role, but there was also interest in indigenous concerns and plant ceremonies such as ayahuasca and other medicinal plants as well as deep ecological concerns. Sometime before my visit there had been a small conference at this ecovillage with 'indigenous women' to discuss plant medicines, (pers. comm., owner of Nature Haven 2015).[15]

The potential of such a 'tourism' situation, but within a Mbyá community, had been discussed with me in Puerto Iguazu by a community leader:

> Yes it could work but not like a hotel — two or three 'cabins', people could learn by living with us, the way of life. We would teach them how to farm, the medicine, the way of life. We are open to those people who really do respect the culture and then we can show them a bit of it. They could then as well talk to the older people and the shaman — the people who have a lot of wisdom — about nature and God, although these things are more private because they carry much more spirituality and energy when someone talks on this theme. For example, someone could talk on this theme, spirituality of nature. This could all be explained but only to those people who come who really feel a respect and who really want to know and who, this is what my grandfather says, who really would keep this knowledge to themselves and not publish. It is not to be written down, it is to be told only. If someone wants to come for a few days in a 'cabin' it has to be someone who respects and loves nature. (Roberto Moreira, Jasy Pora, Puerto Iguazu 11th July 2015 – translation by author)

I was told in conversation with a tourist at the hotel where I stayed that this type of tourism was already occurring informally (and on a very small-scale) in Mbya communities near El Soberbio a border town (with Brazil) in the east of the province close to 'Nature Haven', although some indigenous communities preferred not to invite outsiders.

Collaborative potentials between ecovillages and indigenous communities appear to show some promise and could produce benefits for both of them. Notwithstanding issues of land and territory, could these two types of communities meet and exchange ideas, technology, and knowledge systems, to their mutual benefit? For example, the Mbyá leader I spoke to in Puerto Iguazu showed great interest in solar ovens such as were used in Mamaroja for cooking. He was interested because of the benefits of conserving meagre funds presently spent on gas for cooking and as a way of preserving remaining forest (Interview Roberto Moreira, Jasy Pora, 11th July 2015). Agroecology and permaculture farming techniques shown to produce large amounts of food in small areas (Conrad 2013; and

---

15 There had not been an Mbyá presence at this conference. It was unclear to me why this was so although it may be because of a strong interest in ayahuasca and other similar plant medicine at 'Nature Haven' — types of plant medicine the Mbyá do not use (Cebolla Badie pers. comm. 2015)

see Uphoff (ed.) 2002) could also be usefully taught to interested Mbyá communities. Meanwhile interested and sympathetic parties from the non-indigenous world could respectfully share some of the world views, farming and other practices of the Mbyá and learn ways of managing dwindling forest reserves.

I asked at Mamaroja how they might envisage collaboration with indigenous people.

So what do we have that indigenous groups perhaps don't have? Ok, so we have a connection to enthusiastic people who are looking to help, to learn and to connect with other cultures. So that's the people who come to us. And part of our desire is not only to make this particular space of Mamaroja like a little sanctuary for people to come to and to learn and to grow and to change and to become better people and you know. But also how can we apply the things we are doing here to the other communities. So what if we could take some of our people from here and go out into a Guarani community and spend a few days and say people could be based here in Mamaroja so they don't have to like move into their community for a lot of time but like you know, take a car-load of folks and go out and like help them build a little house for storing their seeds in or help them with their gardening or whatever they're working on. And it could be like they tell us what to do and we help them with the labour which also shows them like oh ok, here there's people from that culture who want to come and support us and they have like an empowerment. They're working with them, we show them that we also want to work with them and then conversations come up. I mean you leave a lot of space for conversation between the people and the joy of sharing the working moments. Get a lot out of that. (Kimberley, Mamaroja 30th July 2015)

After this conversation at Mamaroja I proceeded to interview an Mbyá schoolteacher in a community near Posadas. He agreed with the principle of the idea of a collaboration with *ecoaldeas*/ecovillages but stressed that it would involve a lot of talking, that it would be difficult, and it would take a long time in conversation about such a project, perhaps two to three years (Interview. 1 August 2015). In a previous interview with a tourist provider in Puerto Iguazu who worked with indigenous communities (16th July 2015) I had also been told that the organisation of his tourism project took several years, in this case five, of careful discussion and negotiation before it could be successfully established.

At this point I decided to meet with Dr Mariana Mampaey, a medical doctor and social activist for the Mbyá, who has been working with the Mbyá in Misiones for several decades. I wished to seek expert advice on how to proceed with what I perceived as a possible collaboration between an indigenous community and an ecovillage. She pointed out an important aspect of collaboration:

In this moment the indigenous are in a situation of life and death. So many times when there are collaborations between ourselves and them, in conversation we think that they think the same way as we do, but they have a different way of thinking – a complete and polar opposite to our way of thinking, like for example, we believe in private property, they don't believe in private property; we have evidence based medicine, they think about medicine in a spiritual way. For these reasons communication is very difficult [...] they want to show us but we don't understand what they want to say. (Interview 11th August 2015, translation by author)

Dr Mampaey said that the most important thing to do when working with the Mbyá is "to listen".

Concluding remarks

Collaboration between indigenous communities and ecovillages/intentional/alternative communities has potential. Both are marginal groups, albeit in very different ways. Both intend to live in harmony with the natural environment, in community. Many ecovillages try to incorporate a spirituality that borrows or aspires to an indigenous worldview through learning about indigenous knowledge and rituals. Often, both groups are opposed to corporate greed and exploitation of people and the environment.

Is it too idealistic to consider that such exchanges have the potential to improve profiles and power of both groups? Fundamental inequalities between the dominant culture and indigenous culture remain, but my fieldwork results suggest that there is potential for beneficial interchange on both sides through, for example, the cultural transfer of technical skills and innovations, farming techniques, medicine practices, and 'spiritual' worldviews and knowledge systems. The fieldwork and research needs to be ongoing. There are possibilities but it remains to be seen whether these possibilities will develop into any concrete collaboration between ecovillages and Mbyá communities and, indeed, whether these turn out to be beneficial or not. The history of betrayals and letdowns from the non-indigenous world and the continuing persecution and marginalisation of Mbyá through globalisation are important influencing factors on the success of such a proposal. However, the potential of new solutions must continue to be explored. As Dr Mampaey said for so many indigenous it is a "matter of life and death" (Interview, 11th August 2015).

Regarding research projects of short timescale and working with indigenous people, it may be that such projects must be tailored in such a way as to more realistically appraise what might be achieved (despite the competitive demands of funding bodies) amongst indigenous groups over short time periods. 'Academic time' and 'indigenous time' may be two very different things amid the complexities of the encounter between European intellectuals (for example) and indigenous people.

I would like to end with a quote and request from community leader and research collaborator Roberto Moreira of Jasy Pora, who wished to pass this message on to 'Europeans' (translated by the author):

"We always value the natural world (naturaleza), the sun, this is what we believe, what we value [...]We value our culture – this is our wealth [...] I would like to invite the people of Europe who wish to learn a little more about our culture to come and visit the community of Jasy Pora and if there is perhaps anyone who could pay a passage to Europe, I could explain more of my culture there."

References

Cebolla Badie, M. (2012): "Territorios mbya. Usos del espacio y movilidad", in *Autoctonía, poder local y espacio global frente a la noción de ciudadanía,* Gemma Orobitg Canal (Comp.) Serie Estudios de Antropología Social y Cultural, Departamento de Antropología Social e Historia de América y Africa, Universidad de Barcelona.

Cebolla Badie, M. (n.d.) "Hace 20 años los Mbyas eran casi invisibles", *Misiones Para Todos*, misionesparatodos.com/cebolla-badie-hace-20-anos-los-mbyas-eran-casi-invisibles (last accessed on 25 September 2015).

Conrad, A. (2013): "The benefits of Alternative Farming methods", *The Guardian*, 23 April. Available at www.theguardian.com/global-development-professionals-network/2013/apr/23/farming-methods-agroecology-permaculture (last accessed on 24 September 2015).

De Kadt, E. (1990): *Making the Alternative Sustainable: Lessons from Development in Tourism,* Discussion Paper 272. Brighton: Institute of Development Studies, 1-21.

"Ecoaldeas: comunidades que habitan el monte y comparten una misma filosofia" (2015): *Primera Edición, Información General*, 31 May, 15-17.

Enriz, N. (2010): "Mbyá Children's Knowledge", *Enfance & Cultures.* Paris: Actes du Colloque International, Ministère de la Culture et de la Communication – Association Internationale Sociologues de langue francaise – Université Paris Descartes 9es Journees de Sociologie de l'enfance, Paris. Accessed at http//www.enfanceetculture.gouv.fr/.

Gorosito Kramer, A. M. (n.d.): http://pueblosoriginarios.encuentro.gov.ar/files/docs/MbyaGuarani.pdf Pueblos Originarios Encuentro conectar igualdad www.conectarigualdad.gob.ar (last accessed on 17 September 2015).

International Work Group for Indigenous Affairs 2015 Yearbook. Argentina 2014, 2013, 2012, 2011, 2010. www.iwgia.org/regions/latin-america/argentina (last accessed on 18 August 2015).

Langdon, J. L., I. S. De Rose (2012): "(Neo) Shamanic Dialogues: Encounters between the Guarani and Ayahuasca", *Nova Religio: The Journal of Alternative and Emergent Religions,* 15 (4), 36-59.

Martinez, A. (2009) [1979]: "The Words of Pa'i Antonio", in *The Oxford Book of Latin American Poetry: A Bilingual Anthology.* Oxford: Oxford University Press, 394-399.

Norman, A. (2012): "The Varieties of the Spiritual Tourist Experience", *Literature & Aesthetics* 22 (1), 20-37.

Roberg, J. L., P. Seymoure (2012): *Tourism in Northeastern Argentina: The Intersection of Human and Indigenous Rights with the Environment.* Maryland US, Plymouth UK: Lexington Books.

Rolin, C. H. J. (2004): "Breve Historia de la Provincia de Misiones" Available at www.monografias.com/trabajos15/historia-misiones/historia-misiones.shtml #CONQ (last accessed on 15 September 2015).

Seymoure, P. (2009): "Tourism, Development, and Guaraní communities in Argentina", *Interdisciplinary Environmental Review*, 10 (3&4), 20-34.

Seymoure, P. (2012a) "The Fight for Mbyá lands: Indigenous Rights and Collective Rights", in *Tourism in Northeastern Argentina: The Intersection of Human and Indigenous Rights with the Environment.* Maryland US, Plymouth UK: Lexington Books, 15-44.

Seymoure, P. (2012b) "Special Challenges Facing the Mbya: Land Shortages, Food Insecurity, Children's health, and Education", in *Tourism in Northeastern Argentina: The Intersection of Human and Indigenous Rights with the Environment.* Maryland US, Plymouth UK: Lexington Books, 87-106.

Sy, A. (2013): "Who Defines Culturally Acceptable Health Access: Universal Rights, Healthcare politics and the problems of two Mbya -Guarani communities in the Misiones province, Argentina", *Health, Culture and Society* 4 (1).

Trinchero, H. H. (2006): "The Genocide of Indigenous peoples in the formation of the Argentine Nation State", *Journal of Genocide Research* 4 (2) Special Issue: *Confronting Genocide: new Voices from Latin America,* 121-135.

Uphoff, N. (ed.) (2002): *Agroecological Innovations: Increasing Food production with Participatory Development.* London, Sterling, VA: Earthscan Publications Ltd.

Valente, M. (2006): "Argentina: Silent Extinction of Mbyá Guarani People", *Inter Press Service News Agency: News and Views from the Global South.* http://ipsnews.net/2006/11/aregntina-silent-extinction-of-mbya-guarani-people/ (last accessed on 2 Feb 2016).

Von Hau, M. and G. Wilde, G. (2009): "'We have always lived here': Indigenous Movements, Citizenship and Poverty in Argentina" *Chronic Poverty Research Centre,* Working Paper #46, accessed at http://www.chronicpoverty.org/uploads/publication_files/WP146%20Vom%20Hau-Wilde.pdf (last accessed on 21 September 2015.

Whitehead, T. L. (2005): *Basic Classical Ethnographic Research Methods.*

www.cusag.umd.edu/documents/workingpapers/classicalethnomethodspdf (last accessed on 2 November 2014).

World Data Atlas knoema.com/atlas/Argentina/Misiones/topics/Demographics (last accessed on 15 Sept 2015).

www.mamaroja.org Home page, Mamaroja (last accessed on 12 February 2016).

www.mamaroja.org/what-we-do/yoga/ Site page, Mamaroja (last accessed on 23 September 2015).

Postface

Árpád Szakolczai

We live in particularly turbulent historical times, when the bankruptcy of a civilizational project ruling our lives since centuries has become patently apparent, yet its efforts to radically transform everything in our world, from the core of nature to the infinite varieties of culture are only gaining intensity. Some people identify this project with Europe, Christianity or Western civilisation as such. However, in my view, there is nothing wrong with any of these *per se*; the problem is rather in the turn these took in recent centuries; or, the problem is squarely with *modernity*. This is not the place to elaborate this claim; let it suffice that by modernity I mean the historical confluence of Puritanical Protestantism, revolutionary Enlightenment, colonialism, the governmentalized state and the technologized economy, in the footsteps of Tocqueville, Max Weber, Voegelin, Elias, Borkenau, Foucault and Koselleck, among many others. The central feature of modernity is *destructivity*, a merciless annihilation of everything that exists and that does not serve as raw material or standing reserve for the modern project of universal transformation, substitution, exchange and denaturing of all essences. This is best visible in the convergence between the central ideas of two beacon figures of modernity, Leon Trotsky, the most uncompromising Bolshevik revolutionary, and Joseph Schumpeter, the most uncompromising apologue of capitalism, in permanent revolution and creative destruction. But it is also visible in the fact that the path of modernity at every stage is accompanied by terror – from Calvin's Geneva through Cromwell's Saints and the Jacobins, the Bolsheviks, the Nazis and the Maoists, up to contemporary fundamentalism and the 'war on terror'.

If this is the case, then a central concern for all of us – as we are all deeply involved, to the bottom of our heart, in modern madness – is to keep, maintain, preserve, conserve, guard. Interestingly enough, among others we have a close predecessor here in Plato and his focus on the guardians, who were by no means forerunners of totalitarian police, rather concerned with what is worth maintaining for a contented life, in a similar period of turbulent times, which is even generally identified as a 'crisis of democracy'.

Guarding and maintaining is not identical to keep absolutely and literally everything. To begin with, it cannot be conserving the remains of a previous stage in the same modern madness, in the name of sovereignty, nationhood, class ideology and the like, wishing back the 'good old days' that indeed never were, at least not within living memory. Even further, it cannot even be to keep everything from the premodern past, as modernity has no monopoly over societies going mad, as many anthropologists had to experience during fieldwork, in particular Gregory Bateson in Papua New-Guinea, leading him to return to Plato and coin the crucial term 'schismogenesis'. Yet, whatever exists, and exists on its own, concrete and contextual nature and essence, *thus* on its own 'right', has a value, and is worth preserving. Life is based on chance and error, yet, once something has come to exist, whether a concrete living being or a community, it develops resilience and resistance, *wants* to stay in existence, and the idea to transform it in the name of progress, civilisation, development, and related chimeras is preposterous.

This is why the MEWSC project is such a valuable and worthwhile effort. It has a particularly well-chosen title, and due to several reasons. It evokes an affinity with the project of saving *endangered* animal and plant species, as human cultures are also endangered species – let me add, European culture being very much among them. More specifically, it deals with *marginalised* cultures; those that were pushed on the side by different modalities of modernity; and the *world-views* of these cultures: not simply aspects of such cultures, but the manner in which they envision our natural world as a *cosmos*, a well-ordered and beautiful whole, buzzing with life and contentment, and not simply as an eventually self-organising *chaos*, the privileged perspective of modern technologized 'science'.

The theme, of course, is enormous, limitations being imposed fundamentally by the interests and competence of participants. The book, and the various conferences organised by MEWSC, still managed to incorporate a quite significant variety of areas, each having special importance. This starts with East Europe, from the Balkans up to Siberia. The area vast, while its significance manifold. This includes the long-term symbiosis with the cultures of Western Europe, where relations often and mutually turned parasitic; the experience of various important and particularly oppressive empires, including the Byzantium, the Ottoman Empire and the Soviet Union; and a particularly lethal and recent combination of the previous two, the communist regimes, with long-term effects that still cannot be properly assessed and understood. Here a particularly interesting aspect, evoked in some papers, concerns the possibly Palaeolithic legacies preserved in the immense steppes of Siberia, with a climate recalling Palaeolithic France, in Shamanism, but also in a set of non-Indo-European languages, whose proper study can be a prime example of turning the marginal into liminal. Further areas studied in the volume, and by MEWSC, include prominently India, where the thick layers of remote historical and more recent colonial legacies offer a particularly important and interesting comparison with East-Europe, and also Latin-America, where there is again a strong European presence, combined with rich and variegated historical and colonial layers.

The MEWSC project has manifold affinities both with general concerns in the wider academic community and the concrete place of UCC. Concerning the former, perhaps the most important issue is the intellectual significance of anthropology as a discipline. Traditionally, anthropology was considered a mostly applied and empirical discipline, with its origins outright rooted in studies of 'indigenous people' by colonial administrators, taking for granted modern 'rational' thinking. More recently, however, and relying on the work of a number of more or less maverick anthropologists, like Arnold van Gennep, Paul Radin, Marcel Mauss, Gregory Bateson, Victor Turner, René Girard, or Alfred Gell, it is increasingly argued that anthropological studies that were done with a proper care for understanding, instead of simply applying modern theories, can help to radically re-think the very foundations of modern thinking.

One such undertaking, with close connections to UCC, is the group of scholars around the journal *International Political Anthropology*, founded in 2008 by Ágnes Horváth, Bjørn Thomassen and Harald Wydra, with a number of relevant recent and forthcoming publications, including an edited volume on liminality, based on a 2009 Cambridge conference, a special issue of *Nationalism and Ethnic Politics* on the political anthropology of ethnic and religious minorities, with case-studies including Hungary, Romania, Moldavia, Lithuania, Bosnia, Cyprus and Northern Ireland; a handbook of political anthropology forthcoming by Edward Elgar; or a monograph entitled 'From Anthropology to Social Theory: Rethinking the Social Sciences', to be published with Cambridge University Press. But the MEWSC project is also close to the spirit and orientation of another recently founded UCC research centre, the Centre for the Study of the Moral Foundations of Economy & Society.

Concerning all such affinities and potentially fruitful connections, only one example will be offered here, about the links between marginality and liminality. The term liminality was introduced by Arnold van Gennep in his 1909 classic on rites of passage, but only gained wide acceptance from the mid-1960s, when Victor Turner recognised the significance of the concept. Liminality helps to capture and analyse, with a degree of analytical precision, what happens under ambivalent, ephemeral and fluid conditions of transition. This can be best seen through the three stages of rites of passage, performed in moments of transition in the life cycle or the cycle of seasons, where initiands, like adolescents to become adults or a couple to be married, are first separated from their families, then publicly must pass a trial demonstrating their maturity, and finally are reintegrated into the community in their new roles and identities. The central theoretical issue concerns the potentially transformative aspect of the middle stage of the ritual, when somebody is literally 'on' the limit. This is where the connections between marginality and liminality can be best perceived, as 'margin' and 'limit' mean almost the same thing, except that the 'margin' always stands for an outer boundary, at the edge, while the 'limit' in 'liminality' is the border between two stable states. Yet, the concept helps to understand how it can happen that a place at the 'edge' can suddenly become a new centre, being in the 'midst' of various developments, thus transforming marginality into liminality. A good example is how England became, from an island on the margins of the continent, the new centre for international trade and economic 'progress'. Liminality, however, is an ambivalent condition, implying innovation and creativity on the one side, the potential liberation from a suffocating condition of dependence and oppression; however, it also incorporates anxiety and uncertainty, even homelessness and meaninglessness, and such emotions can even be artificially stimulated and manipulated.

At any rate, the study of worldviews marginalised by mainstream modernity is an eminently important and worthwhile undertaking. It helps us better recognise, cherish and keep the values of traditions and practices that exist. But it can even help us turn our gaze around and – through the eyes of such marginalised cultures – see ourselves and the world around us with new eyes. This is uniquely important in this our historical moment, when the uniform, standardised and technologized vision of the world heaped on us from the medias, by all modernist and modernizing political movements and ideologies, revealed itself as unreal and fake, rendering it evident that the modern utopia of enlightened rationality is just a delirious nightmare.

List of Contributors

GREG ALLES is professor of religious studies at McDaniel College, Westminster, MD, USA. A past president of the *North American Association for the Study of Religions*, he is co-editor of *Numen*, the journal of the *International Association for the History of Religions*. The author of numerous articles, he also edited *Religious Studies: A Global View* (Routledge 2008). His current research interests centre on the Rathvas of eastern Chhotaudepur district, Gujarat.

STEFANO BEGGIORA is Researcher in History of India and lecturer in Anthropology (Indian Tribal Religions and Society) in the Department of Asian and North African Studies at the University Ca' Foscari Venice (Italy), where he received his Ph.D. in 2006. He has conducted extensive fieldwork and specializes in South-Asian shamanism. Dr. Beggiora has published several articles, chapters and books on Indian ādivāsīs (Saoras, Kondhs, Apatanis, etc.), colonial history, constitutional framework and laws for safeguarding the Scheduled Tribes and Castes, contemporary history of political movements in India and postdoctoral research on Indian Economics with a fellowship granted by European Social Fund.

MARINE CARRIN is Director of Research emeritus (CNRS) at the *Centre d'Anthropologie Sociale*, Toulouse. She has published extensively on Adivasis in India as well as on the bhuta cults in Karnataka. She is the author of *La Fleur et l'Os: symbolisme et rituel chez les Santal* 1986); *Enfants de la Déesse: prêtrise et dévotion féminine au Bengal* (1997); *Le Parler des Dieux: le discours rituel santal entre l'oral et l'écrit,* (2016) and co-author of *A Peripheral Encounter, Santals, Missionaries and their Changing Worlds* (with H.Tambs-Lyche 2008). She is the co-author of *From Fire Rain to Rebellion Reasserting Identity through Narratives* (Santal Texts edited and translated by P. Andersen, M. Carrin and S. Soren 2011). She is presently editing the BRILL *Encyclopedia of the Religions among the Indigenous People of South Asia* and is currently working on indigenous knowledge in Middle India and on the Bhuta cult in South Kanara.

LIDIA GUZY is a social anthropologist specialising in the anthropology of South Asia, anthropology of religions, ethnomusicology, museum anthropology and global indigenous studies. She is Lecturer in Study of Religions Department, a Director of the *Marginalised and Endangered Worldviews Study Centre* (MEWSC) and Board member of the *India Study Centre Cork* (ISCC) at University College Cork (UCC), National University of Ireland.

JAMES KAPALÓ is Senior Lecturer in the Study of Religions at University College Cork, Ireland and a Director of the *Marginalised and Endangered Worldviews Study Centre* (MEWSC). His main research interests are minority religions in Eastern and Central Europe in the twentieth century, folk and material religion, and religions in the secret police archives in post-communist states. He is Principal Investigator of the *European Research Council* funded project *Creative Agency and Religious Minorities: Hidden Galleries in the Secret Police Archives in Central and Eastern Europe* (ERC project no. 677355).

LEHEL PETI is a researcher at *The Romanian Institute for Research on National Minorities*, Cluj-Napoca, Romania and a research fellow on the "East-West" Research Group, *Vernacular religion on the boundary of Eastern and Western Christianity: continuity, changes and interactions* (ERC project no. 324214). He is the author of several research articles and book chapters concerning the role of popular culture and religion in the life of Moldavian Csángós, the social changes caused by modernisation, interethnic relations and economic strategies in different communities in Romania. The main common ground of his researches is to analyze the contexts of transformations caused by modernisation, the influence of social and economic changes to religious mentality, strategies of lifestyle and interethnic coexistence.

CLAIRE S. SCHEID is a recent PhD graduate from the Department of the Study of Religions, National University of Ireland – University College Cork. She holds an MSt in Oriental Studies from the University of Oxford, UK, and a BA in Religious Studies from Rice University, Texas, USA. Her doctoral dissertation examined the Donyipolo movement and the formalisation of indigenous faith among the Adi in the Siang districts of Arunachal Pradesh, India, in the far eastern Himalayan foothills. She has previously done fieldwork with the Lepcha and the Lhopo in Sikkim, India. She is interested in the processes by which Himalayan ethnic communities reimagine, restructure, and represent their religious beliefs in modernity.

EVA TOULOUZE is an anthropologist, professor in Finno-Ugric studies in INALCO (Paris) since 2014, and researcher at the University of Tartu. She has worked on the development of a written culture by the Finno-Ugric peoples, both in Central Russia and in Siberia and on the expansion of Christianity in the same areas. Her fieldwork has been focused on one location in Western Siberia and in the areas inhabited by the Udmurt, both in the Republic of Udmurtia and in North-Western Bashkortostan. In recent years, she has mostly investigated the ethnic religion of the Udmurt in Bashkortostan.

TATIANA VAGRAMENKO completed her PhD in Anthropology at the National University of Ireland Maynooth, specializing in religion in post-socialism and indigenous peoples of Siberia and the Russian Arctic. She is currently an affiliated researcher at the *Marginalised and Endangered Worldview Study Centre*, University College Cork (Ireland); and at the *Centre of Arctic and Siberian Exploration*, Institute for Sociology, Russian Academy of Sciences (St. Petersburg, Russia). She conducted research in the Russian Arctic, investigating the phenomenon of post-Soviet Evangelical movements and religious conversion among the Nenets indigenous people. Her present interests centre on the politicisation of religion in post-Soviet Russia and Ukraine, and the legacy of Soviet religious dissent and religious minorities' resistance to authoritarian regimes in postsocialist societies.

MARCELO VIDAURRE ARCHANJO has an MA in Sociology and his PhD in Cultural Anthropology from the Federal University of Rio de Janeiro (UFRJ – Brazil). His main research interests include the Brazilian religious field, Afro-Brazilian religions (macumba, umbanda and candomblé), Western esotericism in Brazil, and embodiment and person theory in anthropology. He is collaborator at the *Marginalised and Endangered Worldviews Study Centre*; research member of CEEO (Centro de Estudios sobre el Esoterismo Occidental) at Unasur (Argentina); research member of Nucleo de Estudos das Religiões Populares (UFPe – Brazil) and visiting research fellow at UCC (Study of Religions Department). He is also a martial artist practitioner deeply interested on the history and development of the contemporary martial arts.

GILLIAN WATT obtained her first degree at the University of Cambridge, UK, in Social and Political Sciences with special interest in Latin America. A Masters at University College Cork, Ireland, resulted in the first study of the presence of the ayahuasca religion Santo Daime in the Republic of Ireland which was published in DISKUS at www.religiousstudiesproject.com. Her main research interest is in the category 'indigenous' and how this coalesces with neo-shamanism, and the use of ayahuasca. She is a PhD candidate at University College Cork, Department of the Study of Religions.

Index

T

U

W

X

Y

Ethnologie: Forschung und Wissenschaft

Laila Prager; Michael Prager; Guido Sprenger (Eds.)
The World of Exchange
Essays in Honour of Jos D.M. Platenkamp
Bd. 27, 2016, 552 S., 79,90 €, br., ISBN 978-3-643-90789-9

Klaus E. Müller
Das Geheimnis
Faszination des Verborgenen
Bd. 25, 2014, 184 S., 29,90 €, br., ISBN 978-3-643-12717-4

Ivo Strecker; Shauna LaTosky (Eds.)
Writing in the Field
Festschrift for Stephen Tyler
Bd. 24, 2013, 240 S., 39,90 €, br., ISBN 978-3-643-90424-9

Tryfon Bampilis; Pieter ter Keurs (Eds.)
Social Matter(s)
Anthropological Approaches to Materiality
Bd. 23, 2014, 240 S., 29,90 €, br., ISBN 978-3-643-90225-2

Werner M. Egli; Lucia Kersten (Hg.)
Kindheit und Jugend anderswo
Ergebnisse ethnographischer Feldforschungen
Bd. 22, 2010, 304 S., 31,90 €, br., ISBN 978-3-643-80044-2

Beata Vidacs
Visions of a Better World
Football in the Cameroonian Social Imagination
Bd. 21, 2010, 232 S., 29,90 €, br., ISBN 978-3-643-10431-1

Irmi Maral-Hanak
Language, discourse and participation: Studies in donor-driven development in Tanzania
Bd. 20, 2009, 288 S., 29,90 €, br., ISBN 978-3-643-50014-4

Friedrich Pöhl; Bernhard Tilg (Hg.)
Franz Boas – Kultur, Sprache, Rasse
Wege einer antirassistischen Anthropologie
Bd. 19, 2. Aufl. 2011, 192 S., 19,90 €, br., ISBN 978-3-643-50003-8

Quentin Gausset
Constructing the Kwanja of Adamawa (Cameroon)
Essay in Fractal Anthropology
Bd. 18, 2010, 312 S., 29,90 €, br., ISBN 978-3-8258-1898-2

Peter Tschohl
Die vervollständigte „Historia de los Mexicanos por sus Pinturas“
Aufbau und Umfang, Autorenschichten und Quellen, Stellung im Vergleich. Bearbeitet und herausgegeben von Angela Brachetti-Tschohl. In zwei Teilbänden
Bd. 17, 2017, 1200 S., 79,90 €, gb., ISBN 978-3-8258-1634-6

Gabriele Rosenthal; Artur Bogner (Eds.)
Ethnicity, Belonging and Biography
Ethnographical and Biographical Perspectives
Bd. 16, 2009, 408 S., 34,90 €, br., ISBN 978-3-8258-1611-7

LIT Verlag Berlin – Münster – Wien – Zürich – London
Auslieferung Deutschland / Österreich / Schweiz: siehe Impressumsseite